The
in

ALSO BY SHARON PAICE MACLEOD

*Celtic Myth and Religion: A Study of Traditional Belief,
with Newly Translated Prayers, Poems and Songs* (McFarland, 2012)

The Divine Feminine in Ancient Europe

Goddesses, Sacred Women and the Origins of Western Culture

SHARON PAICE MACLEOD

McFarland & Company, Inc., Publishers

Jefferson, North Carolina, and London

LIBRARY OF CONGRESS CATALOGUING-IN-PUBLICATION DATA

MacLeod, Sharon Paice, 1960–
    The divine feminine in ancient Europe : goddesses,
sacred women, and the origins of western culture /
Sharon Paice MacLeod.
        p.   cm.
    Includes bibliographical references and index.

    ISBN 978-0-7864-7138-6
    softcover : acid free paper ∞

    1. Religion, Prehistoric—Europe.   2. Goddesses,
European.   3. Prehistoric peoples—Europe.   I. Title.
GN803.M33 2014   936—dc23   2013037361

BRITISH LIBRARY CATALOGUING DATA ARE AVAILABLE

Front cover: a painting (by the author) of a medieval
woodcarving of a "Green Lady" or Spirit-Goddess
of Vegetation, 1300s Britain, with original harvest-
theme colors added back in

Manufactured in the United States of America

McFarland & Company, Inc., Publishers
  Box 611, Jefferson, North Carolina 28640
  www.mcfarlandpub.com

To all the remarkable women in my life —
To my mother, my sisters and aunts,
cousins, nieces and great-aunts —

To friends and students,
colleagues and mentors,
shamans and healers,
wisewomen and teachers —

To my grandmothers and great-grandmothers
from Scotland, Britain, Ireland and beyond,
who passed on their courage, wisdom and strength —

And to my father,
who helped me know that
I could be anything I dreamed

Table of Contents

Preface: To Remember Is to Know

This book is a scholarly exploration of evidence for the veneration of the Divine Feminine in ancient Europe, from the prehistoric era through the late medieval period. It utilizes the most current research in archaeology, anthropology, history, and the study of religion, to bring to light a new and more detailed understanding of the subtle and complex ways in which people perceived, represented and honored spiritual beings in female form. This includes the worship of ancestors, spirits of place, and goddess figures, as well as religious roles of women in those societies.

Each chapter examines a separate time period in early European history, and in some cases focuses on differing regions where the evidence warrants such a division. The reader is provided with historical and environmental background on the time period in question, as well as information about how early cultures lived and interacted with each other and with their surroundings. Their connection to the land, and social reactions to climate change, deeply influenced the forms, beliefs and practices associated with the veneration of the Divine Feminine.

During the prehistoric eras, evidence from archaeology is supplemented with comparative research in sociology, anthropology and the study of religion in order to augment and more fully and accurately explore the physical evidence. Later chapters include additional evidence from written records, including ethnographies, histories, mythologies and other pertinent cultural, social and historical information.

A number of themes run throughout the work and are evident in almost every time period. These include indigenous perceptions about the connection between the physical world and non-physical world(s) of spirit; the importance of living in right relationship or balance with the perceived inhabitants of the spirit worlds; the role of human beings as stewards of the natural world; the importance of honoring and protecting the landscape and the environment; and the existence of female and male spiritual beings (deities, ancestors, and tutelary spirits) within a complex and holistic system of belief.

Each chapter begins with a quotation from a member of an indigenous culture or a relevant scholar that conveys an important theme relating to the events of the time period covered in that chapter. In addition, a fictional narrative is provided prior to the scholarly discussion that is intended to bring that time period to life. The narratives draw on the same scholarly evidence as the discussion and include archaeological, historical, anthropological, and cultural sources of knowledge.

This work is important in that it provides an objective exploration in every time period of the available evidence for actual — rather than theorized — veneration of the Divine Feminine throughout Europe. The recognition that indigenous European cultures included female spiritual beings in their religious practice and theology changes our understanding about the origins of Western culture and civilization. These sacred figures were an important part of varied and sophisticated spiritual traditions, and along with male deities or divine figures, figured in a complementary system of belief and practice.

The existence of these female figures was in many cases (but not all) associated with features of the landscape and the natural environment. However, categorizing all female divinities as "Earth Goddesses" or "Mother Goddesses" would be inaccurate, and an incomplete representation of the widely varied roles they played throughout Europe. Goddesses, tutelary beings and ancestral figures were associated with life, death, fertility, destruction, prosperity, magic, wisdom, knowledge, healing, battle, prophecy, leadership, and many other social and spiritual concepts.

In this day and age, there is an increasing focus on restoring balance in the world, both in terms of preserving and protecting the natural world and in restoring balance to people's physical, mental, emotional and spiritual lives. Religious ideologies that emphasize male deities or holy people can be viewed as biased and exclusionary, and may not provide women (or men) with a balanced view of the totality of sacred life. They may also be found to be lacking in terms of their ability to provide people with role models or spiritual figures to honor or learn from.

Over the last few decades, there has been an increasing interest in women's history, women's spirituality, and women's personal and social empowerment, as well as ancient history, indigenous cultures, and alternative spirituality. These may be seen as understandable reactions to perceived or experienced imbalances in social and religious life, as well as a general disconnection from nature, native wisdom and community.

I became interested in this topic after my undergraduate work as I began to explore my family history, which most recently originates in Scotland, Ireland, Britain and Wales. It also includes Dutch and Norse ancestry, and undoubtedly, farther back, other ancestral European lines. There are many strong women in my family, and even though fathers, uncles and grandfathers were "officially" the heads of families, I could see the myriad ways women in our family influenced the course of events and "got things done" according to the way they envisioned life should be. I began to read about Celtic history and culture, and the farther back in time I went, the more interesting it became.

All around me were women who lived up to their social obligations, but also, with their own brand of wit, wisdom and courage, frequently stepped beyond social norms and accomplished remarkable things. My Scottish great-great-grandmother (a MacLeod) and her daughter were born into economically disadvantaged positions in northeast Scotland. Rather than becoming fishwives, they started a dancing school (or so the family stories say). My Scottish grandmother was a Highland dancer and toured Canada as a professional at a very young age. She and I shared stories about the performing life, as I am a trained professional musician (a male dominated field). My mother was extremely capable and intelligent; there was nothing on earth she could not manifest once she set her mind to it. It was not much of a leap to exploring extraordinary women in history, including the social and spiritual roles women have played in the past.

My interest in the religious roles of women also grew out of my interest in the native religious traditions of the Celts, which has been a major focus in my academic research. The study of Celtic culture and religion necessitates an awareness of social and spiritual elements from other Indo-European cultures, and is facilitated by comparative research in anthropology and the study of religion. My research into the plausibility of shamanic traditions in Celtic culture led to fieldwork and research in indigenous cultures and practices, particularly those associated with shamanism. This research has proven invaluable in rounding out my understanding of Celtic (and other European) native practices and beliefs, which share some commonalities with other indigenous cultures.

Research for this book was primarily undertaken through Widener Library at Harvard University, through the Cambridge Libraries, and the library at the University of Massachusetts at Amherst. Throughout the work I have endeavored to utilize the highest level of research available. I have availed myself of the expertise of top experts in the fields of archaeology, history, sociology and anthropology, particularly in "setting the scene" for each chapter and providing a context for the exploration of religion within a particular era, region or culture.

In my fieldwork, I studied with a number of indigenous shamans, including Don Martin Pinedo of the Andean shamanic tradition, and Tim Swallow, a Lakota holy man from Pine Ridge. In that fieldwork, I was able to ascertain what roles both women and the Divine Feminine play in these cultures, which was a useful comparative framework for the exploration of holy women and goddesses in native European cultural settings.

Over the last number of decades, there has been a proliferation of popular books about the veneration of the Divine Feminine in the ancient world. Many of these books were inspired by the theories of archaeologist Marija Gimbutas and other supporters of a proposed "Goddess Religion" that they alleged existed in the Near East and far eastern parts of Europe. While the archaeological evidence that inspired these books was very interesting, it was also far from conclusive and could not realistically be applied to every part of Europe or every time period.

For some reason, these early theorists did not respond to academic criticisms of their work, and as a result the theories proliferated and were applied to almost every culture in unrelated regions and time periods. Veneration of a monotheistic Goddess figure has been promoted as an historical veracity in popular circles, and sometimes even surfaces in academic writings despite numerous problems with the evidence, theories, and research. The original focus on specific research undertaken in the Near East and Neolithic Eastern Europe has since been applied to any culture one wishes to transform into a "Goddess-worshipping" culture.

In addition to the many detailed and well-written scholarly articles published in academic journals that refute this theory, there have been outstanding attempts to provide accurate information about the veneration of goddesses or female spiritual entities in book form for both a scholarly and a popular audience. One of the most impressive of these books is *Ancient Goddesses: The Myths and the Evidence* (Madison: University of Wisconsin Press, 1988), a series of essays on various aspects of goddess worship in the ancient world edited by Lucy Goodison and Christine Morris. Other excellent works include: *The Faces of the Goddess* (New York: Oxford University Press, 1997), by Lotte Motz; *Through the Earth Darkly: Female Spirituality in Comparative Perspective* (New York: Continuum, 1997), edited by Jordan Paper; *Reading the Body: Representations and Remains in the Archaeological Record* (Philadelphia: University of Pennsylvania Press, 2000), edited by Allison Rautman;

and *Goddesses Who Rule* (Oxford: Oxford University Press, 2000), edited by Elisabeth Benard and Beverly Moon.

These books contain scholarly essays by different authors on specific goddesses or cultures. This book follows a similar academic approach in that its goal is to allow the evidence to speak for itself— to follow a "bottom up" rather than "top down" approach. Many popular books on the worship of goddesses force a particular theory onto the evidence, leaving out anything that does not support the desired outcome. In many of these works, small amounts of historical information are blended with unrelated elements and used as a foundation for entirely new spiritual practices or belief systems. These bear little or no resemblance to the actual cultures and religions of the historical past (or the present, in cases where veneration of the Divine Feminine is still part of the culture).

In this book, the primary focus is ascertaining what evidence we have for the veneration of the Divine Feminine in Europe throughout its history, from the steppes of Russia, through the Continent, and into the Nordic regions, Britain and Ireland. It systematically examines evidence from the Paleolithic, Mesolithic and Neolithic eras; the Copper, Bronze and Iron Ages; and the early medieval period as well. No other work has focused solely on the Divine Feminine in Europe, covering all regions and time periods. It is also unique in demonstrating that early Europeans not only worshipped a wide variety of goddess figures (refuting the single Goddess theory), but that the perceptions, representations and veneration of these figures changed and adapted over time, manifesting in many more diverse forms than has previously been shown.

The early cultures of Europe display a higher degree of sophistication than has hitherto been credited to them, and possessed their own native or indigenous cultural and spiritual traditions. This realization has major implications for understanding the past, as well as the origins of modern European culture and Western Civilization. The book also argues that these cultures developed and focused on their own native traditions, rather than those of the Mediterranean or Near East, an important factor in the development of modern culture (and attesting to the severity of our disconnection from accumulated native culture and wisdom).

In these indigenous cultures, the Divine Feminine played an important role in the social and spiritual lives of the people, and a severing of this aspect of religious life has profound implications for the experiences of every person in the culture. Recognizing and reconnecting with the historical roots of these traditions is important in bringing balance and empowerment into the lives of women of European ancestry and women everywhere. Wherever it is found, the veneration of the Divine Feminine is a significant and integral part of a complex spiritual system. Without this important element, the system is imbalanced and incomplete, and does not represent the whole of society or the totality of sacred knowledge. Restoring that balance is the key to holistic existence, and provides empowerment and possibility wherever it is found.

This book has been many years in the making, and I would like to thank my family and friends for their unfailing support through periods of intensive research, writing and rewriting, and especially the final editing process. Many thanks to the research librarians at Widener and Cambridge libraries, and to James Möbius and Donna Martinez for creating original illustrations depicting the wonderful artifacts that I could only describe in words. The artists may be contacted at *http://mobiusbandwidth.com*.

A very special thanks to Daphne Bishop for editing the book and providing insight, objectivity and enthusiasm during every stage of its creation. I would like to express my gratitude to academic colleagues for their remarkable assistance and support, and to Dr. Carin Roberge and Dr. Michael Verrilli for helping me stay on track, providing balance, inspiration and clarity on so many occasions. Your inspiration has been an enormous gift to me. Finally, my gratitude to the shamans and other members of indigenous cultures who have so generously given of their time and wisdom, illuminating the vastness and depth of native culture and religion, and helping those of us who have lost our own roots to begin to see the way forward.

This preface was given a subtitle: *To Remember Is to Know*, a phrase selected to start the wheels turning, encourage questioning, and open up new avenues of inquiry and discovery. What is it we are meant to remember? I would put forth the idea that memory is the key to knowledge. Without remembering, we would not know who we are, where we came from, or where we are going. Remembering what we have learned or experienced is crucial in living our daily lives, connecting and communicating with others, and growing and surviving on every level. Many traditional societies preserve and pass on their accumulated wisdom through word of mouth, an oral tradition that focuses on remembering and utilizing the wisdom of previous generations. These cultures take great pride in being able to memorize and recite sacred stories, myths, liturgy, parables, legends, genealogies, and vast amounts of practical knowledge with great accuracy over many centuries or millennia.

In this day and age, we have forgotten a great deal about where we have come from, and much of what came before, in our rush to re-invent ourselves and streamline every facet of our existence with technology and consumer goods. The faster we project ourselves into a perfectly engineered future, the farther we find ourselves from our roots, our ancestral memories, and our cultural traditions. We are evolved to live in a much different way than media and consumer models project as the modern ideal, and there is an increasing sense of imbalance and disenfranchisement in many sectors of society. Our souls are quite literally starving in a world of physical "plenty," the acquisition of which never quite reaches a point of satiety or rest.

The achievement of Western cultural "fulfillment" always seems to be just around the corner, but never arrives. For some, these goals or "norms" are not only unobtainable, but are unsustainable. Many look to other cultures — or other periods in history — to gain an understanding of what has been lost. Magazines, books, workshops, CDs, spas and retreats focus on "returning," "reclaiming" and "remembering" — a return to one's roots, a reclaiming of lost wisdom, remembering what we once knew. There is a quiet but steady return to organic and sustainable foods, farming and production practices; re-using and recycling (as our grandparents once did); sharing and bartering; living in communities; taking up spiritual practices; and searching for a meaningful way to live. These issues are gaining ascendancy on the cultural horizon, and represent an increasing social impulse to regain our foothold, our balance and our sanity. Once yoga, meditation, health food, and acupuncture were on the fringes of society, but now are found in almost every town.

One of the most prominent aspects of this resurgence is the desire to explore women's roles in society and religious settings. There is a lingering and unspoken sense that women have been excluded from social positions of respect and authority, power and knowledge, and empowered roles in religious life. These persist even after the decades that have elapsed since women gained the vote, were admitted to universities and the medical field, entered political life, and excelled in every aspect of culture and society. Something still appears to be missing, something less visible or tangible than a position as a doctor, professor, lawyer, senator, artist, scientist or mother. What is missing?

We might ask ourselves what it would be like to participate in a society where the respect and veneration of female powers and energies formed part of daily life and the common spiritual experience? How does it affect people to live in a culture where the Divine Feminine plays an acknowledged role? For as long as cultural memories have existed, most societies have incorporated at least some aspect of the Divine Feminine into their religious belief systems, even if the emphasis the Divine Feminine has received varied in different places and at different times. If there is no sense of (or model for) the Feminine being Divine, women's experience of self-identity, empowerment and sacrality must truly suffer. This imbalance also affects men in the community, creating imbalances within the culture that do not benefit society or the individuals within it.

The existence of female spiritual role models to reflect upon and model oneself after, and to connect with in prayer or meditation, enables both men and women to access a much wider range of personal, cultural and religious potential. It also provides them with spiritual and emotional tools that can increase their understanding of the world and the cosmos (both of which include male and female energies, entities and principles as part of an organic whole). Religious systems that include goddesses as well as gods, and embrace male and female spirits, saints and ancestors, acknowledge, honor and provide access to the entirety of the Divine. In spiritual traditions where many kinds of divine energies each have a place, and where the inherent power of all the sacred elements of this world and the Otherworld are allowed to flourish, then balance is achieved and earthly and spiritual existence can be experienced in all of its fullness.

This is a powerful lesson we can learn from the existence and numinous presence of the Divine Feminine. In a holistic universe, there must be inclusiveness, diversity and balance. We are incomplete without the "Other," and it is incomplete without us. Every member of the tribe is important and sacred, whether their role or appearance is similar to or different from our own. Every living creature has an important place in the web of life. If we remove one element, one being, the web trembles and the whole is forever changed.

Our world is a mirrored reflection, an earthly semblance, of the luminous dance of light, color and sound which exists in the realms of the divine, the ultimate source of wisdom, energy, healing and power. Every rite and hymn, every shrine and prayer attests to our ability to perceive the many faces of the Infinite. And since the Divine is infinite, it cannot be held within any one spiritual tradition — or one gender.

All of these sacred words, rites and teachings, all of this potential, is reflected in the many inspired forms that have sprung forth from the souls of human beings ever since we beheld the Divine — and in doing so, beheld ourselves. In that mirrored pool, we see the reflected faces of grandmothers as well as grandfathers, and of goddesses as well as gods. If we look back at our origins, at our natural connection to the earth, the Divine, and each other, we begin to remember all of this potential. For to remember, is to know.

PART I: ARCHAEOLOGY — SACRED STORIES FROM THE EARTH

1

Through the Past Darkly

"In the words of the Grandmothers from Africa, spirituality is no different among the races.... We all share ancestors, because humanity is humanity."
— Bernadette Rebienot, Medicine Woman, Gabon, Africa[1]

It was the end of the dry season and the ground was covered with short, brown grass that had been overgrazed and reduced to little more than stubble. Two people, a man and a woman, walked side by side through the dry grasslands. They had been walking for some time and still had much ground to cover. Their path led towards the north, away from the smoking mountain. The mountain had always been silent before, but now for some reason it shook with anger. A cloud of fine ash began to pour out from its uppermost peak and was starting to cover the rocks and trees for miles around them.

The birds were the first to leave, followed by the small creatures whose lungs were easily choked by particles in the thick atmosphere. Next came the snakes and lizards, and then fur-bearing animals in great herds. The greens and browns of the landscape were now muted and pale, as if a blanket of snow covered the ground in this very warm place. As the couple walked along, it began to rain. The wet season had chosen this moment to arrive, but it would bring no relief or vegetation this time around.

Walking through the dry ash had not required much effort, but the rain made the ground wet and muddy and walking became laborious. Still the couple persisted, walking steadily towards the north, accompanied by herds of antelope and large birds of prey.

As they walked they heard a deep rumble, followed by the sound of a huge explosion. The companions jumped, and paused to look towards the west where the spirit of the hollow mountain held sway. It was now very angry indeed, and bellowed forth a renewed blast of smoke and dust. After a brief pause to make a small offering to the spirit of the mountain, they turned due north and resumed their trajectory. They seemed to know precisely where they were going, and in spite of worsening conditions they hurried on as best they could. Although they had hoped the rain would provide relief from the thick clouds that hampered their breathing, it only seemed to complicate the situation. Still, they were not deterred.

After quite a long time the rain finally stopped, although the shower of ash continued. Several more inches would accumulate before the mountain ceased its shaking. The intrepid travelers walked for many miles before their footprints mysteriously disappeared. Whether they escaped or reached their final destination is unknown. What we do know is that once the rain ended, the sun emerged — an opaque glow in the dusty sky — and dried the carbonate-rich mud into a hard substance much like cement. With a final puff of ash and smoke, the footprints of these two ancient travelers were sealed into the ground, and preserved for over three and a half million years.[2]

Who were these travelers in time? From the size of their footprints — one pair of which is larger than the other — paleontologists think they may have been a man and woman, or a parent and child. The anatomy of the prints indicates that they were early hominids from Tanzania, a species known as *Australopithecus afarensis*. The most well represented of early hominid species, they lived between three and four million years ago in the eastern part of Africa. It would be another million years before a more advanced genus would evolve in this area, one that would eventually populate other continents. Even more time would elapse before the appearance of modern humans.

The discovery of these ancient footprints in 1978 was a remarkable find, a chance for direct contact with some of the earliest hominids on Earth. Modern human beings (referred to as *Homo sapiens*) probably evolved in Africa between 100,000 and 200,000 years ago.[3] The development of modern human beings, and all the thoughts, words, actions and beliefs which make us who we are, are the result of two developmental processes: cultural evolution and biological evolution. Biological evolution takes place slowly over a long period of time and involves the transmission of genetic information from one generation to another. Genetic information is something we inherit from our parents and ancestors, a pre-arranged code we receive but cannot change or decide for ourselves.[4]

Cultural evolution is the intentional communication of information through teaching, learning and behavior. This is a more active process, one that is eminently flexible and adaptable. Cultural evolution affects individual people as well as whole societies, and can even pass between cultures. Its impact can be much more rapid than biological evolution, although both have profound effects on our development. Our most remarkable achievements — language, consciousness, culture, art and religion — are undeniably the result of the complex and mysterious interplay of both types of human development.[5]

We'll first explore the world of biological evolution, to get a sense of where we came from as organic beings and living creatures in a physical world. Then we will focus on cultural evolution, the ways in which we interact with our world — the environment, animals and plants, other humans, and the world of Spirit. This will help us gain a deeper understanding of how we became the complex beings we are, and why we think and feel and interact the way that we do. Our exploration of cultural development will take us into the world of ancient art and ritual, mythology, ceremony and belief. There we will begin our formal journey, unearthing clues and symbols that will help us understand the meaning behind the many manifestations of the Divine Feminine.

The Branch of Origins

It is a common feature of every society to preserve and transmit creation myths to explain how the world came into existence. This need to understand our origins is one of the universal traits which makes us human, along with cultural organization and traditions, communication through spoken and written language, the creation of representational art, the ceremonial sharing of food, the use of tools, and the importance of spiritual beliefs and practices.[6]

The preservation and transmission of origin stories has always formed an important part of our self-identity as humans. Knowing these sacred stories helps us understand who we are, where we belong, and how we fit into the grand scheme of things. Creation myths are considered to be so sacred that their stewardship and recitation are often the prerequisite of only the most revered elders of the social group.[7] Scientists are also interested in human origins and their quest reads much like a detective story, filled with clues and dead ends, as well as remarkable outcomes and surprises.

After millions of years of primate development and evolution, even when early hominids began walking upright, there was nothing predictable or certain about the eventual appearance of *Homo sapiens* (literally "wise human"). From a scientific standpoint, we were not inevitable. The hominid family tree which led to the development of modern humans was not a single lineage leading inexorably to our appearance. It consisted of many branches, some of which continued to grow, and others that ended. On a certain level, it is fairly remarkable that we exist at all. But then again, some of the best stories are also the most unusual.

Modern humans first appear on the scene about 100,000 years ago. These early modern humans were anatomically similar to us, but evidence of their lifestyle and technology suggests that they were not behaviorally modern. Their bodies were more robust, and they seem to have relied more on strength than intelligence. As we became anatomically modern, we changed not only physically but mentally. The modern human brain is three times larger than the size that would be predicted for a (non-human) primate of our size. Certain parts of our brains have not changed much from those of early hominids (or apes), while other parts have become more well-developed, particularly those associated with language and learning.[8]

Although it is not clear why our brains evolved this way, science can tell us when that change took place. Sometime between two million and seven hundred thousand years ago, hominid brain size doubled, mostly because of a general increase in body size. But about 500,000 to 100,000 years ago (the time period associated with later *Homo erectus* and early *Homo sapiens*), it changed dramatically in both size and shape. This transformation is said to be one of the most amazing shifts ever observed in the evolution of any mammal.[9]

By about 50,000 years ago, the modern capacity for culture seems to have developed, and with it, the existence of totally modern humans who thrived and spread throughout the globe. Modern human beings may have been distinguishable not only by their physical features, but also by their aptitude for language and self-perception. Common traits in the development and use of language around the world suggest that it developed naturally due to similarities in the form and potential of the human brain. It is certainly one of the most significant things that makes us who we are.[10]

Another important aspect of being human is the way in which we are self-reflective. While we cannot know precisely how animals, birds and other creatures perceive themselves and others, we can say that between the species there is a great deal of diversity in terms of methods of perception and the processing of those perceptions. Most indigenous populations speak of the inherent wisdom of animals, which is perceived as being different than our own. In many cases human wisdom is not considered superior to that of animals, but simply a different kind.

What, then, of our specific kind of self-perception? This is what many people refer to as consciousness (or at least, the human brand of consciousness). While a precise definition of consciousness would be difficult to pinpoint, it could be described as (1) the ability to think about ourselves and our world, (2) to reflect upon what we perceive, and (3) to ascertain the meaning in those perceptions. This ability to reflect upon our identity is directly related to our perceptions about the world of Spirit.

Big changes took place in the development of human beings between 50,000 and 40,000 years ago, and this marker is an extremely important one in our history. At that time people began to move around and settle in new places more rapidly than ever before, eventually inhabiting almost every corner of the globe. It is also at this point that new and diverse tools were created for a variety of specific uses. In addition, there is widespread evidence for extensive and sophisticated networks of trade and co-operative social alliances. Language and consciousness are also believed to have become much more highly developed during this time period. During this same era we encounter the first evidence for the creation of art and ritual.[11] These new practices, as we shall see, included representations of the Divine Feminine, which was an integral part of the sacred whole.[12]

A Time of Transfiguration

How did our ancestors survive? What were their lives like, and what can we know about their religious beliefs? Trying to connect with the ancient past is both intriguing and challenging, and a natural part of the human condition. Our curiosity about human origins has led us to explore the ancient places of the earth in order to try and understand the mysteries of our origins, and this impulse has revealed a number of remarkable things. Contrary to popular conceptions, early humans did not always live in caves. Caves were sometimes used for habitation, but early settlements were also created out in the open, frequently near rivers or other bodies of water. Dwellings were made from stone, timber, turf, animal hides, even mammoth tusks. Some houses were easily constructed to facilitate following animal migrations, while others were more permanent in nature. In Europe, huge herds of reindeer, bison, mammoths and wild horses roamed over the steppes and provided early humans with a rich and reliable source of sustenance.[13]

The time period associated with the cultural blossoming of early humans was, strangely enough, during what is now known as an "ice age." There have been eight "ice ages" or cycles of glaciation over the last 730,000 years. During an ice age, glaciers spread and cover portions of the land, and the climate is colder and more severe. The whole landscape becomes more changeable, as glaciers cover and shape the features of the earth, including rocks, mountains and bodies of water. Forests are cleared as a result of the spreading ice, and animal habitations and migration patterns change as well.

People adapted to the changing environment, moving around frequently and reacting to shifting conditions with new strategies and behaviors. Over time, as the ice sheets retreated, temperatures rose and the forests re-appeared. Animals became plentiful in areas where the environment was favorable to their survival. Plant resources were also more abundant in this improved landscape.[14]

How strange, then, that human beings in Europe developed so rapidly during a period of climate change. At the time of these important human developments, the northern and central parts of Europe were experiencing harsh glacial conditions, with a climate similar to southern Alaska or northern Scandinavia. Summers may not have been dramatically different from those of today, but winters would have been longer and harsher, with a great deal more snowfall.

These glacial conditions eliminated a great deal of tree growth, which encouraged the development of open landscape covered by grasses, mosses and rich herbaceous ground coverings. In this environment game is much easier to spot and track than forested settings, where their numbers are fewer and they are more difficult to see. These new open areas were like a rich and productive tundra or steppe, and provided ideal conditions for many species of animals well adapted to colder conditions. Large herds of red deer, horses, bison, mammoth, and woolly rhinoceros grazed out in the open, following fairly regular and predictable migration trails between summer and winter pasturing grounds. Instead of surviving by general gathering and scavenging, people could now predict and take advantage of animal migration patterns. This detailed knowledge of the environment was supported by people's improved ability to communicate this knowledge. Prosperity increased, and population levels began to grow.[15] There were challenges in the environment, but there were also blessings.

During this time there seem to have been innovations in how people lived and organized themselves into social groups. The archaeological record shows that there were now larger settlements, which display evidence of social organization. In addition to the use of caves and rock shelters, homes were purposefully constructed, some with hearths, food storage pits, and areas paved with stone. The ability to co-ordinate social activities also improved, and this benefited the entire community.[16]

This may be the point when the concept of social territory came into existence. Previously, much smaller population groups gathered food and wandered across the wilderness. Now more focused settlements consisting of larger numbers of people worked together on communal tasks, and this may have led to the emergence of social units with specific group identities. Distinct cultural or ethnic groups may have emerged, a theory supported by variations in regional art forms, tool styles, and other practices.[17]

Far from being self-isolating clans, however, these people formed alliances and relationships with other groups to enhance their lives and improve their chances of survival. The sharing of knowledge and development of co-operative networks of exchange helped these groups form bonds that would serve them in times of need.[18] It also enhanced willingness to accept the diversity of our worldwide family, for there is great strength in diversity and in embracing the wisdom of others.

Art, Ritual and Religion

One of the most fascinating developments of the shift into modern human existence is the first appearance of artwork. As humans gained a stronger foothold in terms of their everyday existence, their lives began to include more innovations, such as the use of imagery and ceremony. It may be that as our awareness of our intellectual powers and consciousness increased, our need to express these experiences also grew. And so, as modern humans spread throughout the world, they began to create art.

Some of the earliest artwork comes from Australia and may be almost 40,000 years old. Since these art forms still constitute an important part of Australian Aboriginal people's way of life, this may represent the oldest continuous artistic tradition in the world. Early artwork from Africa dates to about 30,000 years, and the masterful cave paintings of France and Spain were created about 20,000 years ago.

While the precise "language" of these early art forms may elude us, it was undoubtedly comprehensible to members of the groups in which it was created. Some of this artwork seems to have been "public" in nature; it was clearly visible to everyone, perhaps to remind them of important events or reinforce their shared beliefs. Other art was less publicly visible — more "hidden" — and may have been religious or initiatory in nature.[19] We will learn more about the ancient art forms of Europe in the next chapter, and see what clues to the mysteries of human belief they can provide.

One of the difficulties in deciphering this artistic language is that we have no written records or oral testimony to help us understand what it means. Without that advantage, there is a great deal about the religious beliefs of the earliest humans that we may never know. Prior to 40,000 years ago, there is little evidence of ritual or religious activity, except for burial practices. While there is some sparse (and very tentative) evidence for burials among the Neanderthals, it is not until the appearance of modern humans that purposeful burials and symbolic burial customs become commonplace.

What can we ascertain about the burial practices of the earliest modern humans? What might they have been thinking or feeling, in a religious sense? Sometimes the dead were buried in caves. At other times burials took place in open-air locations (where the land was not covered by ice sheets). Both types of burial were evidently acceptable, and may have had religious significance. While the choice of location may have depended upon what sites were available, it may also reflect ideas about the nature of death and what happened to people (or their souls) during this time of transition. Burial in the open-air exposed the body to birds of prey; as the physical form was transmuted, the soul may have been released to the realms of spirit. Burial in a cave may have represented a return to the Earth, which nourishes and regenerates all life forms.

The dead were frequently buried with grave goods, including shells, ivory beads and pendants, animal bones, and tools made of stone or bone. This is the first time we see evidence of personal ornamentation, including jewelry and clothing decorations made from ivory, shell, amber, stone, antler, bone, animal teeth (fox, bear and wolf), and other natural objects. In a number of burials the body was dusted with red ochre, whose exact significance is not known. The color red is sacred in many cultures and has a variety of meanings, including life, death, protection, fertility, good luck, and so on. While we do not know the precise meaning of the color or substance found at these sites, it is likely to have been quite significant.[20]

Some early burials were quite elaborate. In a 20,000 year-old burial from Italy, the body of a man was found dusted with red ochre, and decorated with pendants and a row of shells which may have originally been strung together as a bracelet. Decorated rods made of ivory were carefully laid near the body, and a flint blade was placed in one of his hands. These specially created objects were intentionally buried with the deceased in a purposeful and meaningful ritual.

In another burial from Italy, dated to between 20,000 and 25,000 years ago, the body was decorated with seashells and buried with implements made from deer antlers placed near the persons' shoulders. A burial of two small children from the same time period also included large numbers of shells. A child's burial in Russia contained ornaments made from fox teeth, and bracelets and armlets made of ivory were found in several early Russian burials.[21]

The specific types of shells and animal teeth used in these burial rites may have had symbolic meaning, as did the other unusual objects and ornamentation found at the sites. The burying of the dead with special objects and ornamentation may suggest that the earliest humans believed these objects either honored the memory or soul of the deceased, or were considered necessary for their journey to the afterlife. It also shows that human beings had developed the capacity for ritualistic behavior. They were able to participate in the abstract conception of rituals, and in planning, choosing and creating ritualized objects and ceremonies that had symbolic and spiritual intent.[22]

To this day we still participate in symbolic rituals of many kinds. In almost every known culture, past or present, people gather together to mark the significant turning points of life: birth, adulthood, initiation, marriage, eldership, and so on. There are customs for every stage of the transition into death, both for the person making the journey and for those who remain behind. Special clothes are worn and special objects used in a ritual way. Stories are told about the person's life, and songs, prayers and blessings are recited, whether religious or cultural in nature. Although we do not have access to the specific prayers and rituals of our earliest ancestors, we are still connected to them through our common human experience of life and death, and our need to mark the turning points of our lives.

In these ancient rites — these intentional and meaningful ceremonies — the ancestors enacted and symbolically commemorated their relationships with each other and with the realms of the Sacred. The world of nature (the world that we live in) and the unseen world of Spirit, are reflections of the sacred totality of the Divine. Life and death co-exist and interact in a beautiful, mysterious, terrifying and awe-inspiring dance. As we created our first art and first ritual, we offered to the world of spirit and to each other a symbolic encoding of all we held sacred. In this holistic worldview, the totality of the Sacred — as we shall see — embraced the powers and symbolism of the Divine Feminine.

2

Sanctuaries of Consciousness

The earth is female; she gave birth to all the original creative beings;
She is the initial mother and, by virtue of being original, is now and
forever the mother of everything.

— Australian Aboriginal Tradition[1]

The young woman glanced up from her work as the last rays of a summer sunset spread across the land. From high up on the rock face she could see the floor of the mountain valley. The serpentine shape of the river reflected the sun's golden rays as it wound its way through the tufted carpet of plants and vegetation. She wore a tunic of well-tanned ibex skin and a necklace of brown seed pods and white spiral shells her father had brought back from a multi-tribal gathering.

The afternoon had passed quickly, her attention focused on the object in her hand. Earlier in the week she had spotted an unusual stone on the bottom of the valley floor. Its elongated shape and dark green color stood out among the flat grey stones of the river bed. She placed it in her pouch and returned home.

That night she dreamt of the spirit of the river, a powerful being who brought many blessings into the lives of the tribe's forty-three members. Its waters quenched their thirst and cleansed them, sustained the fish and nourished the herds. In times of drought or flood, however, the river's blessings could be scarce, its powers harsh and unyielding. Just as waters ebb and flow, so did the river goddess' powers bring plenty or scarcity, challenges or growth.

In the dream, the spirit of the river rose out of the waters as a shadowy form. It did not speak, but began to assume a human shape. At first it stood before her, its arms resting on top of a rounded belly. Then it turned around, revealing the other side of its form — a slender woman with a flat belly, arms crossed in front of her. Just as she began to speak a few words the young woman awoke.

She kept the dream to herself for days before approaching her grandmother, whose fifty-seven years made her the oldest of all the elders. At first her grandmother nodded and said little. Finally she spoke, telling her granddaughter that the river had chosen her to receive its message, to understand the cyclical powers of the waters and the need to respect them. She advised her to reflect on this, and make an offering to the river.

By late afternoon she had almost finished her work on the stone when she heard her father and brother emerge from the opening in the rock face behind her. Their hands were stained with red and yellow pigment, and her brother sported a patch of charcoal on his cheek. Her family followed the path of the artisan, a calling inherited through both ancestral lines. Her mother was extremely skilled in preparing skins, sewing them into fine clothes worn by the family and traded at tribal gatherings. Her father and brother were helping prepare a ritual space deep inside the great cave. The elders had been guided by dreams and visions to create a great hall of animals, to show respect and gratitude to the herds who gave their lives so that others could live.

As an artisan herself, the young woman had been permitted to step into the cave to see the initial stages of the artwork. She was thrilled to see images of horses, deer and other animals sketched in charcoal on the walls and ceiling of the cave. Several had been filled in with colored pigment, browns and reds and yellows. By the flickering light of the oil lamps, they seemed to dance upon the walls.

Her brother noticed the chipped pieces of dark green stearite scattered on the ground. The girl showed him the object she had made and told him of her dream. He took the piece in his hand and examined it carefully. It was the image of a woman with her arms resting on top of her full belly. On the reverse side was another image, slender with arms crossed across her chest, and a hole drilled in the top of the figurine.

Her father and brother praised the object with a silent nod of their heads. She thanked them with a gesture of gratitude traditionally used among peers. Her father reminded her that the consecration of the cave sanctuary was in a few days time. Why not wear the image when she attended the ceremony to honor the animal spirits and the abundance of the land and waters? He took a piece of sinew from his pouch and tied the stone around his daughter's neck.

Several days later, the ceremony took place in the unseen depths of the sacred cave. The tribe came together with relatives and friends from neighboring tribes to give thanks to the spirits who blessed their lives in so many ways. In the darkness of this sanctuary of consciousness, they strengthened the bonds of community and reaffirmed their connection with the Divine. The next morning, the image of the river goddess was placed carefully into the waters, where it was held safely in the body of the earth.[2]

In northern Italy, a beautifully carved green stone figurine was discovered identical to the one in the story. One side depicted a pregnant female form and the other side a slender woman with crossed arms. It dates to the later part of the "Old Stone Age" (Upper Paleolithic) era. The figurine is about 25,000 years old and is an example of some of the earliest depictions of the female form. While a pinch of artistic license was used to create the story above, many details were drawn from what we know about the lives of the earliest modern humans in Europe.[3]

Archaeology has uncovered dwelling sites and habitations from this era, as well as tools and weapons, jewelry and religious items, and a multitude of sophisticated artistic creations. Perhaps the most well known art forms from this early period are the cave paintings in southwest France, the Pyrenees, and northwest Spain. These are areas that were not covered over with glacial ice. More than three hundred decorated caves have been discovered in southwest Europe, and more are still being brought to light.[4]

The climate in these regions is believed to have supported enormous numbers of animals. The existence of major migratory routes provided early humans with rich resources for survival and development. These resources are believed to have resulted in a sizeable increase in human population, which may have created a need for ceremonial activities used to bond and co-ordinate social groups in the area. Carefully prepared caves and rock shelters may have served as ritual gathering sites for seasonal gatherings presided over by chiefs, elders or religious leaders, some of whom may have commissioned or sanctioned the creation of the artwork.[5]

In most indigenous cultures, the creation of art is a sacred process, and artwork is considered to have both an ornamental or practical purpose, as well as a symbolic or religious intent. The choice of the site and materials are important, and the process of creation is often accompanied by specific rituals, and carried out with a spiritual or social intent. Tribal art is often divinely inspired or spiritually revealed, and may require blessing or consecration by the religious practitioners of the social group. The artwork of ancient Europe must have been created to fulfill a variety of social and spiritual functions.[6] While cave paintings are the most famous of these early creative endeavors, the ancestors expressed themselves in many other remarkable ways.

Women of the Shadows

On the walls of the cave sanctuaries are some of the earliest representations of the female form. Most were carved into the walls of the caves, sometimes with great care, and at other times rendered with a few carefully chosen lines. In many cases, the images consist of stylized representations of the female form, focusing predominantly on the torso. Sometimes the arms are represented, but there is often little or no indication of the head or legs. While some of the images depict heavy or pregnant women, others show slender women, young women, or older women.[7]

One of the most famous stone carvings was discovered in front of a rock shelter at Laussel, France. Engraved onto a large block of stone was the figure of a heavy or pregnant female with large breasts, a full belly and ample hips. Her left hand rests on her abdomen, while her raised right hand holds an animal horn notched with vertical lines. The image was carefully rendered and may have been polished. Red ochre was used to decorate the figure, particularly the breasts and abdomen. The woman's hand, which rests on her belly, and the notched horn (perhaps representing the moon or a system of time-reckoning) may suggest symbolism associated with women's menstrual cycles.[8]

Two similar engravings of women were also discovered in France. One was found quite close to the figure at Laussel. She also has a large belly and breasts and holds an object in her hand. Her head is covered with a grid of horizontal and vertical lines, perhaps a hairstyle or headdress. The other engraving depicts a similar female form holding an object in her outstretched hand (perhaps part of a skull or a vessel of water).[9]

Another interesting figure from a French cave site depicts a female form with large breasts, whose arms extend down around her body, surrounding it like a wreath. Beneath her is a mirror image of the same form, upside down. These two half-figures joined at the waist have been variously interpreted as a woman giving birth, a sexual encounter, or a woman crouched near a body of water looking at her own reflection. It could also reflect something seen in a dream or trance state.[10]

Another contemporary engraving from a cave wall depicts a number of female torsos in profile. The figures are slightly bent at the knees and hips, with an emphasis on the hip area. Some of the women's bodies are decorated with horizontal stripes or cross-hatching, which may represent clothing or body paint. The stance of the figures, which emphasizes the breasts and hips, may have been chosen to communicate that these are female forms. However, the artist has gone to some length to depict a specific posture, and may therefore denote some kind of ritual posture or dance associated with women.[11]

In addition to these engravings there are a number of carvings described in popular literature (and occasionally in academic settings) as representations of female genitalia. It should be noted that there are only a handful of cases in which female genitals are definitely represented in connection with a female body. In almost all of these, the pubic area is triangular in shape, while those

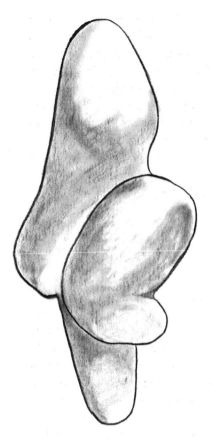

Pregnant female figure carved from amber-colored calcite, originally displayed on a pedestal used to stand the figure upright. 8.1 cm tall, Upper Paleolithic era, Abri du Facteur, Dordogne, France. Artist: Donna Martinez.

of the unidentified carvings are not. In only one instance, a figure unearthed at Bédeilhac, do we see an image modeled in clay which clearly represents a vulva. Several of the symbolic carvings resemble this image, to varying degrees, but many others do not.[12]

Because so many of these "vulvar" images were found without any helpful context or identifying features (i.e. without any connection to a female form), it is difficult to say exactly what they represent. Some look like animal hoofprints, seeds or other objects from the natural world. There may be a reason why Paleolithic artists took the time to differentiate between these various shapes. Studies of rock-art from other parts of the world demonstrate that simple graphic designs can have a wide range of meanings. In any case, the repeated appearance of these forms in ancient Europe indicates that they must have been important, even if their symbolism is not currently understood. Dozens of these images — whatever they represent — are found all over southwestern France, and are among the oldest art forms in the world.[13]

Primordial Icons

A variety of other intriguing objects have been discovered at ancient European sites whose purpose may have been religious or magical in nature. Here we should note that religion and magic are considered to be both sacred and practical endeavors in traditional cultures. At these Paleolithic sites, a great number of cylindrical rods or batons were created from antler or ivory, with a hole pierced near one end. They were frequently decorated with animal forms, including horses, deer, birds, lions, fish, snakes, aurochs, bison and bear. Others were carved with "abstract" shapes or geometrical markings, such as horizontal or diagonal lines, dots, spiral shapes, arcs, leaf shapes and concentric circles.

These beautiful objects have been tentatively interpreted as handles for slings, spear-shaft straighteners, or tent pegs, but their widespread occurrence, their deliberate crafting, and remarkable ornamentation seems to suggest a more symbolic use. In many cultures, special objects with symbolic decoration are often used in religious settings. The carvings on these rods may have indicated that a person was from a particular tribe or social group. Or, they might have served as a ritual scepter or wand in a ceremony or ritual, or used as talismans with a variety of attributed magical or protective powers. The hole drilled at one end of the rods may have allowed the object to be suspended from a belt or costume.[14]

The artwork of the Upper Paleolithic also includes carved representations of animals (although their exact purpose is also unclear). These animal figurines were made from jet, amber, coal, ivory, limestone, stearite and sandstone, or less frequently, molded from clay. This animal artwork is a wonderful blend of realism and stylistic interpretation, attesting to the skill and individualism of these early artisans.

The wide variety of animal imagery reveals a remarkable knowledge of — and even personal or spiritual connection with — the world of living creatures. Deer, horses, bison, fish and other animals were depicted with such realism that one can almost reach out and touch them. Even the character of an individual animal was captured with great skill. Here we are witnessing a "moment in time" — horses running across a field, a delicate ibex poised on three feet, a bison turning to lick his flank as he rests after grazing the vast plains.[15]

In addition to animal images, there are also carved representations of human beings. Sandstone, ivory and calcite were used to create a wide variety of human forms. Not all of the figures can be clearly identified as male or female, and there are many variations in shape and size. For example, an ivory statuette from Germany depicted a male human body with a lion's head. Another ivory figurine, this time in Czechoslovakia, was carved so that the head, trunk and arms of the figure fit together to make an articulated doll of some kind.[16]

Some of the most distinctive artwork from this era are female statuettes which have sometimes been labeled "Venus figurines." These objects were sculpted from a variety of materials, including ivory, calcite, jet, hematite, reindeer antler, bone, ivory, fired clay, sandstone, limestone, green and yellow stearite, limonite, and horse's teeth, and they display quite of bit of regional variation in style. While many are hard to date with precision, it is believed that most were produced during a two- to three thousand year period, between 26,000 and 23,000 years ago. These may be the earliest examples of artwork depicting aspects of the Divine Feminine.[17]

Anatomy of a Goddess

Over 250 ancient female statuettes and figurines have been discovered, from over seventy-five sites (including twenty in southern France, eight in northern Italy and thirty-one in the Danube-Rhine region). Others were found in eastern Russia (at twelve sites) and Siberia (four sites). There is a wide gap of almost 5,000 kilometers between these regions, which may indicate that the figurines were not created or used everywhere in Europe. In addition, the finds at the eastern sites may represent the result of trade, rather than artistic production.[18]

The statues vary widely in shape and form. Some are anatomically proportioned, while others display an emphasis or exaggeration of certain features. In many cases (as with the cave art), facial features are not represented, nor are the feet or lower legs (which often end in a tapered point). It has been suggested that the legs might have been shaped in this way in order to stand the figurines upright in the ground.[19]

Some of the figures appear heavy or pregnant, while others are quite slender in shape. The heavier figures often have large breasts, stomachs and hips. And, while almost all these figures are depicted without clothing, the pubic triangle is indicated in only a few cases. The context of these finds suggests that they may have been used for different purposes. For example, the statues from central and eastern Europe were found at open-air sites, and may have had a special role in the home, symbolizing abundance, fertility, protection, food supplies, the hearth, children, the ancestors, or protection in childbirth. Those from western Europe, however, were found in caves and rock shelters. These may have been associated with religious activities, initiation rites, seasonal ceremonies, hunting rituals, creating or maintaining sacred space, or honoring spirits or deities.[20]

Some of the figurines reflect both male and female imagery, incorporating female breasts and hips in the same object with forms that suggest male genitalia. These may represent sexual union, sacred androgyny, or life generating or sustaining principles. A statue discovered in France displays the dual-sexual nature of some of the figurines. Carved from a pink-colored piece of calcite, the figure has an unusual shape, with no head or arms. The lower section seems to portray the hips and abdomen of a pregnant woman, while the upper part has a conical and potentially phallic shape.[21]

How can we know what the female figures represent? And why are they called "Venus" figurines? The name "Venus" was first applied to the statues by the Marquis de Vibraye in the 1860s, and referred specifically to one of the slender types of figurines. Later, the term was adopted to refer to the more ample figures, and thereafter has been used to refer almost exclusively to the heavier types of figurines.[22]

There are actually four primary types of female figurines from the European Upper Paleolithic era:

1. young, with a firm body, high breasts and a flat stomach
2. of reproductive age, probably pregnant, with a fleshy body and large breasts and stomach
3. middle aged or heavy (but not necessarily pregnant) and
4. elderly or post-reproductive, with a sagging body.[23]

One study of the age and body types represented by the figurines showed that 23 percent were pre-reproductive, 17 percent were pregnant, 38 percent were heavy, and 22 percent were elderly. Other studies reflected a somewhat higher percentage of pregnant forms. One thing is clear: the statues reflect a wide variety of ages and body types, and represent women throughout their lives.[24]

One of the most popular interpretations of the entire range of figurines is that they are fertility figures. However, none of the statues are shown carrying or nursing children, and only one depicts a woman in childbirth. Rather than solely supporting imagery associated with fertility or maternity, they seem to be communicating something about womanhood, something that reflects a wide variety of attributes associated with women's energies, wisdom, power or abilities.[25]

The word "fertility" can refer to human fertility, animal fertility, or the fertility of the land. The concept of increasing or sustaining animal fertility or the productivity of the landscape would certainly have been important to our hunter-gatherer ancestors. Human fertility, on the other hand, is a very different matter. All known hunters and gatherers are more concerned with limiting or restricting human fertility, rather than increasing it. The reason is very simple: survival.[26]

More people means more mouths to feed, and if you are a hunter-gatherer the availability of food is cyclical and sometimes unpredictable. Having some children is necessary (and often unavoidable), but too many children can endanger the survival of the entire group. For this reason, many scholars do not feel that these figurines were associated with or used to enhance human fertility.[27]

The many thousands of years that have elapsed since the figurines were created, as well as the scant evidence from the sites where they were found, make it difficult to ascertain their exact meaning or purpose. However, we can say that far from being just "fertility talismans," these objects are clearly striving to communicate something important about the symbolic feminine, perhaps even the Divine Feminine. Archaeology has provided us with our first steps towards understanding this mystery, but there are also other methods that can help us in our quest.

The Divine Incarnate

Another tool we can use to understand the lives and beliefs of our early ancestors is anthropology, the study of human societies and cultural behavior. More and more, archaeology and anthropology are working side by side to provide deeper insights into the ancient past. In order to gain more information about the symbolism of the female statuettes of the Upper Paleolithic, anthropologists have looked at modern hunter-gatherer societies to see if they use or create figurines similar to those from ancient Europe. Their studies have shown that these types of figures have traditionally been used for a wide variety of purposes, including:

1. personal ornaments
2. educational aids
3. tokens of social status
4. tokens of social relationships
5. portrayals of sexual imagery
6. dolls or children's toys
7. objects used to demarcate ritual space
8. ritual use in special places or ceremonies
9. to represent religious ideas or concepts
10. to commemorate special times (such as birth or initiation)
11. to symbolically depict people
12. as representations of deities
13. as representations of ancestors.[28]

There has been a tendency in popular writing to focus on just one or two of the possible meanings of the Paleolithic female figurines. But by unnecessarily narrowing the options we run the risk of misinterpreting the artwork, as well as missing much of the complexity that was undoubtedly involved in the social and spiritual traditions of these people. It is infinitely more exciting — and more potentially rewarding — if these female images represent a wide variety of possibilities, as they do in other traditional cultures.

Rather than suggesting that ancient people were pre-eminently focused on the polarized concept of "male versus female," these art forms more likely indicate an awareness of the varying attributes, roles and functions that each person played in the social group (or during their lifetime). In tribal settings, every person is important to the survival of the whole.

Whether these figurines denoted status, symbolized sexuality, or indicated a woman had reached puberty, married, or undergone initiation, they are clearly important. Whether they were used as marriage gifts, decorations for the home, or personal ornaments, they are beautiful. Whether they served as amulets to protect a woman during childbirth, sanctify a ritual space, or indicate where a ritual was held, they are powerful. And whether they represented religious ideas, marked the dwelling place of spirits or ancestors, or represented deities or female spirits, they are sacred.

All of these uses and intentions are sacred. In indigenous cultures we do not find the same ideological separation between mundane and sacred as we find in modern western culture. All of life is sacred, and every act, word, and idea can be viewed and experienced in a sacred manner. Everything that exists is part of a sacred whole: male and female, life and death, darkness and light, and so on. The training of a child, the rites of a young initiate, the bond between partners, and the passing of an elder — all are sacral experiences which complete the great tapestry of life. In this worldview, no matter which interpretation of female symbolism might apply in any given setting, most (if not all) of these ancient figurines can be said to symbolize something sacred to the lives of the people who created and used them.

The Magic of Numinous Existence

One of the most popular interpretations of the female figurines of the Upper Paleolithic is that they are goddess figurines. This is certainly possible, but as we have seen, it is only one of a number of possibilities. However, if some of the figurines do represent goddesses or female spiritual entities, these may be the earliest depictions of the energies associated with the sacrality of women's roles and powers, as well as what are called the feminine mysteries. If these figures do represent goddesses, ancestors, female spirits or feminine religious ideologies, how might they have been used or venerated? How do people physically and emotionally interact with iconographic depictions of spiritual entities or symbolic representations of religious concepts or ideas?

One preconception I think we harbor in relation to the religious practices of other cultures has to do with the veneration of holy objects. We are culturally conditioned to view the use of sacred objects as superstitious, or even idolatrous. While elaborate deity statues and shrines are used in many cultures, these are also used in Christian ceremonies and processions around the world.

The veneration of Christian saints' relics, for example, has been very influential throughout the centuries.

Sacred objects are symbols of religious ideas or divine energies, and are not necessarily direct representations of these things. They may be portrayals of sacred entities or ideas, concepts or energies made manifest in physical form, to facilitate the veneration and contemplation of the energies or concepts involved.

Sacred objects can also serve as physical repositories or embodiments of non-physical forms or energies. Here the Divine takes on material form so that we may interact with it in a meaningful way here in our world. These figurines are examples of the universal impulse to interact with the unseen world of spirit in a tangible way. If we respect a belief or concept, ancestor or deity, we can create and utilize a symbolic representation of that idea or figure in a respectful and purposeful manner. Therefore, these objects can be both symbols and containers of the powers of the sacred realms.

One of the less noted but striking aspects of the statuettes of the Upper Paleolithic era is the fact that many can be held comfortably in the palm of the hand.[29] Their size and shape may have influenced the way in which they were used. Religious figurines are used in many spiritual traditions and are sometimes held during prayer vigils or other ceremonies. Celebrants hold the objects in their hands to focus their thoughts and intentions upon the deities or ideas they symbolize, and to connect with their symbolized or embodied powers. Larger figures may be held up in front of an altar or group of people, adorned with necklaces, pigment or garments, or offered food, drink or other gifts in a symbolic offering to the divinities or spirits involved. Smaller religious statues can be used in either formal or personal ritual settings — outdoors as well as indoors — and may be carried about for a variety of spiritual or emotional benefits.

The unusual choice of materials used in the creation of these objects, as well as their portable size, may suggest that they were used for working magic. While in our culture we tend to think in terms of "magic" *versus* "religion" — this is a modern and artificial construct. Most indigenous spiritual traditions fluidly embrace formal worship and veneration, healing, magic, and a wide variety of other spiritual and devotional practices into their religious practices and belief systems.

While we may initially react to the label, many forms of magic are commonly found in our culture. Beyond the obvious example of lighting candles in a church or wedding ceremony, we engage in protective magic whenever we decide not to walk underneath a ladder or allow a black cat to cross our path. Construction companies still sometimes refrain from marking the thirteenth floor of a building. We light and extinguish birthday candles to manifest our wishes and desires, carry rabbit's feet for luck, and knock on wood to avert misfortune, just to name a few examples.

Objects that can be held in the hand, or easily carried about, seem to hold a special meaning in cultural magic and formal religion. These items often have a very personal meaning or significance and are believed to provide blessings, assistance or protection, or symbolize our individual connection with the powers beyond. These attributes may also apply to the female figurines of the Paleolithic. Their portable size and rounded contours, and the unusual materials used to create them can help us visualize the experiential aspects of their use, whether magical or religious in nature.

Some of these portable figures were created in such a way as to permit formal display. Divine statuary is either large enough to be seen by a group of people in a formal ritual setting, or small enough to be placed in a shrine or on a small altar. The base of the figure is flattened so it may be set and balanced upon a level surface. One figurine from France was formed to allow for display in just this fashion. Carved from an amber-colored piece of calcite of exceptional beauty, it has small youthful breasts, a long torso with a small but gently protruding belly, and ample hips and thighs. A vertical hole drilled at the bottom of the figure suggests a pedestal had been used to display it. Another figurine shaped for display from northern Italy was carved from yellow steatite, an almost transparent stone the color of lemon drops. It had ample hips and large round breasts, and a lock of hair carved at the back of its head fell over the nape of the neck.[30]

These are just a few of the remarkable creations produced during the earliest flowering of human religious art. Without inscriptions, texts or other decipherable symbolism to help us unlock their mysteries, we can only guess at their meaning and the ceremonies in which they were used. While advances in scientific development can help unravel certain aspects of these ancient figurines and the societies that produced them, by turning to age-old practices preserved by traditional cultures, we are able to flesh out a more complete picture of the rich and varied customs practiced by our forebears.

3

Voices from the Forest

Nothing belongs to us. We are here for the Universe...
Time goes by. Everything changes, except the land we live on.
And when that changes, we have to accept it...
— Rita Pitka Blumenstein, Yupik Elder, Arctic Circle[1]

The elders of the tribe still told legends about how the forests and mountains had once been open grassland, home to the legendary tusked mammoth and the mythical woolly rhino. Not everyone believed those tales anymore, yet it was difficult to explain the great tusks that occasionally surfaced in the marshes if the stories weren't true. The land was now covered with a rich profusion of trees; where could these ancient herds have grazed?

The brilliant warmth of the midday sun made it hard to visualize walls of ice that had stood taller than the trees. Had hundreds of people really gathered to participate in great ceremonies in times gone by? If so, who would have been left to hunt in the forest or gather shellfish from the ocean? Who even had time to paint on the walls of caves?

On this late spring afternoon, women bathed toddlers at the edge of the water while older children retrieved birds and hares from snares. Women were cleaning animal skins obtained during early spring hunting, preparing them to create garments for an upcoming ritual. Female elders conferred with the men about the construction of deer masks and headdresses that were an integral part of the ceremony. Every year in the spring, a ritual took place that provided strength for the hunters who ventured out into the dark forest.

Before the dance began, storytellers recited sagas of a time gone by when the animals had offered themselves freely to humans. The world was colder and darker, but the abundance of the herds provided balance. Now the world was warmer but the animals hid in the shadows of the forests and were not as willing to give themselves up. It was important to make offerings to show gratitude and ensure reciprocity, as well as to entice them out of their dark hiding places.

The women prepared vessels of pigment used to paint the hunter's faces and arms with patterns symbolizing courage, strength, agility, abundance and success. Into these preparations they mixed a blend of herbs and powdered tree bark whose properties enabled the hunters to connect directly with the animals and the spirit of the forest itself. Their dance symbolized their awareness that their life was dependent upon the world of nature. By making prayers and offerings, they entered into a relationship of mutual respect, creating a cycle of reciprocity that enabled all creatures to flourish. Without acknowledging this sacred relationship, the blessings of the earth might be withheld.

The antlers of the sacred deer glinted in the firelight, and the hypnotic properties of the herbs entered their bloodstream. The dancers danced, the women sang, and the men prayed for abundance. They danced far into the night until they had forgotten both time and place, and the dark recesses of the forest were transformed into a place of wonder and connection. This was the purpose of ritual, after all; to transform human perceptions of existence into a reality in which all of life is sacred.[2]

After the great flowering of human consciousness that took place during the Paleolithic era, Europe also experienced a blossoming of the earth. The cultural achievements that had begun 40,000 years earlier continued for almost 30,000 years. Then, starting around 13,000 years ago, enormous environmental and social changes started to take place. The climate began to warm and the glaciers retreated. Sea levels around the world started to rise as the glacial ice melted into the oceans. As the glaciers disappeared, forests gradually began to grow where the ice sheets had been. The peak of these environmental changes took place about 10,000 years ago, a point that signals the end of the Paleolithic era (the Old Stone Age) and marks the beginning of the Mesolithic era (the Middle Stone Age).[3]

For human beings, the replacement of open grasslands with dense forests was a profound change. Hunting animals in a forested environment is very different from hunting in an open landscape, and requires different skills and strategies. The animals who inhabited the forests did not migrate in the same way as the migrating herds and lived in smaller, more widely dispersed groups. In addition, the forests could only support 20 to 30 percent as many animals as the grasslands had supported. There were fewer animals to hunt, and those that could be found were more difficult to track and pursue. As a result, it is believed that human populations may have declined in many places with people living in smaller, more widely dispersed communities.[4]

Initially, to adapt to the changing environment, some groups followed the herds northward as the animals explored new territories that became accessible as the ice receded. As a result, around 13,000 years ago human beings

began to migrate into northern Europe, moving into areas that had been uninhabited for tens of thousands of years due to the glacial ice. These population
groups spread into the north of France, the south of Britain and parts of Scandinavia. They practiced traditional methods of hunting in an open landscape
until the forests began to spread northwards as well. Others stayed in the
south and adapted to the changing environment with new skills and strategies
for hunting and living, changes that would eventually spread throughout
Europe.[5]

One of the most profound effects of the melting glacial ice was the disappearance of coastline, as large areas of land that had previously been used
for hunting were covered over by the rising waters. Around 6500 B.C.E., the
increase in sea level severed a land bridge that had previously connected Britain
with the mainland of Europe. In many places, the land itself rose, as well as
the waters, as it had previously been weighed down by the tremendous weight
of the ice. This was a very slow process, but one that ultimately had an enormous effect on the shaping of the landscape.

While the environmental changes that took place during this period were
dramatic in terms of geological time, it is not known if they were perceptible
to Mesolithic people themselves during their lifetimes. Mesolithic specialist
Steven J. Mithen points out that we might well imagine that folk memories
existed during the Mesolithic era about earlier times when enormous open
hunting grounds once existed, only to have become submerged by the sea.[6]

The plants and animals that inhabited this new landscape were different
from those that were common during the Paleolithic era. During the early
part of the Mesolithic, the landscape of northern Europe had been covered
with the herbs and plants of the open grassland, as well as trees that can
tolerate the cold: birch, aspen, willow and juniper. As the climate became
warmer, pine trees, and then hazel trees, became quite prominent. After this
came broad-leafed trees that thrive in warmer temperatures: oak, elm, lime
and alder.

The plant life of southern Europe also changed, but somewhat less dramatically. In southern France and the Iberian peninsula, a sparse cover of
pine and juniper was replaced by oak forests, leaving the pine trees to spread
to higher ground. Hazelnuts were the most commonly used plant food, but
a wide range of other edible plants, berries, nuts, roots and fungi would also
have been gathered and eaten. These included water chestnuts, nettles, grass
pollen, wild almond, pear, wild oats and barley, and other regional and seasonal plants and herbs.[7]

As a result of these changes in vegetation, the population and distribution
of animal life also changed. Due to the disappearance of grassland habitat,

several large species of animals that became extinct, including the mammoth, woolly rhino, and giant deer. Reindeer and elk, which had once been widespread and abundant, were now found only in the northernmost regions. Elsewhere, large roaming herds of reindeer and wild horses were replaced by smaller groups of red deer, roe deer, wild boar, aurochs and elk.

Smaller forest-dwelling animals like the rabbit, badger, otter and pine marten also proliferated. Domestic dogs were first kept by humans in Europe during this era, and were used to help track and drive game. Some of these dogs were very similar to German Shepherds, and were so important they were sometimes buried alongside humans.

As sea levels rose and marine environments expanded, the creatures of the ocean also grew in number and diversity. Whales, sharks, porpoises and dolphins thrived and were used as food resources. Shellfish and ocean fish became important sources of nourishment, as did fresh-water fish and water birds that flourished near the abundant lakes, rivers and marshes. During this period wickerwork was first created, as baskets were woven and used for fish or eel traps and other uses.[8]

The remains of Mesolithic dwellings are found throughout Europe, ranging from simple hunting shelters to substantial structures with stone walls and foundations. The floors of these houses were made from earth, stone, wood or limestone plaster, with either round or rectangular shaped central hearths. Temporary hunting camps were used seasonally, as people inhabited lowland areas during the winter months, working together as a community. Fragments of wooden skis have been uncovered which could have been used for winter hunting and gathering. The end of one ancient ski was carved with the head of an elk, a decorative touch whose shape also prevented reverse movement through the snow. During the summer small groups of people moved into upland regions for hunting and other purposes. Boats and canoes were used for travel along rivers, to reach offshore islands, and for deep-sea fishing.[9]

The artifacts from this era were simpler in design than those produced in the Paleolithic era. During the Mesolithic, tools and weapons were frequently made from flint, as well as wood, antler, quartz, bone, quartzite, greenstone and obsidian. Although not as elaborate or diverse as objects from the Paleolithic, they were still beautifully designed and manufactured. In addition, European pottery was first created during the Mesolithic era, the oldest vessels appearing in Scandinavia around 5600 years ago.[10]

Although life in the forest was very different from living out in the open grasslands, the forest was also a sacred place and full of life. The importance of land stewardship and forming relationship with all living beings is part of the natural way of life. As Simon Lucas, Chief of the Nuu Cha Nulth people of Vancouver Island says: "The animals have a right to these forests too. They belong there — it is as much theirs as it is ours."[11]

Under the new climactic conditions, the complex social organization that had supported the art, technology and ritual of the Paleolithic era seems to have disappeared. Most striking is the virtual disappearance of artwork during the Mesolithic age. Apart from a handful of animal figurines and mysterious pebbles painted with geometric designs, little that survives from this era attests to the previous period of cultural innovation.[12] The "age of the forests" was a time of great change for the landscape and all its creatures, as well as the ritual expression of people's inner landscape, including the symbolism of the Divine Feminine.

Shaman, Serpent and Elk

One of the most useful methods for understanding the organization and beliefs of a prehistoric society — one that existed before the advent of written records — is to examine the ways in which people bury their dead. In Europe, the first evidence for the use of cemeteries comes from the Mesolithic era, starting about 6,000 years ago. These formal burial grounds ranged in size from small to medium cemeteries, housing twenty to seventy burials, to larger sites containing several hundred burials. These sites may have also been used to enact rituals honoring the ancestors; recite myths associated with life, death and rebirth; and strengthen the traditions of society. The existence of cemeteries suggests that new thought patterns or perceptions about, life, death, and the afterlife, may have emerged at this time.[13]

During the Mesolithic era, people were buried in a wide variety of ways. In some cases, they were buried lying on their backs in parallel rows. In other cases, they were buried on their side with folded knees. Some people were cremated, and then buried near others in different positions. One of the most widespread burial practices (and a possible symbolic connection with the past) was the continuing use of red ochre. This substance is found in almost all Mesolithic burials, regardless of other variations in ceremony or tradition.[14]

The available evidence from the Paleolithic does not seem to indicate much in the way of hierarchy in society. It is possible (but not verifiable) that the earliest hunter-gatherer societies of Europe were somewhat egalitarian in nature. In the cemeteries of the Mesolithic, however, we begin to see some evidence for social distinctions, possibly based on ancestry, gender, or skill.[15]

A few Mesolithic burials seem to indicate status that was afforded to people based on the circumstances of their birth. This type of hereditary status may indicate the presence of some kind of hierarchy or social distinction. One indicator of "birth status" is the burial of children with objects of value they could not have obtained as a result of their own actions. This might suggest that they were born into a special family or group, perhaps one associated with a social or religious leader, or some other kind of skilled or esteemed person. However, there are relatively few burials of this type, suggesting that the potential for inherited status was probably quite limited during the Mesolithic.

One very dramatic example of this is a Mesolithic burial of a mother and infant in Denmark. The young mother was buried in a dress decorated with ringlets of snail shell beads and a host of pendants. A robe of similar decoration was folded to make a pillow across which her blonde hair was arranged. Her cheeks and pelvis were dusted with red ochre. The baby was buried on top of a swan's wing along with a flint blade.[16]

Social distinction based on personal characteristics such as skill or accomplishment seems to have been more widespread. While some Mesolithic graves contained no grave goods, others contained many objects (or in some unusual cases, hundreds of items). While some of this variation could be gender related, the majority seems to be associated with personal achievement. This suggests a person's actions or abilities could affect or enhance their social standing (both here and in the afterlife).

There are some differences between male and female burials during the Mesolithic, as men and women were frequently interred with different types of objects. Men were often buried with bone tools and weapons, slate knives and daggers, or flint blades and axes. Women were buried with necklaces of deer, beaver or bear teeth. Men were buried with a wider variety of objects than women, but these variations may reflect a difference in social roles, without implying superiority of one gender over the other (a tradition sometimes seen in modern hunter-gatherer societies).[17]

Also, it is not known if these items actually indicate wealth or status, for many of the knives, tools and animal teeth that were uncovered are known to have been plentiful in Mesolithic society. The choice of bear, beaver and deer teeth may have had some sort of symbolic meaning, for these were only three of the many types of animals that were widely hunted at that time. One possibility is that they might reflect a clan symbol or totem animal (personal or community-based). In addition, beaver teeth were frequently buried with men of hunting age, which may indicate that the symbolism of these items is not only related to gender.[18]

Other grave goods, like the boar tusks sometimes buried with young men, may indicate status or achievement because of the rare qualities of the object or difficulty involved in obtaining them. These objects may represent a kind of social status or distinction that was earned or awarded due to skill, achievement or service to the community. Boar tooth pendants were also found in a female burial, along with a flint blade and pendants made from the teeth of red deer, suggesting that the symbolism of these grave goods may not have operated solely along a male-female gender axis.[19]

Overall, there seem to have been relatively few instances of individuals who possessed a great deal of "wealth" or even special objects that might indicate they were social leaders. However, there are some isolated but remarkable Mesolithic burials that may suggest some kind of social distinction based on ancestry or religious service.

At a variety of Mesolithic cemeteries excavated in Russia, some people were buried with carved wooden figures representing snakes, elks or human beings. In some cases, groups of people buried with a certain type of figure were buried in a different part of the cemetery from those associated with another type. In addition, the carvings were found only in some grave sites, perhaps indicating religious affiliation or symbolism, or denoting hereditary leaders of a particular lineage. The carvings may also represent totemic symbolism, representing either specialized religious practitioners or families, or symbolism associated with certain social groups or ancestral lineages.[20]

In addition, at these same cemeteries there are also a few examples of people who were buried vertically (in a standing position). It is thought that these may be the burial sites of some of the earliest known shamans in Europe. Shamans are specialized magical and religious practitioners who exist in cultures all over the world, and are referred to by specialized local terminology. They are renowned for performing ceremonies, healing and divination, and working on behalf of the souls and spiritual lives of their community.[21]

Shamanic cosmology includes three sacred realms: Upper World (Sky Realm), Middle World, and Lower or Underworld. In shamanic cultures there is an almost universal perception of a central tree, mountain or pillar that vertically connects these three sacred realms. The shamans of the Mesolithic may have been buried upright, in a position that symbolically represented the sacred axis or World Tree. It is also possible that the three symbols — elk, human and serpent — may be respectively associated with the three cosmic realms.[22]

The Symbolic Language of a Changing Earth

What about the presence of the Divine Feminine during this era of change? Did the pressures of the Mesolithic push Her into the background, or did some other kind of imagery take precedence? It is hard to know exactly what the varied symbolism of the Mesolithic has to say regarding the Feminine Divine, or any other aspect of existence for that matter. The powers and beliefs connected with the Divine Feminine are not likely to have disappeared completely, even if we do not know how they were perceived or represented. Feminine sacred energies are an integral part of the world, and of perceptions of the sacred, as they have been since earliest times and continue to be.

During the Mesolithic era, the land and the waters changed, the plants and the animals changed, and human society and customs also changed. The appearance of formal burial sites during this era is obviously noteworthy. For some reason it was now considered important to bury the dead in a community setting. This could have been a cultural or emotional response to the relative isolation of smaller social groups.

The artwork created during the Middle Stone Age was also different, and seems to have decreased in quantity and intensity. Perhaps the challenges of making a living now took up more time than they did in the past. There are fewer representations of animals, and far fewer representations of people, possibly reflecting the reduced numbers of animals in the landscape and smaller groups of people scattered across a changing terrain.

Much of the artwork produced during the Paleolithic era was representational in style. During the Mesolithic era, however, direct representations of human beings and animals decreased in number, while the use of abstract or symbolic designs and patterns increased tremendously. Practical objects and animal figurines were decorated with geometric designs created from lines, shapes or dots. There was a widespread tradition of creating symbol stones, round or oval pebbles painted with combinations of geometric symbols and shapes. Instead of depicting the world around them, people were beginning to communicate in a new and interesting way through the use of symbols.[23]

It is possible that the engraved objects and painted stones of the Mesolithic era represent the first evidence of writing in Europe. If we agree that a writing system depicts in symbols, letters or pictograms the communications, words or ideas of a given culture, then the symbolic communications we encounter in the artwork of the Mesolithic may well constitute a system of written communication. These forms and shapes must have been decipherable by other people in that culture or they would not be repeated with such frequency or in so many recognizable patterns.

Artwork is a physical expression of the cultural, emotional and religious beliefs and experiences of the individuals in a particular society. The artwork of the Paleolithic had a very definitive character, and its forms were manifestations of the beliefs and perceptions of the people of that time. It is small wonder, then, that the artwork of the Mesolithic changed so dramatically, reflecting the altered world which surrounded the ancestors and invoking a new series of personal, social and spiritual responses.

One of the most noticeable changes in the artwork of the Mesolithic era is the lack of human representations. The female imagery that had been created during the Paleolithic era disappeared completely, and these particular manifestations of the divine feminine do not, in fact, ever recur or return. It seems as though these early female forms were intended to convey something pertaining to the lives and experiences of that earlier time, something that changed so radically that those forms were no longer created.

Perhaps, then, it makes sense to try and ascertain what the female artwork of the Paleolithic period represented or signified by comparing the lives of these people with the hunter-gatherers of the Mesolithic era. What was different? What did the female figurines or engravings symbolize that was in existence during the Old Stone Age, but which did not exist — or did not exist in the same form — during the Middle Stone Age?

The Mesolithic era heralded the end of relatively easy large-scale hunting of plentiful migrating herds of animals. Now people lived in smaller groups and participated in much smaller organized hunts. Previously the environment had been much colder, but resources were plentiful and predictable. Game was now much harder to track and hunt, and people resorted to hunting and gathering many different types of plants and animals, which required new skills. The relative ease and plenty of the Paleolithic had resulted in an increase in population, new social institutions, the origins of artwork, and the organization of ritual and ceremonial sites that hosted large numbers of people. Much of that culture was now gone, as people struggled with environmental challenges, decreased animal populations, and a decrease in social contact and support.

Perhaps the widely varied female imagery of the Paleolithic celebrated the bounty of the earth and its living creatures, the relative stability of the environment, social co-operation and support, and the inspiration and leisure time to create artwork and large-scale ritual. The subsequent disappearance of female imagery from the archaeological record for many thousands of years may be a profound statement about the powers attributed to the Divine Feminine in the ancient past.

The forces of nature directly affect the daily lives and prosperity of human beings, as well as the need to develop new and improved methods of living in the world. Our relationship with the environment, and its impact upon us, directly affect our daily lives, as well as our cultural and spiritual beliefs and expression. Although many people in the modern era have lost touch with how profoundly nature affects our lives, in truth that relationship does constitute the reality of our existence. We live because nature provides for us. We exist because the world of nature deems it so. If She changes her mind, we cannot survive. The earth is our mother, provider, and protector, but only if we continue to engage in a reciprocal relationship of stewardship and respect.

This truth is well understood by indigenous cultures all around the planet, and would have undoubtedly been appreciated by our ancestors as well. Former *Tadodaho* (High Chief) of the Iroquois Conferederacy, Leon Shenandoah, speaks about the importance of this ancient concept:

> The instructions say that men and women are equal. To have harmony both of them should work together. The woman is like Mother Earth. She brings life. If you hurt her, you are going against the Creator and cutting life down. The Creator is not a he or she. It's just the Creator.... The Creator made everything equal, and gave Human Beings the responsibility to watch out for the rest of creation....
>
> Instead of being guardians, some people have learned how to destroy because of greed. The animals and the fish and the birds don't do that; they just go on with their duties. So we've got to help change people's minds so that they will protect the land, so that their seventh generation from now will have someplace to live.[24]

Ancient Climate Change

The rich artistic traditions of the Paleolithic lasted for more than 20,000 years, and the creative expressions of that time were practiced for more than 800 generations, representing the longest existing artistic tradition in the world. Then, as the environment began to change and temperatures increased, this long-standing tradition disappeared almost overnight, in prehistoric terms. Climate change resulted in the collapse of these traditional social institutions and created a widespread need to rewrite the rules of society, something we should bear in mind as global warming is once again upon us.

The warming temperatures that resulted in the landscape and climate changes of the Mesolithic era also created numerous natural disasters and ecological catastrophes. For example, during the Ice Age the Black Sea had been a fresh water lake. Around 6400 B.C.E., as Mesolithic global warming melted the ice on the Mediterranean Sea, a barrier of silt which had previously blocked a linkage between the great two bodies of water burst. The resulting cascade of salt water that roared into the Black Sea is estimated to have gushed forth with a force two hundred times more powerful than Niagara Falls. The outpouring continued for months and the sound of the water could have been heard 100 kilometers away. Over 100,000 square kilometers of woodland, marshland and fields became submerged, an area equivalent to the size of the country of Austria.[25]

Evidence of another environmental disaster resulting from rising temperatures was found in Inverness, Scotland. During the 1980s, archeologists began to excavate the remains of a 13th-century medieval town that once existed beneath the houses of modern Inverness. As excavations progressed, workers uncovered a layer of stony white sand containing more than 5,000 flint artifacts and pieces of bone. These were the remnants of a Mesolithic population that existed in the area around 7,000 B.C.E., making their living by hunting and harvesting the plants and animals of this coastal region.

Unknown to the inhabitants of ancient Inverness, a massive underwater landslide had taken place in the Arctic Ocean between Norway and Iceland, more than 1,000 kilometers away. An immense tsunami was created whose 8-meter high waves dumped 17,000 cubic kilometers of sediment across the eastern coast of Scotland. Great tracts of coastline were destroyed, and people and animals perished.[26]

The physical form of the world was changing, and in drastic ways. Adapting to physical changes in the environment is a real problem, one that can only be solved by working together. This is something our ancestors understood on a profound level, as do other native cultures, both past and present. The results of this understanding and co-operation are visible in the records of time, for the people both survived and flourished. Anthropologists Richard B. Lee and Richard Daly write about the importance of this ancient wisdom:

> The contemporary industrial world lives in highly structured societies at immensely higher densities and enjoys luxuries of technology that foragers could hardly imagine. Yet these same societies are sharply divided into haves and have-nots, and after only a few millenia of stewardship by agricultural and industrial civilizations, the environments of a large part of the planet lie in ruins....
>
> Hunter-gatherers may well be able to teach us something, not only about past ways of life but also about long term human futures. If technological humanity is to survive it may have to learn the keys of longevity from fellow humans whose way of life has been around a lot longer than industrial commercial "civilization."[27]

What is the message of the Mesolithic? Should we react to our changing world and to warming temperatures with fear and mistrust? The ancestors didn't, and there were far fewer of them. Burnum Burnum, an Australian Aboriginal writer and lecturer states that "Modern ecology can learn a great deal from people who managed and maintained their world so well for 50,000 years."[28] They worked together to create a new way of life, even choosing to be buried together in preparation for the life that exists beyond this one. They learned new skills and co-operated with each other, and adapted their way of life in practical and innovative ways that ensured their ongoing survival and success.

The ancestors did not have access to modern methods of communication, production or technology, and yet they survived for thousands of years under far more difficult circumstances than we now experience. They were adaptable, drawing upon their own resourcefulness as well as the time-tested wisdom of their forebears. Our new way of life has provided us with many conveniences, yet it has also made us almost completely reliant upon these technologies. In the developed world we have become disconnected from the natural cycles and wisdom of the earth, knowledge that our ancestors not only possessed but relied upon.

Siberian hunter and storyteller Vassili Shalugin of the Iukagir people speaks about the beauty of living in connection with the earth and its creatures, and the importance and value of these natural rhythms:

> We used to talk a lot to the fire in the olden days. Addressing our ancestors through the fire. Asking them what to do ... I watch no T.V. The taiga for me is T.V. When I sleep in the taiga I can see what is around me.... Everything is where it should be and like it should be, beautiful and right.... Every beast goes along its own path and everything follows the law.[29]

4

The Ancient Mothers of Europe

Everything that gives birth is female. When men begin to understand
the relationships of the universe that women have always known, the
world will begin to change for the better. Teachings come from the
women...

— Lorraine Canoe, Mohawk Elder[1]

At first it seemed as if the light that shone from the snow-capped mountains was playing a trick. The ridge almost appeared to be moving, rippling
in the glare of the sun like a column of ants. Surely it was only a mirage
created by the light that glinted off the icy peaks. The villagers who lived
between the mountains and the edge of the forest continued to watch the
ridge as they worked collecting firewood or drying fish in the sun. Whatever
this deception of light was, it persisted. As the afternoon progressed, the villagers noticed that the serpent-like image was moving down the side of the
mountain.

One young man, whose eyesight was keen, shaded his brow with his
hand and surveyed the horizon. The dark line on the mountaintop was actually
a group of people who were approaching the village. They must have crossed
over the mountain pass, perhaps in search of good hunting grounds. The villagers were stunned; they had not seen another group of people in several
years.

It was almost dark when the visitors arrived. The two groups stood
motionless, facing each other. Their leaders ritually greeted each other in a
traditional manner, and emissaries stepped forward to present gifts to the
other group. When the villagers motioned to the visitors to step towards the
fires and the food that was being cooked, the newcomers breathed an audible
sigh of relief.

After everyone had eaten and settled the children to sleep, the female
leader of the village and her two husbands stood up. Although it was unclear

if the groups would be able to communicate with each other, she followed tribal protocol and asked the visitors where they had come from. One of the elders of the incoming group drew images upon the ground showing how they had passed over the mountain range following the diminishing herds. One of the village elders shook his head and erased the images of mammoths and giant deer that the newcomer had drawn. These creatures were no more. He pointed towards the forest and showed them wooden carvings of the animals that were found within its shadowy precincts. Some of the animals and plants from the forest were familiar to them, while others were not.

As the evening progressed, the two groups began to notice a number of subtle similarities between their languages. Although many words were quite different, some mutually recognizable terms began to emerge. Once these words were recognized, communication picked up rapidly. One young woman from the visiting group was a storyteller, and her love of language enabled her to recognize the sounds and patterns she heard and reproduce them without hesitation. An elderly man from the village also possessed this skill, and over the next few days the two groups began to learn many things about each other.

First they discussed practical topics — how many people had once been in each group, where they had previously lived, and how they made their living. Once translation skills improved more esoteric concerns could be addressed. At first, short comic tales were shared around the fire. As the nights drew on, the tribal storytellers labored to share the traditional wisdom of their ancestors with those in the other band.

The groups began to notice a number of shared elements in their myths and belief systems. One of the most interesting parallels was a legend concerning their descent from a female elder. This ancestor existed so far back in time that she was now a shadowy figure somewhere between a clan mother and a guiding spirit. Tales existed in both tribes about her name and place of origin, as well as the exploits of her two twin daughters. Sacred stories were shared for several evenings, and a great bond of trust was established between the two groups.

One night, the leader of the visiting group stood up and addressed everyone gathered around the fire. They had left their homes in search of a better way of life and did not know what lay in store for them. On behalf of his people he expressed gratitude for the hospitality of the villagers. The leader of the villagers arose and made a gesture of acknowledgement. She told the other leader that she and her advisors had been discussing their situation. It had been decided that both groups should join forces and became one. Working together they could share resources, wisdom and experience.

The leader of the visiting group sat motionless. Several members of his council whispered quietly amongst themselves. At last he opened a deerskin pouch and carefully revealed a small oval-shaped object. It was a statue of a female figure made from rose-colored quartz. Remnants of red ochre still clung to the stone and the interior of the leather pouch. This was a representation of their ancestral mother, and it had been kept for untold years. Now that the two groups were forming an alliance and becoming one tribe, She belonged to all.

The female chief, and her husbands and advisors, stared in amazement. There was a lengthy pause, and the leader of the incoming group feared he had transgressed some social taboo. With her gaze fixed on the leader of the other tribe, the chief motioned to the most elderly couple in the village. They retrieved a small wooden box from their bundle and handed it to her. Without interrupting her gaze, she slowly opened the lid of the box. Removing some dried herbs, she lifted a small object from inside it. There in her hands was an almost identical figure of a woman, made from amber-colored calcite.

After an eternal moment of silence there was an explosion of sound. Some cried with joy, while others were overcome and began to weep. The elders of both groups recited prayers of thanksgiving. The two communities had lived for so long in isolation and uncertainty. Now their mutual beliefs and common goals would bring them together in a powerful partnership. The two figures were buried in the body of Mother Earth at the center of the village as an offering to the gods and ancestors of all who lived there. Having arisen from the earth in ancient times, the Mothers of the people now returned to the sacred place from which all received their gift of life.[2]

We are lucky, in a sense, to have seen the bones of the ancestors at all. Time, wind, weather and erosion have all played a role in returning the physical remains of our ancestors back into the soil from whence they came. Within that primal darkness, a spark of life mysteriously ignites the energy hidden in the seeds that lay dormant in the silence, awaiting their turn to awaken. Eventually the seedlings uncurl their limbs and raise their heads towards the sun and the rain, all the while experiencing a world of time and perception very different from our own.

Like our ancestors, members of the plant kingdom will eventually return to the soil. They too will live on through the physical incarnations of their offspring, to whom they have passed the wisdom and traditions of their particular way of life. Some will find themselves transmuted into the bodies of members of the animal kingdom. In this way they participate in the never-ending cycles of life, through their death as well as their rebirth. These cycles of transformation have constituted the mysteries of life for as long as any can remember.

We are all profoundly affected by the lives of those who come before us. Our parents and grandparents, as well as our more distant relatives, all play a part in contributing to who we are and what we may become. They bless us with life and culture, songs and stories, and many other powerful gifts of lineage and tradition. In addition to the cultural, spiritual, emotional and intellectual legacy we inherit from the accumulated wisdom and experience of our ancestors, we also receive material gifts. These include physical traits, as well as personality, intelligence, skill and creativity.

One of the most characteristic traits of our species is the universal impulse to understand our existence and learn as much about our world as possible. This intellectual curiosity eventually enabled us to uncover, analyze and even date the skeletal remains of our earliest ancestors. The evidence we have uncovered can tell us many things about the past and about our own history. The great antiquity of these remains, and the many thousands of years which have elapsed since their return to the earth, have resulted in certain gaps in our knowledge which are more prevalent the farther back in time we go.

Researchers and scientists all around the world have followed their intellectual and creative impulses and dedicated their lives to the pursuit of wisdom. The academic rigors they undergo enable them to deeply engage in the quest for understanding. As a result, the mysteries of the universe continue to reveal themselves in many unexpected ways.

The Code of Human Existence

Information about our physical past is recorded in our DNA, which is short for deoxyribonucleic acid. DNA has a very complicated structure and forms the main component of the chromosomes of living cells. Studying DNA is useful in understanding who our ancestors were, where they lived, and how populations groups are related. By mapping out DNA patterns from people all over the world, researchers have been able to find out a great deal about the ancestors of modern humans and trace our modern genetic heritage back in time to the very origin of our species. By examining gene diversity in test subjects from the United States, Europe, Asia, Australia and New Guinea, geneticists have ascertained that the origin of modern humans occurred in Africa about 200,000 years ago, a finding which corresponds with the evidence from archaeology.[3]

The methods used to ascertain this information focus on a particular portion of genetic material known as mitochondrial DNA (or mtDNA for short). Mitochondrial DNA is located outside the cell's nucleus and is responsible for processing food and oxygen to generate energy for the cell. Because it evolves much more rapidly than nuclear DNA, mtDNA can be used to study differences between population groups that are the result of genetic mutations that accumulate over time. The more differences in mitochondrial DNA that exist between two groups, the more time has elapsed since they both shared a common ancestor. For example, population groups in Africa have greater mtDNA diversity than other groups, which reflects a longer period of evolution. How remarkable that a minute physical feature of our cells can serve as a lens which enables us to look back through time to our very origins.[4]

As we may remember from biology class, the DNA that is located in the chromosomes of a cell's nucleus is inherited from a person's mother and father. However, people inherit mtDNA only from their mother. Mitochondrial DNA is always, and solely, a maternal inheritance. Although both men and women have mitochondria in their cells, only women pass this mitochondria on to their offspring (a transference which takes place through the female's eggs). Men can pass on nuclear DNA, but not mitochondrial DNA. By utilizing information encoded in mitochondrial DNA (which is passed down only through the female line), geneticists have been able to determine that all living people can trace their origin to a single, ancient female whom scientists refer to as "Mitochondrial Eve."[5]

One of the many interesting aspects of nuclear DNA is its ability to reproduce itself with great accuracy. Sometimes mistakes in gene copying do occur, and these are what we call genetic mutations. In regular (nuclear) DNA, the mutation rate is extremely low. However, the copying mechanisms of mitochondrial DNA are not as vigilant, and mtDNA mutations occur at about twenty times the rate of regular DNA. The mutation rate for mtDNA is about one mutation every ten thousand years, and that mutation rate can tell us when certain genetic changes took place, and when population groups became to display genetic differences. The more mutations that exist within a branch of the family tree the older it is.[6]

What can mitochondrial DNA tell us about human origins? And how can this information help us understand this ancient, matrilineal inheritance? If two people have very similar mtDNA, they are more closely related than two people who have different mtDNA. The two people with similar mtDNA share a common ancestor who lived more recently than the two people with dissimilar mtDNA. The second pair may still have a common ancestor, but that ancestor will have lived much more distantly in the past.[7]

As mtDNA research progressed, researchers refined their understanding of the human origin story. Ongoing results indicate that the common mitochondrial ancestor of all modern humans lived about 150,000 years ago. It also showed that by about 10,000 years ago, the descendants of the earliest hunter-gatherers had reached almost every part of the globe. Africa and Europe were well inhabited, and people had crossed through Siberia to North and South America, starting around 12,000 years ago. They made sea voyages to Australia and New Guinea, and only Iceland, Greenland, Madagascar and the Polynesian islands were uninhabited at this point in time. The players were ready and the stage was set for the unfolding of a matrilineal wonder.[8]

The Seven Mothers of Europe

One of the most important pioneers in the field of mitochondrial DNA research is Bryan Sykes, professor of genetics at the Institute of Molecular Medicine at Oxford University. An eminent researcher in the field of genetics, Dr. Sykes served as a primary consultant for a number of well-known projects, including the archaeological wonder known as the Ice Man. His pioneering work on mitochondrial DNA eventually resulted in a diagram that mapped out the branches of the entire mtDNA genetic family tree.[9]

In early phases of the work, Dr. Sykes and his research team focused their efforts on genetic patterns or "clusters" they saw in the mtDNA patterns associated with ancient Europe. They noticed seven European genetic clusters dating between 10,000 and 45,000 years ago. These mutation sequences indicated that at the root of each genetic branch or cluster was a "founder sequence," a special mtDNA genetic pattern that would have been carried by only one woman.[10]

In ordinary language, this means that everyone of European ancestry is descended from one of seven women. These seven women are known to us through their genetic code, a code which they passed on to their daughters, who passed it on to theirs, and so on. It also means that each of these women gave birth to daughters, for if they had produced only sons, their mitochondrial DNA would not have survived.[11]

We also know that each ancestress had at least two daughters. The reason for this is quite simple. There are millions of people in the world today who are the descendants of each of these ancestresses. But as we trace the lines of descent back in time, there will gradually be fewer and fewer people. Eventually, there would have been two people (two women, to be specific) whose ancestry converged upon a single woman who was the ancestress of that lineage.

By calling these women "ancestresses" we do not mean to imply that they were the first or oldest women of their eras or regions. Many other women existed before them, and many others co-existed with them as well. These, however, are the seven women who existed at the farthest point back in time in their specific lineage, who, through their daughters and their daughters' daughters, passed on their genetic legacy to become one of the seven ancestresses of Europe.[12]

The continuance of their genetic legacy is all the more unusual because the genetic inheritance of thousands of other women — both ancestors and peers of the seven mothers — did not endure. Their genetic imprint did not survive for one important reason: they had no daughters. So often we think about lines of historical descent in terms of male legacies. In many cultures, men bestow their name, title, authority, status and possessions to their sons. If a man has no sons, he either accedes his inheritance to nephews, grandsons or other potential male inheritors, or passes it on to his daughter(s), if the inheritance laws of his culture permit it.

The inheritance of mitochondrial DNA through the female line is a much less outwardly visible phenomenon, although it has co-existed with male-dominated forms of inheritance for eons. While patrilineal bequests of land, title and power have passed in and out of the hands of countless groups over the ages, the silent legacy of mitochondrial DNA has survived in a continuous and even more cohesive manner. This legacy is also physical in nature and is overall more enduring than physical wealth or titles.

The gifts of the Seven Mothers may seem less obvious to the eye than physical endowments of land or wealth or conceptual gifts of power and status. Yet who can say what effect it has had over the ages for women to participate in an unbroken chain of female-initiated ancestry that stretches so far back into the past? We cannot even imagine all the ways this legacy may have manifested in the experiences and attributes of women. Who knows what additional wonders scientists will be able to reveal in the future? The matrilineal lineage of mitochondrial DNA may have been a quiet and relatively invisible process, but its legacy has been steadfast in its survival, resolute in its endurance, and powerful in its ongoing creation of sacred sisterhoods, each one descending from an unbroken line of female elders.

Who were the Seven Ancestresses of Europe? Where and how did they live? While the precise dates and locations associated with these seven women is difficult to pinpoint with complete accuracy, analysis of the data associated with each group's mutation patterns suggests a general geographical distribution, both in the past and the present. Genetic information associated with mtDNA can show us where a particular lineage probably originated, and where its descendants live today (which may be two different places).

Instead of using numbers, Dr. Sykes and his team chose provisional names for each of the ancestresses. This made referring to each ancestral figure easier and more personal. Each name begins with a letter that had been used in the original classification of the genetic clusters. Using the best information and supporting evidence available, the seven mothers of Europe are believed to have lived in the following times and regions:

1. *Ursula*

The genetic group associated with the ancestress known as Ursula were the first modern humans to colonize Europe, perhaps as far back as 45,000 years ago. Their homeland is believed to have been located in Greece. Today about eleven percent of modern Europeans are the direct descendants of this ancestral figure. Although now found all over Europe, Ursula's group is particularly well represented in western Britain and Scandinavia.[13]

2. *Xenia*

Xenia and her people lived about 25,000 years ago, originally inhabiting parts of Russia south of the Don and Volga rivers. About six percent of today's European population trace their descent back to Xenia. There are three main branches of this genetic cluster now existing in Europe. One branch is located in eastern Europe, while the other two spread into central Europe and as far west as France and Britain.

The genetics shows that an identical twin existed in the early stages of this genetic cluster. The group associated with the twin and her descendants moved eastwards over time, traveling across the steppes of central Asia and Siberia and eventually migrating to the Americas. Therefore, about 1 percent of native Americans can also trace their ancestry back to Xenia, through this unusual circumstance.[14]

3. *Helena*

Helena's ancestral group lived about 20,000 years ago, at the height of the last Ice Age. Their homeland is believed to have been located in southern France, just north of the Pyrénées. This cluster is the largest and most genetically successful of all the mtDNA groups in Europe. The descendants of this ancestral mother exist in every part of Europe, and 47 percent of modern Europeans can trace their descent back to Helena.

The genetic sequence associated with Helena is the reference sequence to which all mitochondrial mutations are compared. It is not currently known whether the group's success is the result of chance, or whether some special

quality in Helena's mtDNA resulted in its widespread existence and conti-
nuity.[15]

4. Tara

The ancestress known as Tara lived during the last Ice Age, about 17,000
years ago, and inhabited the hills of Tuscany in northwest Italy. This was a
period of relative abundance, predictable animal migrations, and Paleolithic
cave paintings. About nine percent of modern Europeans are descendants of
Tara. They now live along the Mediterranean and the western edges of Europe,
but are also especially numerous in the west of Britain and Ireland.[16]

5. Velda

Velda lived about the same time as Tara, around 17,000 years ago. Her
homeland is believed to have been in the north of Spain, just south of the
Pyrénées mountains. Like Tara's group, Velda's cluster enjoyed the bounty of
the Paleolithic era in the southern parts of Europe. About four percent of
modern Europeans are descendants of Velda.[17]

6. Katrine

Unlike the first five ancestresses (who lived during the Paleolithic era),
Katrine's group traces its origin back to the Mesolithic era. Their homeland
was located in the north of Italy. Six percent of modern Europeans are descendants of Katrine. The group is still well represented near the Mediterranean,
and like the other genetic clusters, also has members all over Europe. Ten
thousand years after Katrine died, one of her descendants perished while
attempting to cross the Alps. He is known to archaeologists as the Iceman.[18]

At the end of the Ice Age, the descendants of the first six ancestresses of
Europe — Ursula, Xenia, Helena, Velda, Tara and Katrine — spread northwards
throughout Europe as the herds roamed into land reclaimed from the glacial
ice before the great forests began to spread across the terrain. While most
Europeans trace their ancestry to these early population groups, there is also
a seventh ancestral figure, known as Jasmine.

7. Jasmine

Jasmine flourished some time after the other ancestresses, in an era known
as the Neolithic (which we will explore in the following chapter). This is the

period when farming was introduced to Europe. Jasmine is believed to have lived in Anatolia, near the Euphrates River. Slightly fewer than 17 percent of modern Europeans are descended from Jasmine.

Unlike the other genetic groups, Jasmine's cluster is not evenly distributed throughout Europe. One branch of the group followed the coastline of the Mediterranean into Spain and Portugal, from where members traveled into the west of Britain. This group is especially common in Cornwall, Wales and western Scotland.

The other branch seems to have followed a route through central Europe that is identical to the one followed by the first farmers who cultivated the river valleys and plains of northern Europe. Both branches of Jasmine's clan still live very close to the routes their farming ancestors followed as they traveled from the Near East into Europe.[19]

Adam and Eve in Consensus

The physical remains of the earliest modern humans, and the genetic distribution pattern of modern humans, point to a common origin for modern humans in Africa around 150,000 years ago (give or take several millennia). It is remarkable that two different branches of science — archaeology and genetics — both arrived at such similar outcomes while traveling down different pathways of inquiry.

The research pursued by Dr. Sykes and his team eventually produced a genetic family tree that embraces all known population groups in the world. At the root of that family tree was "Mitochondrial Eve," a woman who can be described as the earliest mtDNA ancestress of all people, past and present. This "Eve" was not the first woman to inhabit the planet, though. Like the ancestresses of Europe, she was the most ancient woman to have had two daughters, who both had daughters, and so forth, through whom she passed her genetic code.[20]

What about the male contribution to things? Logically, any "Eve," whether physical or genetic in nature, requires access to some sort of "Adam" in order to reproduce and set things in motion. Researchers have investigated male genetic patterning to see if it supports the information obtained from mitochondrial DNA. By attempting to identify portions of the Y chromosome (the male sex chromosome), researchers hoped to uncover clues about when and where the founding father of modern humans may have lived.

Once again, genetic mutations have provided a number of important clues about our origins. Much of the material associated with the Y chromosome never recombines with the X chromosome (which is found in both males and females). Therefore, it continues in a relatively unaltered fashion, except for occasional instances of genetic mutation. Much like the mutation rates connected with mtDNA, mutation patterns associated with the Y chromosome can also provide information about the human origin story. Although research results pertaining to dating have varied (anywhere from 40,000 to 270,000 years ago, in some cases), some studies do seem to correlate well with the theorized dates associated with female origins gathered through mtDNA research.[21]

One area of common ground shared by Y chromosome research as well as mitochondrial DNA research has to do with events that took place at the end of the Mesolithic era and the beginning of the Neolithic. Mitochondrial DNA research shows that genetic evidence associated with Jasmine and her descendants constituted a sizeable but not overwhelming percentage of genetic input. This shows that while some early farmers traveled into Europe from the Near East, the technology associated with farming must have also spread through trade and word of mouth. This type of process is called acculturation, and it is known to have taken place at other points of history as well.[22]

Overall, the vast majority of native Europeans trace their roots to the Paleolithic and Mesolithic hunter-gatherer populations of ancient Europe. Genetic research into humans origins is still a lively area of research, one that will undoubtedly continue to produce illuminating results. As work on the human genome project continues, our growing body of knowledge is likely to result in more scientific convergences as well as deeper human understanding of our common origins and connections.

Who are the genetic "mother" and "father" of modern humans? Despite Old Testament allegory, we are not all descended from a co-existing pair of individuals. Mitochondrial Eve is not the first woman, but the carrier of an ancestral mtDNA molecule that gave rise to all modern human mtDNA. Likewise, Genetic "Adam" does not refer to the first man, but to the earliest male figure who provided genetic material which was passed on to the population groups of the world.[23]

Many other women and men would have been alive at the same time as our genetic foremother and forefather. While we cannot claim to descend directly from a cohabiting primordial couple, we can say that all people developed from a founding group of people who lived in Africa about 200,000 years ago. According to the genetic research, after flourishing in Africa for many millennia, modern humans journeyed from the northeast corner of Africa into the Middle East. Then, around 100,000 years ago (a date that corresponds well with archaeological evidence), some population groups moved westward into Europe while others spread east into Asia and the rest of the world. This scenario is one that many people agree upon, including historians, archaeologists, geneticists and anthropologists. And that is quite a story in and of itself.[24]

The Gifts of the Primordial Tree

It is remarkable to reflect on the idea that after a certain point in time, somewhere between 150,000 and 200,000 years ago, all people in the world — past, present and future — are the descendants of one woman and one man. Mitochondrial Eve and Primordial Adam probably never met each other, and our existence is not the product of their union. Nevertheless, as a result of their pairings with others, and the subsequent twistings and turnings of the human family tree, at some stage these two people unknowingly stepped into their role as progenitors of all who were to follow.

The family trees of the children of these two primordial ancestors developed according to unpredictable patterns of descent, much like the growth of a real tree. Some of the branches grew for many years and then grew no more, while others continued on, pivoting and diverging in their pathways throughout the ages.[25] A tree does not grow upwards from a seed in a single direction, but branches out in many directions. The branches change both form and course, following different pathways to make best use of resources provided by the environment, displaying their innate intuition and intelligence.

In the female line of descent, the ability to produce daughters rather than sons was the most important factor contributing to these changes, whether or not the women involved were aware of their genetic contribution. While it is unlikely that people would have had any sense of their cellular contribution to these ancestral patterns, one has to wonder about the results of our intimate connection with these ancient lineages.

The similarities and variations that exist within our genes are an ancient code that geneticists are working hard to read and decipher. By mapping out the patterns that exist within this biological code, they are able to understand more and more about the extraordinary ways in which we have chosen, at a cellular level, to grow and transform. These patterns are reminiscent of the geometric expansion of ice crystals or the profusion of buds that emerge from tree branches, a testimony to the natural processes that govern and guide us all.

Hidden within the recesses of our genes is a veritable cellular archive of the past, a tangible way to connect with the physical lives, experiences and wisdom of our ancestors. This knowledge is part of many indigenous wisdom traditions, and is now supported by scientific methodologies. Australian anthropologist T.G.H. Strehlow speaks about a traditional Aboriginal belief of the northern Aranda people that states: "Every cell of the original ancestor is a living human being."[26]

What have we inherited from the Seven Mothers of Europe, as well as from the Fathers of our lines? In different places, and in different times, these ancestral figures encoded the blessings and challenges of their lives into their genetic makeup, passing their wisdom and experience on to us in a very physical way. In addition to outwardly visible family resemblances, we have inherited other subtle and more powerful gifts as well. We may be skilled at weaving or horseback riding, growing crops or composing poetry, running great distances or deciphering the patterns of the natural world. How far back do our gifts of song, dance and artwork originate? Who is to say what other unseen but nonetheless tangible gifts the seven ancestresses have given us?

There is one thing we do know. All of us are connected to a great pool of ancestral knowledge that encompasses all of the physical, intellectual, creative, intuitive and spiritual wisdom and skill that our ancestors developed and passed on to us. Perhaps this is the origin of what Carl Jung called the 'collective unconscious,' an unseen network of energy, perception, potential and archetypal imagery to which every person has access, both past and present.[27]

Vickie Downey, a Tewa elder from Tesuque Pueblo in the southwestern United States, talks about this innate and inherited wisdom:

> In the beginning there were the Instructions. We were to have compassion for one another, to live and work together, to depend on each other for support. We were told we were all related and interconnected with each other....
> So that was the beginning. The Instructions during that time were to love and respect one another even with all the differences, different cultures, different languages. We were told we were all from the same source ... from the same mother, same parents.[28]

In many traditional cultures, women are charged with preserving and transmitting sacred knowledge from one generation to the next, as well as with overseeing the respectful and harmonious balance of society. Traditional African healer Bernadette Rebienot speaks about the importance of this traditional knowledge: "Our culture acknowledges that the gentle power, the gentle strength, the conserver of our beliefs is woman. Therefore, nothing in our country is done without consulting the women. Our wise people, our elders are like libraries. We consult them whenever we have to make big decisions."[29]

Amongst the Six Nations of the Haudenosaunee (Iroquois), clan mothers are chosen for each traditional clan within the tribe. Janice Sundown Hallett of the Seneca describes the religious roles of the women and the clan mothers:

The clan mother selects the chief for that clan. The chiefs do most of the decision making, with the consent of the clan... The ultimate decision with a clan comes from the clan mother. Whatever the clan mother decides, goes. The role that women play in the Longhouse is they carry through with the traditions and ceremonies. The faithkeepers are like the overseers to make sure it does get done. We make sure it is passed on to the little ones.[30]

The concept of ancestral memory is a powerful one, and something for which many perceive a great yearning in modern Western culture. Carl Jung, in "The Structure and Dynamics of the Psyche," speaks about this ancestral inheritance:

Man's unconscious ... contains all the patterns of life and behavior inherited from his ancestors, so that every human child is possessed of a ready-made system of adapted psychic functioning prior to all consciousness.... If it were possible to personify the unconscious ... it would be exalted above all temporal change.... It would be a dreamer of age-old dreams ... and it would possess a living sense of the rhythm of growth, flowering and decay.[31]

Looking back at the history of our ancestors we can sense some of the richness and complexity of their lives. History books frequently describe prehistoric people (as well as modern primal or traditional cultures) as "primitive" beings living in fear and ignorance and struggling to survive. The ancestors' lives were clearly much more sophisticated than this overly simplistic picture.

Their ingenuity and skill not only facilitated and informed their own lives but have enriched our lives as well. Inside this ancient patterning of tradition and innovation, we may be able to discern an encoded inheritance of seven blessings that the ancient Mothers of Europe have passed down to us: courage, skill, strength, adaptability, creativity, intelligence and intuition. These are things they inherited from their ancestors, which for thousands and thousands of years enabled them not only to survive, but to flourish.

Over the last few decades, a few academic theories about possible matriarchal cultures in the past have given rise to a torrent of popular books about widespread "goddess cultures" and their alleged extermination at the hands of patriarchal societies. As we can already see, the past is infinitely more complicated than that. Genuine examples of social matriarchy (and to a lesser degree, instances of matrilineal succession) are nigh to invisible in any sort of verifiable historical sense.[32] However, the genetic, cultural and spiritual lineage of the Seven Ancestresses of Europe (and countless other ancestresses around the world) may be the best example we have of a true matrilineal inheritance. This inheritance has existed since earliest times and continues in an unbroken line — and on an ever-changing path of transformation — right up to the present day.

5

The Sickle and the Hearth

In our original Instructions, we were told that nobody owned the land
except the Creator.... But Europeans decided the land they lived on
was theirs. That was funny to our people because we knew that
nobody owned the land. Then the Europeans decided that all of Great
Turtle Island was theirs to own. That wasn't funny to us anymore.
— Chief Leon Shenandoah, Former Tadodaho
Chief of the Iroquois Confederacy[1]

It was the time of year when the daystar's power reached far into the evening, illuminating the fields of barley and millet that spread across the landscape. The dirt lanes that wound between the houses were uncharacteristically
quiet. There was a hushed sense of anticipation as each family in the village
prepared for the evening's festivities. This was the Summer Solstice, the longest
day and shortest night of the year. Inside the modest dwellings, people washed
their hands and feet before putting on special linen garments made for the
occasion. Some wore copper pendants shaped like double-edged axes or the
sinuous body of a woman, while others adorned their heads with small wreaths
of yellow grain and crimson poppies.

As the sun began to set, the villagers poured out of their homes and began
to congregate on the streets, and the sound of bone flutes emerged from various
points in the crowd. The procession grew larger and began to move in a synchro-
nous motion to the beat of goat-skin drums and the clatter of ornaments made
from trimmed animal hooves many of the women wore around their ankles.

The high-spirited crowd approached the center of the village where the
lanes became wider and were intermittently paved with large, flat stones. As
they approached the central lodge, a closely tiled pathway of red brick indicated that they had entered sacred communal ground. Voices and instruments
were hushed, and the villagers gathered in quiet expectation in front of the
newly constructed shrine.

This was by far the largest building in the settlement, and its well-crafted walls and newly thatched roof stood out among the small, weathered houses of the village. The walls of the shrine were painted red and white, using pigments from the soil. The front of its imposing doorway was elaborately carved with spiral and triangular symbols. Only the elders of the village were able to decipher the origin and meaning of all the symbolism.

The sun began to sink closer to the horizon. At last they heard the sound of a clay drum echoing from inside the building, and all bowed their wreathed heads in silence. The doors of the building slowly opened and a man and a woman emerged from within, wearing gold neck rings and copper armbands that shone in the waning sun. Both held a polished stone axe in their right hand and a female figurine made of alabaster in their left.

The couple was followed by a group of young initiates who had been selected from the community for their outstanding character and special abilities. They stood proudly behind the priest and priestess carrying armloads of summer blossoms, pottery vessels full of grain, and copper bowls filled with water. When their speeches were finished, the drums rang out and they turned and walked back through the temple doors.

One of the initiates played a melody on a large ceramic flute as her companions motioned to the villagers to process into the building. The front chamber of the temple was a great open space with benches built against the walls where older people and women with infants could sit. Symbolic markings had been painted around the upper edge of the walls. The initiates distributed offerings of grain or flowers to the members of the waiting crowd.

A rounded archway led from the front chamber into the main area of the shrine and its edges were painted with double-edged axes, female forms and other symbols. One by one, the community was ushered through the archway and into the temple. The great chamber was a masterpiece of design and artistry, elaborately decorated with curved and angular patterns painted in cream and red. The contrast between the rich ornamentation in this room and the simple artwork that decorated the small family shrines was astounding; the people had never seen anything like it before.

In the back of the hall was a large, raised altar made of clay. On top of the altar were ceramic statues representing the spiritual guardians, ancestors, and deities of the community. In the center of the altar stood an imposing female figure whose arms were raised towards the skies. Her upper body was ornamented with spirals and her lower body was decorated with a striped pattern. Next to her was a robust, seated male figure, calm and beneficent. The front of his body was covered with symbolic markings and he carried a large sickle over his right shoulder.

Other female figurines had been carefully placed on either side of the altarpiece. On the left was a tall, slender female figurine dressed in a long robe and wearing a mask shaped like the head of a bird. Nearby was a pottery vessel decorated with the highly ornamented form of a male figure, his eyes closed in contemplation. Other figurines of female forms made from smooth white stone were set up around the altar.

The villagers were ushered toward the central platform. The front of the altar was decorated with beautiful red and cream spirals. Two cream-colored pillars stood in front of the altar painted with red patterns that curved and intertwined from floor to ceiling. As each member of the community stepped between the pillars and approached the altar, it was as though they had entered another realm of existence. There they stood in prayer, making offerings of grain and summer flowers and paying respect to the ancestral protectors and deities of their community.

It was dark outside by the time everyone had passed through the main hall. Many of the villagers re-assembled in the courtyard. The muted sound of flutes and drums once more rang out, but in a more somber and reverent mood. The procession moved quietly through the streets until they reached the fields of grain, whose gently waving stalks swayed in the moonlight. Libations of goat's milk with herbs, and sheep's milk with honey, were poured along the edges of the fields.

Some of the villagers remained in the fields throughout the night, dancing or praying under the summer stars. Others returned to their homes to feed their children and ensure that their hearth fires and animals were safe. Still others spent the night of solstice in quiet devotion, sitting in prayer inside the shrine where the light of clay lamps illuminated the sacred images painted on the walls. Farmers and weavers, mothers and smiths, children and grand-parents, had all come together to sit in communion with their gods and ances-tors at the time of the sun's greatest power. They gave thanks for their crops and herds, for the bounty of the earth and for each other, and asked for guid-ance and protection in this time of abundance and change.[2]

After the challenges of the Mesolithic came an era which historians refer to as the Neolithic ("New Stone Age"), when farming was first introduced into Europe. The technology associated with agriculture and domesticated animals spread slowly throughout Europe in a gradual process over about three thousand years. For this reason, the date when the Neolithic era begins is different in various parts of Europe.

Like other chapters of prehistory, the story of the Neolithic period is varied and complex. Starting around 7,000 B.C.E., and continuing until about 4,000 B.C.E., the knowledge associated with this new way of life traveled from south-east to north-west, spreading across the entire continent of Europe and eventually reaching Britain, Ireland and Scandinavia. However, the word "Neolithic" does not necessarily refer to the appearance of new population groups but to communities of people who adopted the practices of farming and herding as their primary mode of economic survival.[3]

Around 7,000 B.C.E., much of Europe was covered with forests and was inhabited by Mesolithic groups who hunted and fished, and gathered plant resources to support themselves, using a very intimate and sophisticated knowledge of the land. At this time farming societies had already become established in the Near East. Through contact with small groups of incoming farmers, trade networks and word of mouth, the skills and technologies associated with farming and raising domesticated animals were introduced into Mesolithic Europe from the Near East.[4]

Not all communities were interested in farming, however, and Neolithic and Mesolithic communities continued to live side by side for quite some time. Some foraging groups supplemented their hunter-gatherer lifestyle with small-scale farming, and initially this may not have altered their lifestyles a great deal. However, by about 5500 B.C.E., the spread of agriculture is evident in Central and Western Europe. These new technologies resulted in the creation of distinctive networks of small villages that survived for a very long period of time.[5]

The first farmers of Europe grew a variety of crops and raised several kinds of domesticated animals. Wheat, barley, oats, spelt, millet and rye were cultivated, and people grew or gathered legumes (peas, beans and lentils) as well as flax and hemp seeds that provided oil, as well as fiber for clothing and many other uses. Many types of fruits and nuts were also grown or gathered: hazelnuts, acorns, walnuts, beechnuts, crab apples, cherries, plums, pears, rosehips, haws, sloes, raspberries, blueberries and strawberries. Wild plants were also gathered, making use of leaves, buds, stems and roots. Many of these edible plants are now considered "weeds," including wild mustard, field cabbage, wild carrot, Scotch thistle, water pepper, common sorrel, curled dock, ribwort plantain, common chickweed, tufted vetch and field pansy.[6]

Early farmers used the cereal grains they grew to make porridge or bread. These early forms of bread could be light and porous, or harder, more compact loaves or biscuits, depending on the amount of sun and rain received in the area. Grains were also used to feed the herds of domesticated animals. Eventually people discovered that sprouted grains could be used to make alcoholic beverages as well.[7]

Newly domesticated sheep, goats, cattle and pigs provided meat, milk and hides. Domesticated oxen were used to pull ploughs and carts, a role later filled by the horse. Domesticated dogs were kept, and people continued to hunt large game like red deer. They trapped fish, birds and small game animals, and gathered shellfish of many kinds.[8]

The kinds of domesticated plants and animals that were raised in Neolithic Europe, as well as the types of wild animals and plants that were utilized, varied a great in different areas and eras. As a result, archaeologists are not entirely sure whether plant cultivation or animal husbandry was more important as a source of food. In many cases, people may have tried to rely on as many different types of resources as possible (both Mesolithic and Neolithic) in order to serve as a buffer against crop failure. This means that farming may initially have been just an adjunct to hunting and gathering, rather than constituting a completely new lifestyle. Over time, however, the practice of farming gained ascendancy and created a new way of life that changed our history forever.[9]

From Forest to Field

During the Neolithic era, as people prepared the land for planting of crops, they cleared enormous amounts of woodland and natural vegetation. This resulted in major (and totally unprecedented) man-made changes in the natural environment. As traditional farming plots were utilized season after season, the soil became depleted and soil erosion became an enormous problem. In addition, grazing animals stripped away centuries worth of ground-covering plants that had previously maintained water levels and protected the nutrients in the soil from the effects of sun and wind. From this point onwards, the integrity of the landscape would never be the same.[10]

In previous eras, the activities of human beings had little or no effect on the land or its features. During the Neolithic era, however, humans had a monumental effect on the land. This was the first time in European history that human beings displayed the potential for dominance over — rather than a harmonious co-existence with — the world of nature. This was especially true where farming practices were intensive and the amount of acreage involved was large.

This is not to say that growing food necessarily involves the destruction of the environment. The combination of hunting and gathering with small-scale farming practices may not have had an adverse affect on the landscape. Many traditional cultures in the modern era and recent past have lived in a respectful manner in the environment while practicing a combination of low-level farming along with hunting and gathering.

However, the dramatic conversion from low-impact subsistence farming to widespread land clearing and utilization by a rapidly growing Neolithic population had a far greater effect on the land — and the development of culture and society — than most people realize. As farming became more widespread and increased in intensity, the growing need to clear more land (and subsequent soil depletion) had a profound impact on the environment.

This is a lesson we need to re-learn in our modern age. Nowadays, huge agricultural corporations produce food for mainstream supermarkets without concern for the environment or long-range land use. They utilize unhealthy and non-sustainable methods of production and ignore impacts upon human health, spraying "conventional" food with toxic (and in many cases, carcinogenic) pesticides. Agribusiness pollutes the earth and the water through widespread application of toxic chemicals. Conventional meat and poultry are often raised in an inhumane fashion and their meat frequently contains large amounts of steroids and antibiotics.

Other large organizations are involved in the destruction of the ancient rainforest that is being cut down to make room for the herding of beef cattle and non-traditional coffee bean production. Innumerable species of sentient, living beings are being displaced and destroyed as a result of this catastrophe. In addition, large numbers of potentially life-saving medicinal plants are being lost before biologists can learn about their health-promoting properties from the indigenous people who live in the rainforest (and who are themselves being displaced and adversely affected). The effects of this deforestation are so profound that they can be seen from outer space. These are lessons we must re-learn and teach our children, even if our Neolithic ancestors were not able to foresee the consequences of their new way of life.

Eventually, as farming became the primary economic activity in Europe, people increasingly lost touch with the wisdom of their hunter-gatherer ancestors. This practical knowledge of the local environment, including the identification of edible and medicinal plants and the behavior of birds and animals, became less and less of a focus in society. This resulted in a profound loss of traditional knowledge as well as the decreased ability to be self-reliant in the natural world.[11]

In modern society, our disconnection from the natural world and the loss of our ancestral wisdom are profound. Most people are hard pressed to identify the living things in their local environment. Hunter-gatherers can walk through the landscape and recite from memory the names, attributes and behavior of animals, birds, fish and insects, as well as the edible and medicinal properties of trees and plants. They live in a state of appreciation for the bounties of the earth, and have at their disposal the natural equivalent of supermarket, pharmacy and convenience store.[12] We, on the other hand, can scarcely envision life without cell phones, computers, video games, portable music devices, and a host of other luxury items without whose presence we seem to have survived perfectly well up until a few years ago.

There were benefits to the hunter-gatherer lifestyle. Although hunter-gatherer societies are often described as having "subsistence economies," the fact is that people in modern foraging societies enjoy a relatively large amount of leisure time. Members of society hunt and gather for the benefit of all members of the tribe and resources are commonly shared, leaving time for others to rest, create, pray and foster relationships.[13]

Hunter-gatherers tend towards peaceful societies and relationships, are respectful of nature and other living beings, and have a deep relationship with the natural world. They are independent rather than coercive, practice sharing and co-operation, and value sharing, honor and truthfulness. They are often quite egalitarian, honoring all members of the tribe, male and female, with little hierarchy. In terms of religion they tend towards animism (the belief that spirit is inherent in all things), honoring both female and male deities in a polytheistic system that honors gods, spirits and ancestors. They live in a numinous world where there is no boundary between culture and nature, or between (what we would consider) the mundane and the sacred.[14]

Many modern hunter-gatherer societies have consciously chosen not to adopt the ways of western culture. They experience pride in their self-reliance and report a deep sense of happiness and well-being. Their traditional ways of living serve them well, as they served their ancestors for thousands of years.[15] Anthropologist Richard Lee describes hunting and gathering as a way of life that was — until the advent of agriculture 10,000 years ago — the universal mode of human existence around the world, and the most successful and persistent adaptation human beings have achieved to date.[16]

The success and integrity of the hunter-gatherer way of life may have been an important consideration in Mesolithic groups when faced with the prospect of setting aside a way of life that had sustained their ancestors for thousands of years. These time-honored traditions and their benefits had long formed part of a sustainable and interconnected way of being in the world.

We Are Forever Changed

The image of a peaceful farming village is one many people cherish. Peaceful farming communities do exist all around the world, as they have for many eras. However, for several decades it has been popularly theorized that the inhabitants of Neolithic Europe were peaceful, earth-honoring people who existed in complete harmony with their environment, were matriarchal in terms of social organization, and were custodians of an ancient culture focused on the Divine Feminine. Is this theory actually true?

The only part of the Neolithic period that could have been both peaceful and earth honoring was the early portion, and this depended on whether people engaged in small or large-scale farming and how many people lived nearby. We have no way of knowing if any of these cultures were patriarchal, matriarchal, or any other type, because of the lack of written records. It is also difficult to know with any certainty what their religious beliefs were, for the same reason.[17]

What we are able to understand is that as farming practices increased, the competition for land — and for authority over that land — also increased. This led to social tensions, and eventually to internal violence. By the fifth millennium B.C.E. purposely constructed enclosures surrounded by banks and ditches were being built in Neolithic Europe. Some of these enclosures may have been used for controlling herds of animals or for ritual purposes. Some, however, were clearly built for defense.[18]

Houses were built closer together and surrounded by wooden fences or palisades, some of which contained watchtowers. It has sometimes been argued that these structures were used to keep out wild animals. No such enclosures were built during previous eras, nor are they used in other traditional cultures for such a purpose. The only animals against whom all societies tend to build defensive structures are human beings.

There is other indisputable evidence of violence and warfare during this period as well. Hundreds of thousands of arrowheads have been discovered at Neolithic settlement sites, rather than in woodland settings where one might expect their presence if they were used for hunting. In many cases, people were the clear and obvious target of these projectiles. Arrowheads were found embedded in numerous skeletons, and evidence for death by axe blows is also well attested.[19] Wars are frequently fought over land and resources, and Neolithic people were apparently not immune to this human tendency.

However, in spite of growing social tensions, the threat of violence, and the unforeseen ecological effects of the new farming practices, the Neolithic era was also a period of immense growth and development. Textiles were first woven in Europe during this era, although it would be some time before garments made of cloth replaced hide and skin garments that had been worn for so long, especially in outer parts of the Continent.[20]

Although pottery was first created during the Mesolithic era, this important craft grew tremendously and spread throughout Europe during the Neolithic period. Early pottery wares were fairly simple in terms of design and ornamentation, but soon evolved to include a variety of sophisticated shapes and designs. Some of the symbolism seen on Neolithic pottery and ceramic wares seems to have been associated with specific population groups or particular regions, perhaps indicating pride in group identity.[21]

People continued to mine stone, including flint and obsidian, and produced fine tools and stone axes that were traded with other groups. Trading networks were in existence, fostering barter and communication between communities and regions. Trade goods included raw materials like flint, stone tools and axes, fine pottery wares, and seashells used for ornaments.[22]

One of the most remarkable developments of the Neolithic period was the introduction of metalworking. Copper was the first ore to be mined and smelted in ancient Europe, followed by gold.[23] The ability to create entirely new objects from the stones of the earth was undoubtedly perceived as a truly remarkable skill. The sheen of copper and gold must have seemed as though it reflected the luminous quality of fire, or of the sun itself.

The powerful symbolism attributed to metal objects is attested by the widespread production of highly specialized objects from these materials, including those associated with ceremony and ornamentation. Fine axes of jadeite and other prized or unusual stone were also produced during the Neolithic era. Many of these objects were non-practical in nature, and must have been used for ceremonial purposes or social display. Jewelry and ritual ornaments, symbolic pottery wares, metal and stone tools, ornate weapons and ceremonial paraphernalia continued to be produced throughout the Neolithic.[24] This demonstrates a finely developed sense of intentional and spiritual symbolism in the creation of objects whose very forms constituted a symbolic language unto itself.

The Ritual Landscape

Houses and villages continued to develop during the Neolithic, and communal buildings were constructed for the benefit of all members of the community.[25] In many traditional societies, the planning of dwelling sites and ritual sites is considered extremely important and can be a ritualized activity involving the entire community. In many cases, the family home is created to reflect beliefs and perceptions about the organization of the cosmos. At some settlement sites, special buildings were constructed which are believed to have served as lodges, meeting houses, temples or shrines. These too would have reflected and incorporated cosmological symbolism.[26]

The changing world of the Neolithic resulted in a number of other developments and innovations in the material culture of the people of ancient

Europe. The introduction of copper and gold, as well as the increasing sophistication of pottery wares, affected the daily lives of people as well as rituals for the dead. Mesolithic groups had displayed a wide variety in terms of burial practices, but the people of the Neolithic were not to be outdone. Almost every type of conceivable burial practice is found in Neolithic Europe, and attests to the many types of belief systems that must have been present at this time.

Regional burial patterns are found in many areas. In southeastern Europe, burials were sometimes made inside of settlements, probably near the family home. External cemeteries also existed, and burials at these larger sites included people who had lived in smaller settlements in the nearby region. Some burials were quite formal. In many cases graves were set out in rows and contained fairly large quantities of grave goods.[27]

The variety of burial practices, as well as the varied distribution of grave goods, indicates a great deal of diversity in terms of beliefs and perceptions associated with status. In some cases, there is very little difference between the burials of men and women, or between the young and the old. In other cases, however, certain people seem to have been distinguished due to age, gender, skill, experience or social status, and were given special or elaborate burials. This is the first time that really lavish grave goods are seen in Europe. In spite of this, the burial practices of the Neolithic do not seem to suggest any sort of clearly definable or widespread distinction based primarily upon gender or any other social factor.[28]

In addition to new burial practices, there were other developments related to communal religious practices. During the early stages of the Neolithic, the family home appears to have been the focus of religious activity. Over time, however, that focus seems to have shifted towards groupings of houses, and eventually to larger buildings (lodges, meetinghouses, temples or shrines that served the community as a whole).

The early ceremonial sites of the Neolithic contained many remarkable objects, including flint blades, stone tools, jadeite axes, gold ornaments, ritual pottery, copper beads and daggers, and ceremonial drinking vessels. These reflect new developments that took place during this era, especially those associated with ceremony and ritual display. These widely found objects of power and prestige may have been associated with an increasing transference of religious activity from the home to community (although some ritual must still have taken place in family dwellings).[29] The cultural and religious developments of the Neolithic period exhibit an increasing concern with land, territory and the use of sacred space. And it is within this setting that the Divine Feminine once more reappears.

The Re-Emergence of the Divine Feminine

Many unusual artifacts have been found at a number of distinctive Neolithic settlements in southeastern Europe. Some of the most interesting objects are clay figurines depicting animals, domestic objects and human beings, both male and female. In this part of continental Europe, numerous female figurines were created during the Neolithic era in a wide variety of

Marble figurine of female figure, northeast Bulgaria, mid–5th mil. B.C.E. Artist: Donna Martinez.

shapes and forms. Some were anthropomorphic in design — part female and part bird or animal. Others were highly stylized and elaborately decorated representations of female forms. Most of the figures are fairly small and portray women sitting, standing, squatting, or reclining.[30]

For some reason, after an enormous lapse of more than 20,000 years, people in ancient Europe once again began creating female figurines. These objects were different from those created during the Paleolithic era, although a few parallels may be seen. Like the female images created in the past, facial features are usually absent or very simplistically rendered. In some cases (but not all), the lower limbs and sexual parts are exaggerated. As in the Paleolithic, heavier female forms are seen, but many of the images depict more slender forms. Earlier figurines were often crafted from stone or ivory, a fairly time-consuming activity. Neolithic figurines, however, were often made from clay, which required less time and effort. Their enormous variety of shapes and forms attest to the new social and spiritual impulses that led to the creation of these figurines.[31]

The production of female figurines during two prehistoric eras has often tempted writers to conclude that they represent an ongoing belief system. However, the new objects were only produced in very specific region of Neolithic Europe, and during a very specific window of time (between 4500 and 3200 B.C.E.). They also differed in many ways from those that had been produced in the past. These changes must certainly reflect the changes that had taken place in the lives and beliefs of the people who created them.

We also cannot ignore the fact that no female figurines were created for an enormous period of time (over 20,000 years). This discontinuity must say something about the challenges associated with the time period that fell between these two disparate eras. The symbolism and practices associated with the figurines must have changed tremendously once they re-appeared. However, the very fact that female figurines were once again being created is clearly of great significance.

We have already explored the many ways the female figures of the Paleothic era were created and utilized. What do we know about the female imagery of the Neolithic era? In archaeological excavations, the place where an object is found can often tell us a great deal about how it was used and what it may signify. The female figurines of south eastern Europe were often found inside or next to domestic dwellings, and are likely associated with the members or identity of the household.[32] In many traditional societies, the house is considered a sacred enclosure; there is no perceived boundary between the mundane and the sacred. Over time, as specialized ritual buildings were created for community use, religious ritual seems to have shifted towards these more communal ceremonial sites.

In addition, with the appearance of more ritual objects and activity comes the possibility that there was an increased emphasis on ritual, as well as more restricted

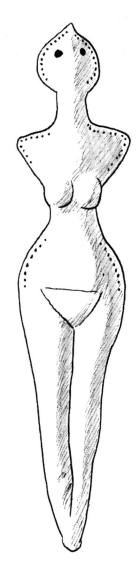

Slim female figurine with bird-like beak at top of head, 15 cm. tall. Southern Moldavia, mid–4th mil. B.C.E. Artist: James Möbius.

access to its practice and control. This suggests increased religious specialization and the emergence of religious specialists or elite, as certain buildings were increasingly used as shrines or temples.

Without the aid of written records, we do not have enough information about the varied religions of Neolithic Europe to be able to say what people believed, and how these ritual objects helped them express or enact those beliefs. However, by looking at the forms of those objects and carefully considering the world in which their creators lived, we can begin to develop some informed ideas about what these female figurines may have signified. Whether or not we can fully decode the message embodied within these figurines, they must contain some information about how people perceived the world, the realms of the sacred, and the power of the Divine Feminine.

Goddess, Magician and Ancestor

Like the statuary of the Paleolithic era, the female figurines of the Neolithic are generally quite small, of an appropriate size to be held in the hand. This must have influenced the ways in which they were used. Large statuary is often placed before an assembly of people so it may be seen and venerated by all. Smaller statues, on the other hand, are more appropriate for personal veneration or use by a smaller group of people, perhaps in the home or in a smaller shrine.

Indeed, domestic dwellings are some of the places where these Neolithic figurines have most frequently been found. In some cases they were discovered next to the oven or central hearth, or near stones used for grinding grain. This may suggest a connection with baking, a skill that developed during the Neolithic as a result of cereal crop

Painted clay vessel with example of female figurines, Northern Moldavia, early 4th mil. B.C.E. Artist: James Möbius.

production. Some statues may have served as guardians of the oven or hearth, or symbolized goddesses or ancestors credited with the invention of these domestic innovations.[33]

Some female figurines were also found seated on small ritual platforms, or near small clay replicas of animals, houses, furniture and domestic objects.At first glance, these miniature objects look like children's toys, which may be what some of them are. They could also be educational aids, for domestic or religious instruction (perhaps even explaining to children the attributes associated with female roles or symbolism). These figurines may have focused on domestic concerns: the maintenance of the house, the preparation of food, and the care of domestic animals, as well as symbolic concepts like fertility, abundance, healing and protection.[34]

Another possibility is that the objects were used for magical purposes. Miniature houses, animals, furnishings and female figures would be well suited for use in household magic and ceremonies. In many cultures, miniature replicas of objects or divine figures are used in rituals and magical rites associated with fertility, abundance, healing, protection and other purposes. In some cases, once the object has been used in a working of this kind, it is set aside — thrown away or buried — symbolizing that it has served its intended purpose and is not to be used again. Interestingly, the vast majority of Neolithic female figurines were recovered from garbage heaps located next to domestic houses and ritual buildings. This does not mean that they were not considered sacred or important, but strongly suggests that their period of magical or religious use had been completed (one that hopefully resulted in benefits for the family or community).[35]

The female figurines of Neolithic Europe and those of the Paleolithic past share one particular trait in common — variation. Neolithic figurines sometimes focused on the body, perhaps suggesting that they represented an abstract concept that did not need to be depicted as an identifiable character. In some instances, however, deliberate care was taken to outline the eyes and nose, and stylistic choices were made by the artists to create specific facial expressions and other characteristics. One type of facial pattern seen in a number of figurines consists of a highly stylized face with a small pointed chin, a wide elongated nose and almond-shaped eyes that almost suggest a cat-like appearance (at least to our modern perceptions).[36]

Specialized facial features were also molded into highly ornamented pottery vessels, some which have a cat, bird or owl-like appearance. Some of the Neolithic figurines have little or no decoration, while others are ornamented with elaborate patterns and symbols. Some statues seem to portray skirts or garments that may have been worn by women of the era. Others even depict free-flowing hair or elaborate hairstyles that may have been fashionable at the time.[37]

On some level, it would be more convenient for us if the Neolithic figurines of southeastern Europe consisted of just one or two clearly identifiable types. It would also be helpful if they were accompanied by clearly decipherable symbols or explanatory frescos that could tell us what their attributes were and how they were used. Clearly, this is not the reality of the situation. However, there are a number of methodologies that can help provide us with a glimpse into the beliefs of the ancient past, including examination of the shape, size and context of the figurines.[38]

We have seen that some of the female figurines may have been used as toys or served as educational aids for religious or secular purposes. They may have also represented guardian spirits of hearth and home — goddesses, tribal or community spirits, or ancestors. It seems likely that some of the figurines were used for personal, household or community-focused magic. A multitude of purposes can be envisioned: a mother hoping for a successful birth, concerned parents with an ailing child, a household praying for the fertility and protection of fields and animals, an old man praying for the spirit of his departed wife, a young woman performing love magic.[39]

Another strong possibility is that some of the figurines were connected with the ancestral dead. With the increasing emphasis on land use and ownership during the Neolithic period, and the attendant need to continually re-assert the rights to the land, people were more and more concerned with territorial authority conceptually granted to them by their ancestors. In other parts of Europe, these concerns resulted in the creation of enormous monuments to the dead. In southeastern Europe, these concepts may have found expression in rituals performed in dwellings, and later in communal temples.[40]

There is no reason to envision the fast-growing communities of Neolithic Europe practicing only one religion, or practicing a religion focused primarily or solely on fertility or reproduction. All around the world, traditional cultures display varied and sophisticated religious beliefs and practices that focus on a wide array of theological concepts and ideals. As fully modern humans (like ourselves), the people of Neolithic Europe were capable of perceiving, experiencing and interpreting the many innate aspects of the Divine with sophistication, diversity and finesse.

The female figurines of this distinctive era were undoubtedly created to symbolize a wide array of concepts and intentions, and it was apparently fitting to represent many of these intentions in female form. During this period of increased agriculture, and the beginnings of ideas pertaining to land ownership (rather than land stewardship), the figurines may have represented the physical abundance of the land, as well as ancestral authority to work that land. These powers were mediated through powerful female figures who could potentially grant people the right to inhabit a specific territory, and whose blessings and power provided them with abundance, well being and protection.

The Seeds of Change

It is remarkable to reflect on how much the lives of ancient Europeans changed throughout the prehistoric period. Many thousands of years have

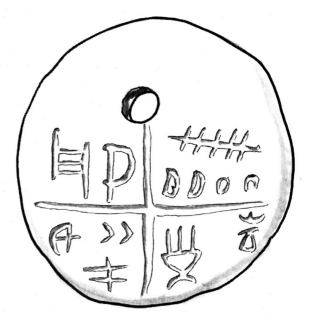

Inscribed clay disks with symbolic markings, possibly the earliest known form of writing in Europe. Tartaria, Eastern Europe, c. 5000 B.C.E. Artist: James Möbius.

elapsed since that time, and there are many challenges involved in attempting to understand the lives of other people almost exclusively through the lens of physical objects. As a result, it is tempting to distill the idea of "ancient times" into a golden age of peace and harmony, or a hazy period of darkness, superstitious fear of the powers of nature, and lack of sophistication. As we can see, not only were prehistoric humans intelligent, complex, and innovative, they adapted their lifestyles and religious practices to resonate with their environment and the current conditions of their lives.

It is interesting to note the many types of divine feminine imagery produced during the earliest phases of prehistory, as well as during subsequent eras, when the lives of ancient Europeans were quite transformed from what they had been. The symbolism of the Paleolithic era expressed the concerns and beliefs of that particular time, as did the symbolism of the Neolithic, thousands of years later. Instead of lumping these two eras together as representing a continuous belief system focused on fertility and the veneration of goddess figures, we are now able to perceive the varied and sophisticated impulses that led to these powerful but distinct forms of religious and cultural expression.[41]

Some of the artwork seen during the Paleolithic and Neolithic may have been connected with fertility (or perhaps more accurately, abundance and prosperity). In addition, some of the female figurines may be goddesses. But the images of these two disparate eras do not necessarily represent the exact same thing, especially when found so far apart in space and time. In addition, all the available evidence points to their connection with a far richer system of beliefs than has hitherto been assumed.[42]

One popular belief about the female figurines of prehistoric Europe is that they were created by peaceful, matriarchal cultures. We can see that without the verbal or written testimony of these cultures, we cannot possibly confirm this type of information about their social organization or beliefs. In addition, the indisputable evidence of violence and warfare seen during the Neolithic period speaks of cultures in transition that were experiencing increasing social pressures.

Another point to be considered is that the existence of female imagery does not necessarily correlate with peacefulness, prosperity or female rule. In Hindu culture, for example, the imagery associated with powerful goddesses like Kali and Camunda symbolizes their dynamic powers of life, death, transformation and destruction. Women in Hindu society, however, did not necessarily share in that power. In addition, the idea that male energies are associated with aggression and female energies with passivity is not only an outdated perception, but an inaccurate one as well. If we think about all the men and women we know, we will notice that they possess a wide variety of energies and attributes, many of which do not line up conveniently on one side or another of a male–female axis. The same is true of the deities, spiritual beings and belief systems of the world's religions, past and present, where variation seems to be one of the primary rules.

There is, however, one perceived aspect of the prehistoric past which may be quite accurate (at least in terms of the pre-farming or early farming period). In studying the social organization of hunter-gatherer societies of the present and recent past, anthropologists have noted a tendency towards what we would consider a more peaceful and egalitarian way of life. Egalitarianism does not mean a lack of hierarchy, but refers to a social structure in which personal autonomy is highly valued. People in these societies are concerned with maintaining individual autonomy and therefore wish to avoid being subjugated (both from within and without). These are not only practical concerns, but constitute a set of moral beliefs about how life "should be."

In these traditional cultures, the importance of developing a relationship with the land is considered paramount. Failure to take care of the land constitutes a potent spiritual danger.[43] Fostering a reciprocal relationship with the environment involves both practical concerns and spiritual realities, which are not perceived as being separate from each other. Harvard scholar E.O. Wilson writes about the importance of caring for the land: "The drive towards perpetual expansion — or personal freedom — is basic to the human spirit. But to sustain it we need the most delicate, knowing stewardship of the living world that can be devised."[44] This awareness has formed part of the traditional wisdom of indigenous cultures for millennia. Thomas Banyacya, the spokesperson for Hopi religious leaders, states:

> Through religion we are going to find those who are searching for the right way of living the truth and the peaceful way of harmony with each other and with nature all around, the clouds, the rain, the animals and the plant life. We are all a part of Mother Earth. We cannot break away from that. We are going to have to understand that so that we can look at each other. We are just like the trees out there — all different people with different languages, different colors and ways of expression. We are just like any other part of nature that is around us. This, we must understand.[45]

Humans are always adapting to the world around them, and when life is challenging, so too are the choices with which we are faced. It is not always easy to see the long-term outcomes of the choices we make on a daily basis. Native wisdom tells us we must consider the results of our actions on the lives of the next seven generations, and this is good counsel. We now have more choices than ever before. Our ability to transcend the current trend of materialism, environmental destruction and cultural elitism reflects our potential to make the personal and social choices necessary to create and maintain a harmonious relationship with the land, the environment and each other.

The female imagery of the earliest prehistoric eras attested not only to the blossoming of human culture and vision, but also to our ancestors' acknowledgment of the land as provider and sustainer and their ritualized gratitude for that bounty. Many thousands of years later, sacred imagery associated with the Divine Feminine re-emerged, embodying a variety of powerful attributes in a society that was completely transformed. The Divine Feminine symbolized the earth that provided for our needs, as well as other complex ideas and concepts that enhanced the lives of human beings.

Once the land had become a possession, human interactions became critically challenging. Even though our relationship with the landscape profoundly changed, the Divine Feminine once again stepped forward, demonstrating that she had the power to serve as a balancer, teacher and guide. She could be provider and destroyer, a magician or guardian of souls. She could be entreated as a beneficent mother or angry warrior, an ancestral figurehead or guardian of the land. Her watchful gaze brings about an increased awareness of the consequences of our actions in the great network of life.

The transformations of the Neolithic era deeply affected society, the landscape, and people's religious beliefs. And all of this took place as the result of a plough blade passing through the earth and the sowing of a few grains of wheat. Steadfast in her wisdom and powerful in her adaptability, the Divine Feminine bore witness to it all. During this period of diverse cultural expression, divine and ancestral female figures served the people in a multi-aspected guise of Guardian, Goddess and Ancestor. These principles form an important part of our cultural and spiritual inheritance, in the present moment and in the eternal echoes of time.

PART II: ANTHROPOLOGY — TRANSFORMING DIVINE WISDOM

6

The Power of the Inner World

In the ancient languages of our traditions, we believe that our people love the land so much that when we "die" or transition, we merely enter another dimension ... so we can always call upon our ancestors, who are always with us ... for their guidance, wisdom, and help....
— Nalani Minton, Indigenous Hawaiian Activist and Educator[1]

The sun had not yet risen above the horizon as a small group of people began to gather by the side of the river. Several men and women stood beneath a willow tree whose leafless branches were coated with frost. As a pre-dawn breeze swept past them, they gathered their cloaks around their necks. The icy fingers of the willow brushed each other in the wind, ringing out with delicate, hollow tones that resonated like small bells.

The wind died down and a heavy silence surrounded the group. At last they heard footsteps approaching from a small embankment that led to the sheltered vale. Seven cloaked figures made their way towards them, their pace stately and dignified. No one spoke in the pre-dawn stillness, but bowed their heads in a gesture of greeting. Every year at this time, three high priests and four priestesses gathered with secular leaders, elders and seers from the tribes who inhabited this region to perform an ancient rite.

The groups joined together and began processing up the hill that guarded the banks of the river. As they climbed, the imposing form of the great mound came into view. The contours of the stone monument on top of the mound were indistinct in the early morning haze, but as the group approached the sacred precinct they could feel the strength of its powerful embrace.

They reached the entrance to the great tomb where they paused and set their staffs and bundles upon the ground. Foreheads and fingertips were washed in vessels of water gathered from the sacred river. The head priest ran his fingers along the smooth edges of a grey stone scepter engraved with spiral designs. The head priestess prepared a copper vessel similarly decorated with spiral patterns. She stood up and adjusted a polished stone blade that hung from her belt. Carefully crafted from light-green jadeite, it had been entrusted to her by her great-grandfather, a celebrated priest and elder.

Two small vessels of pigment were produced from inside one of the bags. The men dipped their fingers into a vessel of red ochre and painted their foreheads with rows of triangular patterns. The women gathered around a vessel of dark-blue pigment and placed three small circles on their foreheads between their brows.

As they prepared, the faint purple glow that had appeared on the horizon deepened in color and intensity, and in its light the outline of the great stone monument began to take shape. In front of the doorway was a long, low stone carved with triangular and spiral patterns similar to those that adorned their faces. A clay vessel was set in front of the great stone and a blend of sacred herbs placed inside it. Using a pair of firestones, one of the women lit a spark and ignited the dried plant materials inside the bowl. A rich, earthy smoke rose from the vessel and the members of the group stepped forward to inhale its scent and powerful effect.

The group sat quietly and focused their attention on the symbols carved on the face of the stone as they waited for the herbs to take effect. In silence they waited for the transformation of mind and spirit they knew would take place as they began to merge with the ancient energies of this place. At last, out of the stillness, a small bird let out a short resonant call. Three or four sweet, hollow notes floated through the air, answered by another call farther away. Time had taken on a new meaning and several minutes passed before the group acknowledged the subtle but unmistakable signal of the dawn.

Finally a gentle amber-colored light glowed with promise at the base of the eastern sky, heralding the approach of the white ember of the winter sun. The group rose to their feet and stood in a formation facing the east. This was the sunrise of the Winter Solstice, the point at which the sun's period of diminished power was transformed into a new cycle of growth. Having prayed and fasted throughout the night, the power of the solstice vigil was renewed; the group had once again passed through the darkness of the longest night of the year.

Silently and majestically, sunlight broke over the edge of the land. The birds, who had held back their songs in anticipation, responded with an exhalation of joy. The bright rays of the new dawn illuminated the outer façade of the monument, which was covered with shining white quartz stones. The great sanctuary showed itself in all its power, a beacon of ancestral memory and sanctuary of remembrance for all who had gone before.

High priest and priestess lifted scepter and blade towards the sun, chanting a hymn of praise and welcome. They turned and faced the doorway of the monument, and the assembly bowed towards the sacred mound. At that moment, the sun's rays passed through a small stone portal above the doorway and flooded into the sacred passageways of the tomb. Every year, for seven days before and after the winter solstice, the sun turned its visage towards this holy place and sent its blessings into the house of the dead.

Sacred symbols carved inside the tomb were illuminated by the light. A triple spiral was engraved inside on one of the walls, a symbol that had many meanings. It represented the powers of the three realms that made up the cosmos: the Sky Realm, Earthly Realm, and the Realms Below us. It symbolized spiritual power, transformation, and the eternal cycles of life, death and rebirth that had been celebrated here for millennia. The sun had returned and the power of life continued on.[2]

During the Neolithic period, the cultural and spiritual innovations of northwestern Europe rivaled those of the southeastern regions. Both areas displayed a remarkable capacity for creativity, growth and transformation. In the northerly parts of the region, the artwork and monuments of this period display an increasing focus on concepts associated with sacred time and space, as well as the importance of social relationships and an intensification of respect for the dead. In many cultures the dead are revered as elders, teachers, leaders and ancestral figures who provide guidance and assistance to the living. They are symbolic representatives of family or community who provide a sense of traditional authority to established and continuing lines of descent.[3]

As the importance of maintaining the community's right to own and cultivate the land increased, so did the importance of maintaining those rights through an ancestral line. In order to emphasize this sense of authority (whether associated with land stewardship or land ownership), the Neolithic inhabitants of northwestern Europe began to build elaborate monuments to honor and house their ancestors. As in the southeast, over time ritual emphasis shifted from the house and village towards the larger settlement or region as a whole, where large burial monuments represented the entire community.[4]

At first, mortuary houses were built from timber or stone, and were enclosed in long, earthen mounds that became the focal point for the ritual life of the community. Over time, these ceremonial sites grew in size and complexity. Their distinctive design and characteristic ornamentation is unique to this part of the world. These elaborate and unprecedented stone monuments are without parallel in the ancient world, and are older than the Egyptian pyramids. The Neolithic monuments of northwestern Europe were bigger than anything built before, and loomed large in the environment as imposing and very prominent features of the social and religious landscape.[5]

The size and existence of these monuments sent a message to those who lived in the region (whether Neolithic or Mesolithic in lifestyle); this area was under the control or ownership of a particular group of people. The size of the monuments suggests that they served as ongoing ritual sites where people could meet to hold religious ceremonies, perhaps associated with the agricultural cycle. Some ritual sites were constructed with a specialized courtyard in the front, an ideal place to enact religious ceremonies.

In many cases, monuments were constructed in areas where farming communities encountered Mesolithic populations. These encounters could be peaceful or otherwise. The permanent nature of the monuments seems to reflect a longterm perspective associated with planting and harvesting as Neolithic communities settled in one place to work the land. As the construction of these tombs spread throughout Europe, the inhabitants of each region developed their own variations on the original designs.[6]

In northern France, early mounds evolved into another type of stone monument that was eventually constructed in many regions that bordered the Atlantic coast. The new design consisted of round mounds containing burial chambers that were approached by a long corridor. These "passage graves" allowed for repeated access into the central chamber so that new burials could be placed inside the tomb over time. This type of distinctive burial site, and later forms that were derived from this design, eventually became the symbolic marker of farming communities all over northwestern Europe.[7]

Throughout the centuries of the Neolithic era, many different types of tombs were constructed. The construction of these tombs would have required enormous amounts of human labor, which the expanding population of Neolithic Europe was able to provide. These efforts necessitated management and organizational skills, probably facilitated by authority figures or groups, whether political or religious in nature.[8]

In some areas, tombs were used for very long periods of time and were clearly imbued with a sense of power and sanctity. However, as change and development seem to be inevitably associated with human activity, starting around 3800 B.C.E. some of the early monuments began to be reconstructed. In some cases, stones were removed or even broken into different shapes for re-use in the construction of new passage graves. A shift in local power and authority, or new developments concerning beliefs associated with death and the proper organization of sacred space, may account for these changes.[9]

Many different types of tombs were built throughout Neolithic Europe and the spread of monument types attests to ongoing contact between communities and the sharing of ideas and technology. In some cases, certain types of tombs were favored in particular areas. In Neolithic France, for example, passage graves, dolmens, and chambered tombs (tombs with multiple chambers) were traditionally used. The dead were either buried or cremated, and grave goods included flint knives, pottery, stone axes (sometimes made of jadeite), bones, grindstones, stone pendants shaped like small axes, and beads made of copper, bone and shell.[10]

In Britain, monuments for the dead included passage graves, portal dolmens, long barrows, round cairns and long cairns. Early tombs contained few grave goods, usually just a few personal items like beads, pendants, necklaces and the occasional pottery bowl or cup. In the later part of the Neolithic, however, grave goods increased and included polished flint blades, arrowheads, stone tools, shale beads, stone or flint axes, antler tines and maceheads, and jet and shale ornaments.[11]

Irish Neolithic sites were rich in variety and grave goods. Irish passage graves often contained the cremated remains of the dead along with personal ornaments and heavily ornamented pottery. Beads and pendants made from semi-precious stones were carved into shapes that imitated the form of larger, everyday tools: miner's hammers, pestles, and axes. Pins made of antler were often buried with the dead, and their mushroom-ended shape may have had a phallic significance. Many Irish sites also contained mysterious spheres or balls made from stone or chalk. These were found singly and in pairs, and may represent an attribute associated with male fertility. Interestingly, no flint or stone tools or weapons were found at Irish sites.[12]

Travelers to Britain, Ireland and France often visit the many well-preserved Neolithic settlements and monuments that have been discovered. Some of the most famous examples are located in Britain and Ireland, and their remarkable construction and ornamentation have inspired the curiosity of historians, antiquarians, artists, writers, and spiritual seekers for centuries.

In Ireland, the first phase of Neolithic tomb building focused on three massive mounds or *tumuli* located near the River Boyne in County Meath. These tumuli were built on prominent locations on top of three knolls about a mile apart, encompassing an area of about 6,000 square meters. Smaller tombs were clustered around each of the larger ones, and over time passage grave cemeteries of this kind became quite common in Ireland.[13]

Interestingly, these pre–Celtic sites found their way into the mythology of the Celtic people, whose culture did not arrive in Ireland for thousands of years after the sites were built. The mystery and sanctity associated with them was so timeless that the power of the monuments was preserved in the legends of medieval Ireland, a culture far removed in time from the first farming communities in the island. The most famous of the three sites is Newgrange, known as *Brug na Bóinne* in the legends. One tale describes how the Irish god

Oengus mac Óg was instructed to take possession of Newgrange so that he would possess land or territory, although it was already occupied. It is interesting to note themes of land ownership and authority, as well as the marking of time:

> Oengus is to go to Elcmar and threaten to kill him unless he obtains his request. That request is that Oengus be king in the Bruig for a day and a night.... Oengus is to argue that the land is his by right in return for his sparing Elcmar — that he requested the kingship of day and night, and that it is in days and nights that the world passes.[14]

At Newgrange the huge tumulus has a diameter of about 80 meters and weighs about 200,000 tons. The construction of the monument would have required the intensive labor of several hundred workers. Around the edge of the mound are a number of oblong boulders, many of which are carved with elaborate designs comprised primarily of spirals and diamond shapes. The entrance stone in front of Newgrange is a masterpiece of stone working. It is decorated with five spirals (a group of three and a group of two) surrounded by lozenge shapes and nesting arcs. Inside the tomb is a passageway leading to several burial chambers, capped by a corbelled stone roof. An elaborately carved triple spiral design was carved on one of the walls. A small rectangular opening above the doorway was positioned so that the rays of the Winter Solstice sunrise illuminate the inside of the tomb.[15]

A number of other well-known Neolithic monuments are located in the north of Scotland. In the Orkney Islands, at the Neolithic settlement of Barnhouse, a group of stone huts were arranged around a central circular building whose entrance faced the rising sun on the Summer Solstice, the longest day of the year. Some of the larger tombs in the Orkneys exhibit similarities in design and orientation with Newgrange.[16]

At Maes Howe, for example, a fine chambered tomb was built containing a large, square central chamber. The passage that leads inside the tomb was oriented towards the southwest, the direction the sun sets at the Winter Solstice. A stone was set up to block a portion of the passageway, thereby allowing the rays of the setting solstice sun to shine on the back wall of the chamber (reminiscent of Newgrange).[17]

Many Neolithic sites are oriented along a northeast–southwest axis, an alignment associated with the Midsummer sunrise (northeast) and Midwinter sunset (southwest). This orientation may have been connected with a ritual interpretation of symbolism associated with light and dark; life, death and rebirth; and the transformative properties of the cycles of life as reflected in the annual journey of the sun and other celestial bodies.[18]

Evidence for specific ritual activities has been discovered at a variety of

Neolithic sites. Inside an Irish tomb at Knowth, excavators uncovered an object that has been described as one of the finest works of art ever created by the Neolithic passage-grave builders of northwestern Europe. At the entrance to the eastern alcove of the tomb was a ceremonial macehead made from beautiful white and brown marbled flint. The mace-head, which looks like an oval-shaped axe head, was elaborately carved on every surface in patterns of extreme elegance and precision. It would have originally been mounted on a wooden handle and probably carried in procession or wielded during ceremonies.[19]

The front and back of the mace-head are decorated with lozenge motifs, while the top and bottom each bear a double spiral. On either side of the macehead (the areas which would have been most visible to onlookers) were large, perfectly carved spiral designs. We can only imagine the visual impact of this ritual object as it was carried and used inside the monument in rites of dedication, burial or initiation.[20]

Another interesting find was discovered at a Neolithic site in Wales known as *Barclodiad y Gawres,* first excavated in the 1950s. The name means "The Giantesses Apron" and comes from a later folklore tradition in which a supernatural female figure was said to have dropped a pile of stones from her enormous apron onto the landscape. Indeed, the mound at Barclodiad y Gawres looks much like a pile of stones that was dropped onto the ground.[21]

Inside the mound is a narrow passageway that leads to a series of inner chambers. The cremated remains of two adult males were found inside the western side chamber along with the charred remains of bone or antler pins (probably used to hold their garments in place). Excavations showed that a fire had been lit in the center of the monument that had burned for quite some time. While the blaze was still burning, a strange concoction had been poured onto the fire. Afterwards, the flames had been extinguished and the central area was covered over with soil, shells, small flat stones and smooth pebbles, many of which were made of quartz.[22]

The brew that had been poured onto the fire contained the bones of fish, eel, frog, toad, grass snake, mouse, shrew and rabbit. The ingredients in this strange concoction are reminiscent of the witch's brew described in Shakespeare's *MacBeth,* which include ingredients like "eye of newt," "adder's tongue," "toe of frog," and so on. It is interesting to note that many of the animals whose bones were uncovered at Barclodiad y Gawres inhabit the lower regions of the earth and the waters. This may reflect a belief in three spiritual or cosmogonic realms — the Sky Realm, the Middle Realm of Earth, and the Lower World — a perception that exists all around the world, particularly in cultures in which shamanism forms part of the religious or spiritual tradition.[23]

The Art of the Spirit World

One of the most alluring and mysterious aspects of the megalithic tombs are enigmatic symbols carved onto the stones inside and outside of the monuments — designs that together seem to form a complex and elaborate system. Some of the most common shapes are: spirals, concentric circles, nested arcs, rounded rectangles, lozenges or diamond shapes, zigzags, triangles and meanders (snaking or river-like lines). A wide variety of circular forms are also found, including dots or small circles surrounded by an outer circle or a series of rayed arms, evocative of a sun symbol or flower pattern. In many cases, a combination of shapes, both curved and rectilinear, are found together on the same stone.[24]

One of the most remarkable things about the patterns on the stones is the precision with which they were made and the intensity of the patterns formed by adjacent designs. Many theories have been put forth regarding the possible interpretation of these symbols. One thing is clear; the designs must have been of great cultural or spiritual importance to have been so carefully rendered and so widely used. Many of the carvings would have been very time consuming to create, requiring the skill of one or more artists (and possibly the input and approval of religious or secular leaders). At some sites, certain patterns are more common than others which may indicate that they were associated with a particular group or area, or represented an idea that was important to the creators of that site.[25]

Perhaps the most compelling theory concerning the significance of this artwork is that the patterns are "entoptic" in nature. Entoptic designs are those that can be seen with the eyes closed while in a meditative or altered state of consciousness, or which in and of themselves induce an altered or meditative state. Entoptic patterns are often experienced by shamans and other spiritual practitioners during meditative states, whether those visions are induced through the use of entheogens (sacred plant substances used for religious purposes) or arise spontaneously as a result of a profound trance state. Patterns seen during an altered state can be drawn, carved or otherwise reproduced, and then used in subsequent rituals to help induce or reproduce these altered states of consciousness.[26]

Anthropological studies have provided a number of documented cases in which traditional cultures intentionally use designs similar to those found in Neolithic European artwork for these same purposes. For example, studies of the rock paintings made by the *San* (Bushmen) of South Africa show that their sacred artwork frequently depicts actions performed during the shaman's trance dance, as well as visions experienced by shamans, symbols of supernatural potency, and symbols that are clearly understood to be entoptic patterns. In an early stage of the trance experience, *San* shamans report that they experience a neurological phenomenon in which they "see" certain geometric shapes.[27]

A similar study was undertaken with a cultural population from South America known as the *Tukano*. Members of the Tukano were asked to draw pictures of their mental imagery after taking an entheogenic-based preparation known as *yajé*. They subsequently filled sheets of paper with rows of reduplicated geometric motifs. When asked what the motifs represented, they stated that the motifs were derived from what they themselves recognized as the first stage of their trance experiences. Many of the images were also said to form part of the group's mythological belief system.[28]

Especially interesting was the way in which the artists packed the repeated entoptic patterns into every portion of the available space. This is reminiscent of the Neolithic stonework of Europe, in which designs are often placed very close together and covering the entirety of the stone's surface. Some of the most common entoptic designs found among the Tukano were spirals, nesting arcs and lozenge shapes, designs that are also widely used in European settings. Spiraling and curved entoptic patterns were sometimes reported by the Tukano to be associated with transitions between the spiritual realms, an interpretation that fits the Neolithic artwork of northern Europe perfectly.[29]

Other studies have explored similarities between the rock art produced by various indigenous cultures and entoptic images experienced by study participants in altered states (induced or produced under laboratory conditions). After noting a widespread correlation between visionary experiences and religious symbols, Cambridge scholar Jeremy Dronfeld explored the symbolism found at Irish Neolithic sites. After examining the passage grave art at Newgrange, Knowth, Dowth, Loughcrew, Sess Kilgreen and Lochmany, he concluded that eighty percent of Irish passage-tomb art was fundamentally similar to artwork derived from subjective visions experienced during various types of consciousness-altering practices.[30]

The ritualized artwork used at these sacred sites appears to function as a bridge between the worlds, as Joseph Campbell so eloquently describes:

> The temple is an enclosure wherein every feature is metaphorical of a connoted metaphysical intuition, set apart for ritual enactments. The function of the ritual is to bring one's manner of life into accord with non-judgemental perspective ... of synergetic participation in a phantasmagoric rapture.[31]

This type of ritual symbolism is utilized in many shamanic and traditional cultures. The Chewong of Malaysia describe the symbolic associations of the shaman's visionary states: "The shaman is able to see, when in the different non-human and superhuman worlds, in the same ways as members of those worlds see their reality, without losing the ability to see as a human being at the same time."[32]

The mysteries associated with sacred perception were also described by Nobel-prize winning biologist George Wald when he wrote: "That is the problem of consciousness. It is altogether impervious to scientific approach."[33]

All cultures engage either directly or indirectly with the symbolic wisdom of the sacred, and find ways to express that which cannot be put into words. The importance of relearning this symbolic language is described by African elder Bernadette Rebienot: "Humanity must enter a reconciliation with nature if we wish to create a new reality, a new alliance. We must learn the essential and mysterious language of nature that is always speaking to us, the language the great initiates have always understood."[34]

Talismans and Entheogens

Some of the entoptic patterns in northwestern Europe were depicted on portable objects as well as large stones and monuments. Remarkable finds of portable entoptic art were discovered at Neolithic sites in the north of Britain. A series of unique objects, found almost exclusively in Scotland, were unearthed at several locations, primarily in the northeastern region between the River Tay and the Moray Firth. Almost four hundred carved stone balls were discovered, most about two and three-quarters inches in diameter. They were carved with a variety of rounded or pointed knobs protruding from the surface of the sphere. The number of protrusions, and the accuracy of the carving, suggests they were intended to represent geometric concepts (perhaps similar to the Platonic solids).[35]

In some instances, however, the stone spheres had just three or four rounded faces extending from the surface of the sphere. These flat surfaces were carved with precisely rendered spiral patterns very similar to those seen at the Neolithic ritual sites. Some years ago, during a visit to the National Museum of Scotland, I had the opportunity to examine these remarkable stone objects. These had long been some of my favorite Neolithic artifacts, and it was a great privilege to be able to inspect them so closely. In addition to their smooth, polished forms and the geometric precision with which they were carved, I noted that they were a perfect size to be held in the hand. This underscores the possibility that the portable stones were used for trance induction or other spiritual purposes, as they could be carried around by religious practitioners and potentially used to induce an altered or meditative state, regardless of where a person might be.

In addition to the entoptic or otherwise spiritually related artwork found inside and outside the tombs, the shape and construction of the monuments themselves seems to reflect specific symbolic intentions. Passage-graves generally consist of a mound that is entered through a specially constructed passageway. This tunnel acts as a portal, leading from the outside world into the darkened space of the internal chambers. Once inside the body of the earth, people leave the mundane world behind and enter an internal universe outside the boundaries of ordinary space and time. To facilitate this experience, religious symbolism was placed near the entrances as well as at strategic points along the passage. These designs would have assisted people in transitioning between mental, emotional and spiritual states as they entered the sacred sanctuary, a place that constituted a symbolic cosmos and contained its own form of reality.[36]

Another indication of the sacred nature of the sites and the spiritual activities that took place within their precincts is the use of specialized materials in the construction and formation of the monuments. One of the most intriguing aspects of the site at Newgrange is the proliferation of white quartz stones found near the entrance to the mound. Lead archaeologist Michael O'Kelly believes that these were originally used to decorate the outer walls of the tomb. Using only stones found at the excavation site, he was able to embellish the entire façade of the tomb with shining white quartz pebbles. Similar stones were also found at Knowth and Loughcrew. The Newgrange stones, which contain flecks of white mica, come from the Dublin-Wicklow mountains more than thirty-five miles away. They would have been mined in the mountains and then brought by boat (first by sea and then up the River Boyne) to the site at Newgrange.[37]

Quartz stones and crystals are connected with spiritual beliefs and practices in a number of cultures around the world. They are often used by shamans or other religious practitioners who specialize in the ability to use altered states of consciousness for the purposes of healing, transformation, or the acquisition of hidden or sacred knowledge.[38]

Among Australian Aboriginal people, holy people and elders often carry quartz crystals around with them. They speak of these objects as "solidified powerful water" that can be metaphorically used to sprinkle their powers upon neophytes. In these cultures, quartz is believed to bring about a transformation that enables people to experience soul flight. In some areas, crystals are used in shamanic healing rituals and initiation rites, as well as to create mystical weapons of protection. The most important qualities associated with quartz are life energies and ancestral beings, the latter concept being particularly appropriate to the Neolithic tombs.[39]

South American shamans also utilize quartz stones in their practice. They often wear polished quartz crystals on their bodies and carry smaller pieces in their purse. In some instances, shamans report seeing bright geometric forms during their vision states which glisten and shine with their own light. For these shamans, the crystals symbolize sacred space, the place where all essential transformations are believed to occur.[40]

Regardless of the means of induction, the visions and experiences reported by people in altered states of consciousness exhibit a number of commonalities. Some of the most common experiences include:

- a sensation of flying, floating or otherwise traveling through a tunnel or passageway
- the ability to see vividly
- transformation into animal forms
- objects transforming into other things
- the perception of bright geometric patterns.[41]

These experiences may have formed part of the ritual activities that took place at the sacred sites of northwestern Neolithic Europe. This possibility is strengthened by the archaeological discovery of several types of plants capable of inducing a trance state that have been discovered at various Neolithic sites. Hemp seeds were found at Neolithic sites in Germany, Switzerland, Austria and Romania, and carbonized henbane was also discovered at one location. A gravesite from Neolithic Spain contained a still-clothed skeleton that had been buried with a number of baskets containing the blossoms of poppy flowers. A number of French Neolithic sites contained highly decorated ceramic burners, perhaps used to burn sacred or entheogenic herbs or resins. Mushroom shaped pins are widely found in Neolithic gravesites, and while these may have had some sort of phallic significance, it is also possible that they actually represent mushrooms. A number of hallucinogenic mushrooms grow in Europe, including the Fly Agaric or *Amanita Muscaria* mushroom that is well known from Siberian shamanic contexts.[42]

A variety of methods are traditionally used around the world to help human beings connect with the realms of the Divine. Some of these may have been utilized by the religious practitioners of Neolithic Europe to facilitate and empower their religious ceremonies. These visionary techniques may have resulted from the use of entopic patterns, the mastery of meditative practices, or the respectful use of entheogens. The widespread presence of religious artwork that fits the criteria for entoptic patterning suggests that these ritual specialists had developed and mastered the art of trance induction. They may have enhanced their religious experiences through the use of song, chanting, prayer, fasting, drumming, music and other widely utilized methods to facilitate their spiritual journeys into the realms of the beyond, spiritually transforming the lives of the living and symbolically honoring the souls of the dead.[43]

The Dark Goddess of the Tombs

As in southeastern Europe, after many thousands of years with no trace of female imagery the inhabitants of northwestern Neolithic Europe began to once more create symbolic representations of the female form. These were quite different in shape and design than those of

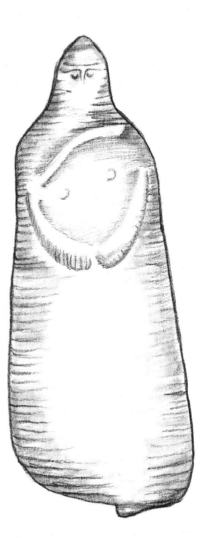

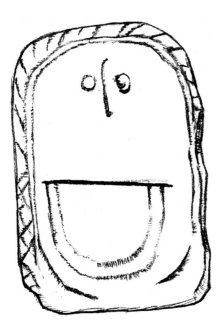

Left: Carved stone menhir of female figure with owl-like eyes, wearing neck ornaments, 50.3 cm tall, Late Neolithic period, 4th to early 3rd mil. B.C.E., Crato, Alentejo, Portugal. Artist: Donna Martinez.

Right: Late Neolithic tomb goddess or ancestress, depicted with hook (possibly a sickle), 163 cm tall, Late Neolithic period, 4th to early 3rd mil. B.C.E., Mas de l'Aveugle, Collorgues, Gard, southern France. Artist: Donna Martinez.

their southerly neighbors, however, and may have symbolized a very different set of religious beliefs and ideas.

Artwork found inside some of the tombs suggests the presence of a female divine figure who may have guarded, protected or inhabited the monuments of north-west Neolithic Europe. Depictions of this spiritual entity and clearly recognizable portrayals of female figures were widely created in the north of France between about 3,000 and 2,500 B.C.E. They were also found at sites in Spain, Portugal and the south of France.[44]

These female images are found engraved on standing stones outside the tombs, as well as on stones connected with the monuments themselves. In some cases, the female figure is represented by a pair of round eyes with a piercing gaze, sometimes augmented by a nose or the outlines of a face. Beneath these features are representations of necklaces (either single- or multiple-strands) or what appears to be a series of ornate neck ornaments or breastplates. A pair of small round breasts is frequently depicted beneath the necklaces. A few figures also contain a pair of arms that hold a curved or hooked object of some kind, perhaps a scythe or ritual sceptre.[45]

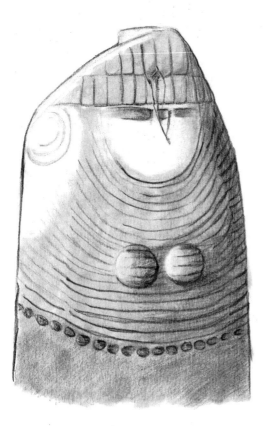

The shape of the face and unblinking gaze have led some archaeologists to compare these images with the face of an owl, a bird associated with the night (and in some, but certainly not all cultural traditions, with death). The intensity of the figure's gaze may reflect the use of entoptic patterns and the induction of altered states of awareness. Another possibility is that the watchful eyes of a deity, spirit or ancestral figure may

Carved stone stelae of grave goddess or ancestress, with headdress, owl-like facial appearance, breasts and elaborate cloak and head covering or neck ornaments. Arco, Trentino, 3rd. mil. B.C.E. Artist: Donna Martinez.

have been set up to guard the tombs or watch over the souls of the dead (as well as the lands and activities of the living).[46]

Anthropomorphic designs were also found on a number of standing stones or *menhirs* in Brittany and the Isle of Guernsey. These stones do not portray facial features, but do depict a pair of breasts, frequently a necklace or belt, and sometimes a pair of arms. These stones are part of a wider tradition of menhir carving also found in southern France, Italy, the Alpine regions, and parts of Eastern Europe.[47]

Male images are also found carved onto menhirs, and these are often depicted with stone axes or hammers, daggers, maces and curved objects which look very much like a bow. In a few cases, female images were also depicted with axes or daggers, indicating that these might represent social authority or spiritual power of some kind.[48]

We do not know if the female figures depicted on the external standing stones

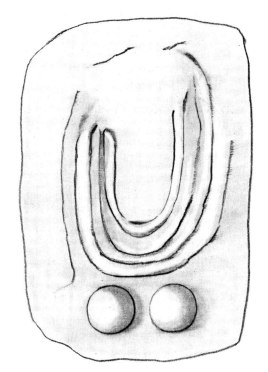

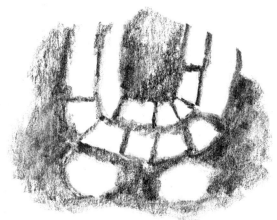

Top: Detail of grave goddess/ancestress, carved stone representation from a megalithic tomb showing outline of breasts and three neck ornaments. Boury, Oise, France, circa 3000 B.C.E. Artist: Donna Martinez.

Bottom: Neolithic grave goddess or ancestress as represented by breasts and neck ornaments. Late Neolithic gallery grave, La Pierra Turquaise, Paris Basin, France. Artist: James Möbius.

are the same as those portrayed inside the tomb monuments. The standing stones were found in outdoor locations where all members of the community could conceivably see them and participate in associated rituals. The female images found inside the monuments on the other hand, may not have been viewed by everyone in the community, suggesting that they represent a different set of figures or concepts.[49]

One of the most common theories about the tomb-goddesses is that they represent ancestral figures. If this is true, it is strange that relatively few male images appear in this context. Both men and women were buried inside the tombs, and if their ancestral presence lent spiritual authority to the ownership and use of the land, we would expect to see both male and female images depicted inside the tombs.

One possible explanation is that some Neolithic societies may have practiced a matrilineal form of descent. This is a practice in which the ancestry of a particular family or group is either traced through the female line (a less frequent occurrence) or where the determination of kingship or leadership is determined by following lines of descent back through the female line (a more common practice). Matrilineal descent in a social context is not the same as a matriarchal culture (a culture led or dominated by women), which is historically a very rare occurrence. Also, a tradition of matrilineal descent does not imply the existence of matriarchal practices or of male–female social equality.

What matrilineal descent does indicate is an awareness of women's contribution to the ancestral line and a very practical set of solutions to one of society's oldest problems. When a queen or noblewoman gives birth to a child, the event can be witnessed by others. Therefore, that woman is known to unequivocally be the birth mother of the child. The father of the child, however, is not always certain. A king or chief may hope he is the father of the child, yet for biological reasons cannot be sure.

The group or community is therefore faced with the possibility that the child's biological father is not of a royal or noble line. They can, however, be certain that the child carries royal blood through the mother, and for this reason status or nobility may be determined through the female line. In this form of matrilineal descent, successors to the throne or other positions of secular or spiritual power may include nephews, grandsons and other relatives who are related through the female side, and not just the man's sons.[50]

If matrilineal descent was practiced during the Neolithic era, the female figures in the ancestral tombs may represent female ancestors (biological, spiritual or symbolic) whose presence and authority lent power to the group's territorial claims or ancestral line of descent. Although we have no way of knowing if this theory is true without the corroborative testimony of written records, it is a plausible suggestion which may help us begin to understand some of the complexity of the social and religious ideas of the time.

The monuments of Neolithic Europe were likely used for a variety of purposes, and the religious or social concepts that the female figures embodied may also be quite varied. Ancestral spirits associated with the monuments may have been entrusted with the protection and authority of the group and its land, as well as ensuring the prosperity and wellbeing of crops and herds. The female images could have represented social or spiritual concepts that were considered so important or sacred that it was necessary to safeguard their symbolic depictions inside sacred sites. These might include complex ideological concepts associated with life, death, transformation and rebirth; initiation and magical power; mystical vision or religious authority; and social ideals like courage, honor, compassion, strength or will.[51]

Another possible interpretation is that these female figures were spiritual figures or deities. They could have represented goddesses or spirits associated with life, death and rebirth who guided the souls of the dead or protected them in the afterlife. This theory is strengthened by the southwest alignment of many Neolithic monuments, the direction of the Winter Solstice sunset and darkest point of the year. We know that these hallowed sites were used as tombs and probably for other religious purposes as well. Therefore, the tomb-goddesses may symbolize a female creator or spiritual caretaker who presided over the realms of the dead and the world of the spirits, in whose domain souls were transformed and prepared for the next cycle of life.[52]

Representations of these figures were stylistically varied in different regions, perhaps indicating differences in local or regional belief. The highly stylized artwork used to depict these spiritual entities may suggest that it was not customary to depict spiritual beings in a realistic fashion. It might have been considered inappropriate or unrealistic to portray a spiritual being through the auspices of the human form. Or, these sacred figures may have been seen as an embodiment of certain forces or energies, rather than a specific, personified individual. Both of these suggestions would account for the highly stylized artwork and sparing use of human features that are seen in so many of these images. The Divine Feminine was certainly present, but her powers may have defied direct representation.

One thing we can say with confidence is that the most common anthropomorphic images of the Neolithic period were female. While we cannot say for certain who or what the images represent, the variety of female carvings and large statuary found in north-western Europe attest to the importance of this symbolism during the Neolithic period. After a lapse of more than

20,000 years, the inhabitants of both southeastern and northwestern Europe, each in their own unique ways, once again created powerful and evocative female images, figurines and stone carvings. Far different from those created by their predecessors (who lived in an entirely different world) these new female forms represented the symbolism and concerns of the New — rather than the Old — Stone Age.[53]

As before, some male imagery was also produced, and it too must also have been significant. Perhaps the male figurines of southeastern Europe symbolized the role of men in bringing the new technologies to fruition. The stone axes depicted on the stone stelae may have symbolized the physical strength needed to clear and prepare the land for planting. Stone daggers or knives served as practical items and could also function as ritual objects associated with power, status or ritual practices. The bow could have symbolized the need to defend the land and its resources, a Neolithic social function of increasing importance as time went along. The male images of the Neolithic era may have been guardian spirits, deities or ancestral figures associated with agriculture, protection, authority, defense, resourcefulness or the potency of ritual practices.

The female figures carved inside the monuments and on external standing stones are sometimes depicted with objects that could be interpreted as sickles. These objects were associated with the reaping of grain, and perhaps also with the symbolic reaping of life. The location of these figures and their highly ritualized ornamentation strongly suggest an interpretation associated with death, passages, transitions, and religious ceremonies. If the male symbolism represented the preparation of the land in order to propagate life and the physical protection of the land, the symbolism of the female images may have been associated with the social or spiritual authority necessary to maintain the rights to the land and sacred transitions between this world and the next.

Like the female images of the Paleolithic era, the female imagery of Neolithic Europe seems to embody a number of sacred principles or energies existing within a matrix of ancestral, spiritual or goddess-based forms. These goddess figures may have been associated with life, death, abundance, power or protection. As a local or tribal goddess associated with the land, she reigned over the world of natural abundance, weather, animals, and the harvest. She guarded and protected the community, ensuring or withholding their right and ability to earn their bread. She protected and nourished their territory, and considered their claims and desire to utilize these environmental resources.

Inside the passage graves, she dominated the internal ritual landscape. An ancestral figure or goddess who validated the community's claim to use the land, she was associated with matrilineal descent or other ancestral concerns. She may even have been a shaman or priestess-figure associated with spiritual practices and ceremonies involving trance work and entheogens, whose very presence enabled spiritual practitioners to bridge the gap between the worlds of the living and the dead. By invoking and honoring these powers and attributes, the inhabitants of Neolithic Europe were engaged in a complex spiritual tradition in which the Feminine Divine played a powerful and yet mysterious role, displaying more and more of her sacred potential as the world continued to grow.

7

The Vessel and the Sword

The goal of the hero's journey is finding yourself...
The return is seeing the radiance everywhere.
The warrior's approach is to say "yes" to life: "yea" to it all...
The sword is usually a benevolent instrument that clears the way....
— Joseph Campbell[1]

A small group of children scrambled up the cliff-face and climbed to the top of a rocky hill. It was a fine, sunny day with only a few thin clouds floating overhead on the mid-autumn breeze. The younger children sat down to rest, while the eldest of the girls stood and scanned the horizon. She spoke a few words to the other children who scrambled to their feet and looked where she was pointing. Out on the open grasslands they could see something moving in the distance.

They had often heard tales of strange people who lived out in the open grasslands, who built no houses and grew no crops. They wore strange costumes and rode mythical creatures who flew like the wind. Strangely enough, the image out on the steppes seemed to be moving at a rapid speed, but it was better to be cautious as the children were alone.

The little group sat down to confer on the far side of a cluster of birch trees, and after some deliberation decided that the strange apparition was far too enticing to pass up. They began to climb down the far side of the hill, staying hidden behind trees and bushes. Finally they came within sight of the apparition, and from their hiding place they could see a group of people the likes of which they had never seen before.

A number of men and women were standing around a fire and laughing. They wore brightly-colored costumes with checked or striped shawls or cloaks held at the shoulder with metal pins. Many of the men, and several of the women, wore thick leather belts around their waists from which hung a leather sheath. The blades inside the sheaths were made from some kind of strong, shining metal.

Two of the men rose from the fire and began to engage in a mock combat, playfully encouraged by their companions. After a while, a resilient looking woman stepped forward, throwing back the folds of her cloak. She held a sturdy looking weapon, much longer than a flint blade or copper dagger. As she approached, the men lowered their blades. Then one of the men, sporting an enormous grin, took up with the woman.

She was swift and decisive in her movements, and her opponent was quickly unarmed. He seemed chagrined, but she threw him back his weapon. Eventually they halted and dropped to the ground in a breathless fit of laughter. The crowd who had been watching the duel dispersed, clearing an area in front of the children hidden in the grass.

Standing next to a large tent was a herd of remarkable animals different from any they had seen before. They were about the same height as cattle, but more slender and graceful with flowing tails and long hair that ran down the length of their necks. The animals stood about peacefully and regally, occasionally stamping their feet or letting out a cry that sounded both joyful and defiant.

Several men and women walked up to the animals and slid their hands over the creatures' long, elegant necks. They wore beautiful coats dyed in rich blues, reds and greens. Thick pads were placed upon the animals' backs and, much to the amazement of the children, they permitted the people to jump on their backs. With a few soft words and clicks, the animals began to move around, apparently in communication with the riders. The group moved away from the encampment and the animals began to race across the open grasslands at a remarkable speed. It was true! These must be the people they had heard about in the stories passed around the hearth.

Suddenly, the children heard a strange noise behind them. Towering above them were two of the mysterious people on top of their swift animals. For a long moment, the children and the strangers locked eyes, each sizing up the other. The riders spoke to each other briefly and then peered around the landscape diligently. Without a sound, they slipped down from the back of their mounts.

They looked directly at the children and said something in a language the youngsters did not understand. The riders put their hands out in a comforting gesture and motioned for the children to stand up. They silently obeyed and stood huddled together in a bunch. Sensing their fear and curiosity, the riders gently patted the noses of their mounts and motioned for the children to do the same. They were surprised at the softness of the animals' muzzles and the warm, sweet smell of their breath.

Soon the children were patting the animals' necks and stroking their manes. These were no monstrous beings at all, but sensitive, intelligent animals. One of the children, besotted with the whole experience, asked the riders what the animals were called. When her question received no reply, she pointed repeatedly to the animals with a questioning look. The woman rider said "*ek-wo*" which the children eagerly repeated. An "ek-wo," eh? They couldn't wait to go home and tell their families about their adventure!

After a while, the children realized they needed to return to the village. They pointed in the direction of the hill, using hand gestures to indicate that they lived on the other side. The riders seemed to understand. They nodded and leapt back on their mounts before ambling back across the grasslands. The man began to sing a strange melody as they rode. The children walked away reluctantly, turning frequently to catch a last glimpse of the ek-wo's and their intriguing owners.

A few minutes later, the children were surprised to hear the animals running up behind them. The mounted riders extended their hands down to the children. Within moments, they were packed onto wool saddle-pads in front of the riders. When they arrived at the base of the hill, everyone dismounted and walked up the steep, rocky sides.

Once they reached the summit, the children eagerly pointed out the village to their new friends, but the riders remounted and encouraged them to walk quickly, as the sun was setting. The children's faces fell. They were not going to ride into the village on top of the magical animals. No one would ever believe their story.

Early the next day, however, their tales of adventure were confirmed when a large group of the riding people approached the settlement in ceremonial formation. They carried a pole with a small flag onto which was sewn the image of one of the ek-wo's. Elders from both groups approached each other with caution and respect. At the end of the day, they returned home and spoke excitedly about what they had seen and heard. Each was changed by their contact with the other, although the villagers seemed most impressed by the flamboyant strangers and their strange animals. Imagine! They grew no crops and lived where they pleased. Not only did they ride and communicate with the ekwos, they also raised smaller animals with thick hair that could be used to make coats, tents, rugs and shawls.

Foreign words for new things — like "horse," "wool" and "bronze" — danced on the tongues of the villagers for weeks after the meeting. These were not the last riding people they would encounter. Before long, the culture and language of these intriguing strangers would have a profound effect on their lives, changing their ideas about society and religion, as well as the words they used to talk about these things. Sometimes, from the most unexpected encounters, the most amazing ideas are born.[2]

During the Neolithic period, as the inhabitants of Europe adopted the technologies associated with farming and herding, the foraging way of life all but disappeared. In its place, a wide variety of regional cultures sprang up all over Europe. These diverse tribes and cultures began to think of themselves as individual groups with unique identities. Contact between groups varied widely, from the friendly exchange of goods, ideas and information to tense or violent interchanges involving competition for land and resources.

Late Neolithic and early Copper Age Europe consisted of a melting pot of cultural traditions, and its inhabitants created many types of settlements, artifacts and monuments that were uniquely their own. After the introduction of farming and herding technology, Europe remained relatively unaffected by Near Eastern influences for millennia. Instead, it evolved into its own specialized cultural domain, one that served as a foundation for the many traditions that followed.[3]

The period of history that followed the Neolithic era and Copper Age is known as the Bronze Age. This phase of prehistory lasted for about two thousand years, from 2,500 B.C.E. to 600 B.C.E. At this time, urban-based societies existed to the south in the Aegean, but these societies had little effect on the internal development of European culture until the very end of the era. The mobile, pastoral societies of the steppe-lands to the east, on the other hand, had a tremendous influence on Bronze Age Europeans, as we will see.[4]

Metalworking continued to develop during the Bronze Age, and white gold and silver were used to create symbolic and ritual objects and ornaments that were placed inside tombs and burial sites. In addition, a new type of metal was developed, one that was much more practical and durable than any that had come before. Since copper is a very soft metal, in order to produce more functional objects it was alloyed with a small amount of tin. This produced a new metal known as bronze that was widely used to make tools, weapons, ritual objects and personal adornments. These objects were part of a new type of material culture and reflected social changes that took place during this era.

Bronze was especially popular in the production of items used for elegant display, and to denote wealth, status or achievement. It was also used to make specialized objects that were buried with the dead, and also offered to the gods or supernatural powers. Some of these objects and symbols reflected the presence and power of the Divine Feminine, who had also begun to take on new forms. These forms would continue to develop for many years, maintaining their power and resonance in the eras that were to come.[5]

Circles of the Sun

One of the most interesting developments of the late Neolithic and early Bronze Age is the construction of what are known as "henge monuments" (commonly known as stone circles). Initially, many of these monuments were created from turf rather than stone, and consisted of earthworks in the form of banks and ditches. In some cases, simple monuments made of timber were erected on top of these earthworks.[6]

In the early period, wood was used to create a wide variety of henge-type constructions, as well as other types of ritual sites. Near an English village called Holme-next-the-Sea, a ring of 55 timber posts was discovered underneath a layer of peat. In the center of the circle, an oak tree had been buried in the ground in an upside down position, perhaps as an offering to the spiritual inhabitants of the Lower World. This site has been called "Seahenge" by archaeologists, and the dendochronology of the tree-rings shows that it was constructed in 2,050 B.C.E.[7]

In Britain and Ireland great stone circles were created, as well as individual standing stones, stone rows and alignments, and many smaller stone circles. In the south of Britain, a combination of monuments was used to create a great ceremonial center at Avebury. Northern Britain also boasts a number of remarkable sites. In the Orkneys, the impressive stone circles of Brodgar and Stenness were built in connection with a series of banks and ditches. Many ritual sites were constructed with "kerbs" surrounding them (borders of low-lying stones), a later development of the round passage grave design.[8]

This type of monument eventually became quite widespread in parts of Britain, and some circles were created with large ceremonial entrances. Stone circles must have served as spiritual home to many types of religious ceremonies, and could accommodate many more people than the inner chambers or forecourts of the passage tombs. The larger circles often dominated the landscape around them, and their silhouettes evoke a memory of the rituals once held within their sacred boundaries.[9]

In Scotland, two other types of ritual monuments were also created during the Bronze Age: the Clava cairns (Inverness) and the Recumbent stone circles (in the northeast). The Clava cairns consist of stone circles built around a ring cairn or round cairn. A ring cairn is a stone mound or cairn with a small, open central space. A round cairn contained an inner chamber connected to the outside world by a passageway. The recumbent stone circles were built of standing stones of varying heights, either arranged in a gradated fashion with the tallest stones in the southwestern quadrant, or with one enormous recumbent stone (a stone laying on its side) in the southwest.[10]

During the Bronze Age, stone circles and standing stones were also built throughout Ireland. There are more than 200 henge monuments in Ireland; almost half are concentrated in the southwestern portion of the island (Counties Cork and Kerry). These circles are fairly small in size, and like the Scottish recumbent stone circles often have a horizontal stone situated in the southwest. There are also a great number of stone circles in Ulster, located in the northeast of Ireland.[11]

In addition to the creation of stone circles, other types of ritual monuments were also constructed in Bronze Age Ireland. The most common type of monument was the wedge tomb, which is the most widespread megalithic construction in ancient Ireland. Between 400 and 500 wedge tombs have been discovered so far. They consist of a long narrow gallery of large upright stones covered with capstones. Wedge tombs are generally aligned with the same northeast-southwest orientation as stone circles and other megalithic constructions.[12]

Perhaps the most famous of all the henge monuments is Stonehenge, an imposing stone structure built on the windswept plains of Wiltshire in southern Britain. The first phase of this site was built around 3,000 B.C.E. and consisted of a circular earthwork that probably served as a tribal or ceremonial meeting place. The earthwork had two entrances, a main causeway in the northeast aligned with the midsummer sunrise, and a smaller secondary entrance located in the south. During the second phase of construction (2,900 to 2,600 B.C.E.), timber settings were erected in the center of the monument as well as in the entranceways.[13]

During the third and final phase of its construction, Stonehenge began to acquire the appearance for which it is so famous. Bluestones from the Preseli Mountains in Wales, each weighing up to four tons, were set up to form a double crescent in the middle of the enclosure. Several centuries later, huge sarsen stones weighing over 25 tons each were transported from the Marlborough Downs, about 20 miles to the north. Then, at the center of the site, five huge trilithons were raised. These were comprised of two upright stones with a crossing lintel stone on top. Around these stone portals, 30 upright sarsen stones were erected. These were capped with a continuous line of lintel stones, each one mortised and shaped to fit the curve of the circle.[14]

The main entrance of Stonehenge was located in the northeast and was marked by three portal stones, only one of which now remains. Outside the main entrance was a second stone that marked an alignment with the Summer Solstice sunrise. Inside the earthen bank, four Station Stones were set up to mark alignments with the Winter Solstice sunset and various points of the lunar cycle. A great processional avenue was created leading directly to the main entrance. The construction of such an impressive edifice of stone must reflect the grandeur of the ceremonies that took place at this site.[15]

A great deal has been written about the planning, construction and alignments of the henge monuments. Indeed, one can find a theory to support almost any type of possible purpose or cosmic alignment. While there is a quite a bit of variation in the alignments of the tomb monuments and stone circles, overall there is a marked predilection for a northeast/southwest orientation. Archaeologists from Britain's National Heritage point out that this particular axis is aligned with the midsummer sunrise and the midwinter sunset. This same alignment is seen in connection with a variety of Neolithic monuments, including Maes Howe and Newgrange, as well as Bronze Age stone circles and wedge tombs. The recumbent stone circles of Scotland and Ireland also pay special attention to the southwest quadrant, and many of these stone monuments are even concentrated in the northeast and southwest parts of the country.[16]

This traditional alignment, which runs diagonally from the northeast to the southwest, appears to have played an important role in the spiritual beliefs and practices of our ancestors. It was undoubtedly associated with the rising and setting of the sun at various points of the annual cycle. The point of the Summer Solstice sunrise, which marks the longest day of the year and apex of the sun's light, may have been associated with waxing or increasing life energies. Conversely, the point of the Winter Solstice sunset, the shortest day of the year and the time of greatest darkness, may have been associated with waning energies or concepts associated with death and transformation.

Without the aid of texts or inscriptions, however, the exact beliefs of our Bronze Age ancestors continue to lie just beyond our reach. We can say that these sites clearly served as an important focal point for a variety of complex ritual activities connected with personal, family or community spiritual needs and beliefs. These may have been associated with the earth, the celestial realms, the gods and ancestors, and the worlds that exist beyond.

Theology, Music and Ritual

During the later part of the Bronze Age, a number of new burial practices began to appear in Europe. Contrasting with the communal burial practices of the Neolithic era, single or individual burials became more prevalent during the Bronze Age. Later still, cremation was the most common practice. In some areas, the ashes of the dead were placed in pottery urns and buried in large well-defined cemeteries. Because of this practice of placing urns in large fields, this sub-phase of prehistory is sometimes referred to as the "Urnfield" period (approximately 1300 to 700 B.C.E.). At many of these sites there does not seem to be a focus on social differentiation or segregation of the sexes.[17]

In Northern Europe, other types of burial rites were practiced. Cremated remains were sometimes buried in graves that were (paradoxically) large enough to accommodate a full burial. In some areas, large mounds or barrows were placed on top of the cremation burial, serving as a clearly visible marker for future generations. Very rich grave goods were sometimes placed inside the mounds. Some gravesites were outlined with stones, and even shaped like boats, perhaps symbolizing the soul's journey to the beyond.[18]

The shift from burial to cremation is believed to signify a change in spiritual perceptions about death and the afterlife. When a person's remains are buried in full, the wholeness or entirety of the physical body may be considered necessary to the spirit of the deceased person or for them to accomplish their journey to the afterlife. When people are cremated, on the other hand, it suggests that the soul or spirit is of primary concern, and that the body is understood to be a temporary physical repository of the person's spiritual essence. Once the spirit leaves that physical body, it can journey to another realm, or even phase of existence.

One religious symbol that played an increasingly important role in Bronze Age Europe was the image of the bird. Bird figurines made of bronze or clay have frequently been found, including individual statuettes or smaller images forming part of a larger object like a cauldron or pottery vessel. In many traditional cultures, birds are associated with the journey of the soul, both during trance states and during the soul's journey to the afterlife. The possibility that this type of symbolism was represented in Bronze Age settings is suggested by the existence of small bronze carts, wagons or chariots that carry figures of birds (perhaps symbolizing the journey of the soul). These miniature vehicles are believed to be replicas of actual carts or wagons used in religious rites or processions.[19]

One of the most interesting developments during this period is the ritual use of music. Archaeological evidence from Bronze Age Europe shows that a variety of musical instruments were created, many of which are known to produce sounds that have the potential to affect a shift in consciousness or awareness. In Ireland, bronze horns were created which were either played from the side or end of the horn. Both straight and curved horns have been found, the latter type probably reflecting the shape of a bull's horn. Experiments with these horns showed that they produced a variety of sounds similar to the Australian *didgeridu*. The didgeridu is used by Aboriginal people in religious ceremonies to contact and work with spiritual beings, and its distinctive sound is well known for its trance-inducing properties.[20]

Elegant bronze trumpets were also found in Denmark. The trumpets were discovered in pairs and are believed to have been used in ritual performances. The horns were found to have a very pure and resonant sound, capable of producing eight or nine notes in the overtone series (a naturally occurring acoustical phenomenon renowned for its trance-inducing capabilities).[21]

Pottery and metal drums were found at a number of central European locations. In some cases there is evidence to show that pottery drums were utilized in ceremonies; they were also left inside tombs.[22] Bone whistles and panpipes have also been discovered, as well as an instrument called a *tintinnabulum*. This is a type of percussion instrument made from circular rings of sheet metal, which hang from a small metal rod. Smaller metal rings also hang from the rod and act as clappers, producing a series of rhythmic ringing tones.[23]

Other unusual musical artifacts were discovered at lakeside settlements, habitation sites that became increasingly popular during the Bronze Age. These include long bronze tubes to which metal rings were attached. When shaken, these objects produced a very resonant rattle-like sound. Small, hollow pottery globes were also found at lakeside sites that contained a small piece of hardened clay inside them. These would have made a jingling or rattling noise when shaken.[24] Egg-shaped metal rattles known as *crotals* were also discovered at a number of northern European sites, including Ireland and Scotland.[25] At Bronze Age sites in Switzerland and Poland, archaeologists uncovered beautiful pottery rattles shaped liked birds.[26] In many traditional cultures, drums, rattles and wind instruments are frequently used to provide music for religious ceremonies. People in these cultures are well aware of the consciousness-altering properties of certain rhythms, tones and scales, particularly those produced by instruments that emit sounds rich in overtones.

Another fascinating ritual object from Bronze Age Europe with possible female connections comes from late Bronze Age Germany. Dating to the ninth–eighth centuries B.C.E., it is a ceremonial percussion instrument known as a *sistrum*. This particular instrument consists of a narrow metal handle on top of which is a U-shaped frame. Across the top of the frame is a thin bar of metal from which a small bell-shaped disk of metal was suspended. Several more metal disks were fastened to the top of the handle by a series of small metal rings. The sistrum is played by rhythmically shaking it, producing a series of resonant sounds similar to a rattle but much richer in overtones.[27]

The sistrum is familiar to most people from its use in ancient Egypt. When I first discovered a sistrum in a Bronze Age German context I was astonished, but assumed it somehow made its way into Europe through trade routes. However, the dating of the find did not seem to correlate with this scenario, and so I began to research the forms and uses of the sistrum in ancient Egyptian contexts.

In Egypt, the sistrum was not only a practical musical instrument but also a cult object in its own right. Of all the instruments used in ancient Egypt, none has more specific sacred associations than the sistrum. There were two different kinds of Egyptian sistra. The first, which dates back to the Old Kingdom (2686 B.C.E. to 2181 B.C.E.) was the "*naos*-shaped" sistrum. It was made from faience (an early type of glass) and consisted of a papyrus-shaped handle with a square frame on top shaped like a naos (miniature chapel). Inside the frame were bars of metal onto which metal disks were strung. On either side of the naos were objects thought to symbolize the horns of the Goddess Hathor. While this type of sistrum was certainly usable, it was also somewhat fragile and would have had only moderate acoustic potential.[28]

The second kind of sistrum is the "arched sistrum," mentioned in Egyptian texts as far back as the Middle Kingdom (2030 B.C.E. to 1786 B.C.E.) although depicted only in the artwork of the New Kingdom (1567 B.C.E. to 1085 B.C.E.). It was made of metal and had an arched frame on top (rather than the square frame of the *naos*). Inside the arched frame were several bent metal bars onto which metal disks were strung. Some instruments were quite simple in design, while others were decorated with a wide variety of ornamental motifs. The decorations frequently consisted of the head of the goddess Hathor, which was placed between the arched frame and the papyrus shaped handle. In the Late Period other motifs were added, including cats and uraeus serpents.[29]

One of the most fascinating things about the sistrum is that it was almost exclusively played by women. It was considered to be essentially a female instrument (although in the Middle Kingdom there is a depiction of a male priest instructing priestesses in the art of sistrum playing). Female court musicians played the lute, the lyre, the double oboe or the boat-shaped harp, but the sistrum was considered to be an instrument appropriate for a woman of noble birth. The sistrum was also the cult rattle of priestesses and princesses. The purpose of the sistrum was in all cases the same: it was shaken in front of the image of a deity to propitiate and invoke the divine presence.[30]

As I continued my research into the origins of this fascinating instrument, I realized something quite remarkable. None of the Egyptian sistra looked anything at all like the German sistrum. Even the simpler Egyptian models looked nothing like the German example. The width and form of the handle, the shape of the frame, the placement of the metal bars, and the design and arrangement of the metal disks or clappers were all quite different.

The European sistrum was created several centuries after the last depictions of the instrument in the New Kingdom period. Although there is the possibility that these images may have somehow been seen in Europe and the instrument reproduced, it is also possible that the inhabitants of Bronze Age Germany came up with the idea on their own at a later date. Many other types of unique musical instruments were produced in Bronze Age Europe, and there is no reason to think that these were all the result of outside influence. However, it must also be said that one of the most appealing prospects about the existence of a sistrum in ancient Europe is the possibility that as in Egypt it was used by priestesses or noble women in ceremonies that venerated goddess figures.

In addition to the use of musical instruments, the people of Bronze Age Europe were apparently fond of ritual costumes and adornment. Gold was used to create a wide variety of symbolic ornaments, many of which must have been used as religious regalia. In Bronze Age Ireland, several kinds of specialized ornaments were made from thin sheets of hammered gold. The first type is known as a "sun-disc," and consists of small, round discs of gold decorated with an equal-armed cross motif that is believed to be a symbol of the sun. Two small perforations were made in the center of the disc which suggest they may have been sewn onto robes or garments.[31]

The second type of ornament is the lunula, a ceremonial neck ornament shaped like a crescent-moon. These were often decorated with small lines, zigzags and triangular designs around the edges. About eighty gold lunulae have been found in Ireland and others in Scotland, Cornwall and Wales. A third kind of ceremonial ornament from Bronze Age Ireland is the *gorget*, a large, elaborate neck ornament shaped like a multi-tiered collar. These were decorated with concentric circle designs, and were probably worn by leaders or spiritual practitioners during rituals or processions.[32]

Ritual headgear has also been found at a number of Bronze Age sites. A small, polished conical gold cap was unearthed in south central Britain and probably worn by a priest or priestess. Several gold circular ornaments found in Belgium and the Netherlands may have been worn as either headdresses or neck-rings. Some of the most remarkable examples of ritual wear from the Bronze Age are enormous gold headdresses discovered at French and German sites. These consist of tall, conical brimmed hats up to 75 centimeters in height that could have been seen from a great distance. Each was made from a single piece of sheet gold and decorated with rows of concentric circles, stripes, dots, eye-shaped objects, ovals and half-moon shapes. The tops of several headdresses were also decorated with multiple-pointed stars.[33]

Other types of special materials were also used to create ritual objects and ornaments. In some areas, especially parts of Scotland, elaborate necklaces were made of jet beads, possibly simulating the shape of the lunula but utilizing other valuable (but perhaps less costly) materials. Jet and amber beads, ornaments and necklaces have also been uncovered at a number of Bronze Age sites in Britain.[34]

Ornate wooden scepters up to sixteen inches long were found at lake dwellings in Central Europe. These were carefully engraved with triangular and zig-zag patterns and must have been used in some sort of religious setting.[35] Bone mounts for ceremonial scepters in a zigzag or lightning motif were also found in Wiltshire, England.[36] A ritual cup made entirely from amber was found in Britain, as well as small pottery cups from Ireland with small perforations in their sides, perhaps used as incense vessels.[37] These remarkable objects help create a visual image of the complex rituals that must have taken place throughout Europe during this time.

Overall, bronze was the most widely used prestige and ritual material utilized during this phase of history. The most common objects created from the new prestigious metal were vessels and bladed implements. Beautiful cauldrons were made from sheet bronze, some of which had rounded handles so they could be suspended from poles and ceremonially carried into a feast or ritual gathering. Daggers and swords were also made from the new alloy, and like the cauldrons and vessels, these appear to have possessed both practical and symbolic functions and meanings.[38]

These two symbols — the vessel and the blade — would continue to play an important role in European society and religion, exerting a powerful influence on cultural and mythological traditions that lasted well into medieval times and the modern era. In order to understand how these symbols developed, we must examine the development of Bronze Age ritual.

The Cauldron and the Sword

One of the most important innovations of the European Bronze Age at first seemed little more than a new burial practice. However, the ideologies and cultural traditions associated with this practice, and its subsequent influence on almost every part of ancient Europe, came to symbolize an entirely new way of life that eventually formed the basis for much of native European culture and religion.[39]

As we have seen, in many areas burial rites shifted from group burials at communal sites to single or individual burials. Grave goods became much more common and new objects were now buried with the dead. These included bone, antler, flint, stone and metal tools and weapons, as well as copper, bronze, silver and gold ornaments. These practices varied to some degree from region to region. In Bronze Age Spain, men were buried with copper or bronze weapons and jewelry. Women were buried with metal knives and tools and silver adornments. In the Alpine regions and Poland, men were buried with metal blades and ornaments, and women with clay vessels and jewelry.[40]

At various sites in Denmark, bodies were buried in thick oak coffins. Some of these bodies were exceptionally well preserved. Men were buried with weapons, carved wooden bowls, and jewelry, and women with metal daggers, birch-bark vessels, and bronze and gold jewelry. In Britain, grave goods were rich and varied between the sexes. Although certain objects were buried primarily with one gender or the other, both men and women were

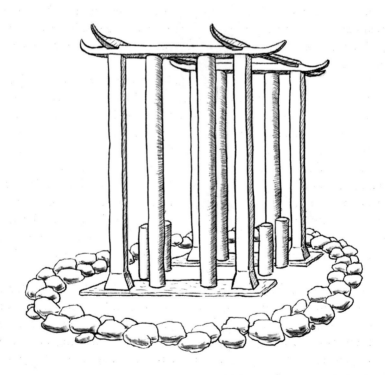

Reconstruction of wooden "horned" temple from Bargeroosterveld, Drenthe, Holland, Bronze Age period. Artist: James Möbius.

buried with flint blades and bronze daggers, tools made of antler, flint and bronze, and jet and gold ornaments.[41]

In many cases, these grave goods included symbolic objects that seemed to imply social distinction, perhaps based on skill, ancestry, wisdom or some other factor. They also seem to suggest a change in societal focus away from communal projects (like megalithic tombs) towards a society in which individual achievement was celebrated.[42]

In the early Bronze Age, a new type of pottery vessel called "Corded Ware" was placed in some of the earliest single grave burials. These vessels were often accompanied by a stone axe. Over time, a variation on this type of vessel developed, known as a "Bell Beaker," a tall drinking vessel that held about a liter of liquid. These vessels became extremely prominent all over Bronze Age Europe and were found in gravesites from Scotland to Italy. Beakers were frequently accompanied by other grave goods, the most widespread of which was the blade (first made of flint, then copper, and then bronze).[43]

The custom of burying people with a vessel and a blade symbolizes the beginning of a new way of life for the people of ancient Europe. Previous settlements and social structures began to shift to a more mobile and adaptable way of life that reflected the opportunity to join a new cultural community with unique traditions, beliefs and rituals.[44]

What do these two ritual objects signify? The pottery vessels, at least in some instances, appear to have been associated with the ritualized use of beverages, some of which contained alcohol. These would have included rites of feasting and hospitality, as well as religious rites and ceremonies, perhaps including concepts associated with the afterlife. Ritual beverages could be made from wild fruits or honey, as well as grain. Remnants of mead have been found inside pottery vessels at some sites, as well as pollen from fruits and an herb known as meadowsweet, probably used to flavor the mead.[45] In later European spiritual tradition, sacred vessels figure prominently in religion and folklore. In these contexts they symbolize attributes like nourishment and abundance, healing and transformation, and the attainment of divine wisdom.[46]

Like the vessel, the blade also involved two-fold symbolism, both practical and esoteric. During the Neolithic, competition for farmland may have reached a level that necessitated the development of a group of people charged with protection and defense. The previous strategy of building large monuments whose authority supported claims to the land may have no longer been able to serve its original purpose.

In this social and ritual context, the appearance of weapons does not necessarily equate directly with violent action. The very presence of a weapon can be a deterrent to violence, and therefore it can function in a symbolic manner. In fact, some of these objects were not entirely functional, showing that their suitability for use in action was secondary to their elaborate appearance.[47]

A trained warrior class — as well as other specialists like metalsmiths, potters, weavers and so forth — probably began to form part of European society at this time. The presence of symbolic and ritual blades, both in social and religious settings, may suggest that those responsible for protecting their people would have focused on concepts like courage, honor, loyalty, and skill. These ideals continued to play an enormous role in the legends and beliefs of Europe for centuries to come.[48]

Sacred vessels and blades also played an important role in another widespread practice that developed during the later Bronze Age. This was the deliberate offering of metal objects — including weapons, cauldrons and ornaments — to the supernatural powers. From Ireland to Czechoslovakia, single items, as well as huge hoards of votive offerings, were buried in gravesites, placed under earthen mounds, or offered into bodies of water. These objects were usually made of gold or bronze (although amber, tin and other materials were also sometimes used). In northwestern Europe, swords, spears and shields, gold and bronze tools and ornaments, ritual horns and rattles, and metal vessels and cauldrons were widely offered in rivers, lakes and bogs.[49]

The pattern suggested by these activities is that these offerings were being presented to the gods of the Lower World or other spiritual beings who inhabited the regions beneath the earth and the waters. It is believed that these may have been offerings to appease water gods, weather gods or other chthonic divinities, for during the late Bronze Age, the climate began to deteriorate.

Temperatures dropped, and rainfall and flooding increased, both of which could have a devastating effect on crops. This would have aggravated conditions like soil erosion and lack of soil fertility that were already present (or prevalent) in some areas. Bogs, heaths and moors, which seem like natural parts of the landscape, are actually the result of intensified settlement and farming practices that began during the Neolithic era. While some of the environmental changes that took place during the Bronze Age were the result of naturally fluctuating climactic cycles, a good deal of it was caused by the misuse and overuse of the land.[50]

Perhaps the most evocative objects associated with these offerings to the Underworld powers are the blade and the vessel. From early flint blades to copper daggers and bronze swords; and from pottery drinking vessels and burial urns to large metal cauldrons; these objects were utilized and offered at countless sites all over Europe. The widespread use of the vessel and the blade in burials and offering ceremonies attests to their cultural and spiritual significance. As the Bronze Age progressed, swords began to be offered into bodies of water in many parts of Britain. This practice continued for many centuries, and its symbolic importance would echo in the myths and legends of the island for centuries to come.[51]

Dancers, Birds and Sword-Bearers

The Bronze Age was an incredibly rich period of European history, and the Divine Feminine makes a number of bold appearances during this era. In Eastern Europe and the Danube region, a number of human figurines were made from clay. Most are female and wear elaborately decorated skirts or dresses, the lower portions often formed into cylindrical or bell-like shapes. Facial features are usually not very prominent, but the women wear belts, jewelry and headscarves and are sometimes depicted with a long braid of hair at the back of the head.[52]

In Denmark and Germany, numerous bronze figurines have been discovered which depict women engaged in various types of ritual activity. A knife from late Bronze Age Germany was carefully crafted into the shape of a female figure. She is dressed in a skirt made from woolen cord similar to women's garments found in the oak-coffin graves of Northern Europe. She wears two neck rings and holds a vessel between her hands.[53]

A bronze figurine of a female dancer was found in Denmark, also wearing a woolen cord skirt. She is arched backwards, perhaps as part of a ritual dance or acrobatic display. Other bronze figurines of female dancers or acrobats were also discovered, as well as male figurines who wear horned helmets and carry ritual axes. One bronze figurine depicts a kneeling female figure involved in prayer or enacting a religious ceremony. She was buried with a number of bronze animals, including a long snake with a curved tail that wears a horse's bit and reins, and four horned animal heads.[54]

A number of miniature cult wagons made of bronze have been discovered at many Bronze Age sites. They are frequently drawn by birds, ducks or swans, and sometimes carry a divine figure inside them. One chariot bore a figure wearing a robe covered with sun symbols, while another contained a female figure with a bell-shaped skirt and a bird's head.[55]

In the later part of the Bronze Age, human figures were also depicted but in a very different style. Male and female images were carved onto large standing stones during the fourth and third millennia B.C.E. These were widely produced throughout Europe, from Britain to the Black Sea. Archaeologists believe the figures on these stones may be Bronze Age gods and goddesses, heroes and heroines, or biological or divine ancestors.[56]

Male figures are frequently depicted with daggers, axes and shields, and sometimes with bow and arrows. They often wear pendants and neck ornaments, as well as a bag suspended from a belt. The female figures do not usually have weapons (although in some cases they do), and are depicted with small round breasts, combs, neck ornaments and elaborately decorated bodices or robes. Both male and female carved stones sometimes wear a double-spiral pendant and the back of male and female statues may depict a striped or checkered mantle or cloak.[57]

One of the most famous of these carved stone statues is a female figure from Bronze Age France. Carved from a single piece of red-brown sandstone, her face is depicted solely by the presence of her eyes and nose. Above her small, rounded breasts is a great ritual collar or multiple-stranded necklace. Some of the most intriguing details of this carving are the unusual motifs depicted on the woman's face. On either side of her nose are three small horizontal lines believed to represent ritual tattoos. A set of tattoo needles was uncovered at a Bronze Age gravesite, and so it is entirely possible that this technology was known and used by Bronze Age European cultures.[58]

Another interesting feature of the statue is an unusual object engraved on the front of the figure, just between her breasts. On many of the stone statues, male and female, the arms are depicted bent inwards at the waist, in some cases holding an object (in male statues, an axe or blade). The object depicted in this female carving has been tentatively described by archaeologists as a "Y-shaped pendant."

However, the object is clearly too wide to be a pendant. It seems to be some sort of object that is being held or symbolically presented by the female figure. It may be a sword or ritual blade, the end of which is hidden beneath the edge of her belt. The upper part of the object has a curved shape almost identical to the curved sword pommels on some of the other statues. Those blades appear more angled than the straight blade seen in this representation, but this may reflect the tapered tip of the sword, as opposed to the straight upper edge of the blade visible above the woman's belt. Bronze Age women were sometimes buried with flint blades, or copper or bronze daggers (as evidenced in the examples given above from burials in Spain, Denmark and Britain). Accordingly, there is no reason to suppose that this female warrior or divine figure did not also have the power to wield such an object.[59]

The symbolism of the examples above suggests that the divine female figures of the European Bronze Age may have been associated with dancing, offering ceremonies, the powers of the earth and the waters, and the symbolism of both vessel and blade. These were formidable divinities whose forms and attributes would continue to grow. Eventually they manifested as well-known deities and supernatural women, like the river goddesses of Iron Age Europe or the medieval figure of the Lady of the Lake, divine women whose archetypal powers and legendary names still resonate in our day and age.

The Spiritual Ancestors of Europe

At this point, the observant reader may be wondering about the origins of the great social and spiritual changes that took place during the European Bronze Age. It would not be inappropriate to think of this era as having two phases: (1) an earlier phase in which henge monuments and stone circles were created, with a focus on communal burial, and (2) a later phase with individual gravesites and ritual sites containing vessels, weapons, tools and jewelry. Indeed, the introduction of cultural innovations like burial mounds, horses and drinking vessels into western and northern Europe has been the subject of a great deal of historical speculation.[60]

Many of these innovations are believed to originate from inter-cultural contact, sharing, trade, and the linguistic and social influence of small influxes of population groups who arrived in Europe from the eastern steppes sometime in the early third millennium B.C.E. They initially seem to have settled primarily in the open plains, far away from farming settlements. Over time, their presence and influence spread into the Danube region, where goods and ideas like metalworking, chariots and horse culture traveled by river into other parts of Europe.[61]

These people were characterized by traditional practices of herding and riding horses, as well as the creation of distinctive burial sites. These consisted of single graves which often contained wooden wagons or wagon wheels, and which were marked with an anthropomorphic stone pillar. Due to the nature of the evidence, historians have experienced difficulty determining whether these changes are the result of incoming population groups or simply the result of adopting new ideas and technologies.[62]

Radiocarbon dating shows that for about two hundred years, the people associated with horses and burial mounds initially lived nearby (but outside of) communities involved in the building of megalithic monuments. Were these new groups utilizing innovative methods to compete for territory? Or were they simply traveling around in search of new pastureland (and possibly adventure)?

Over time, through processes that are somewhat unclear, the culture of the steppe inhabitants became the dominant social element in many parts of

Europe. Their traditions spread into the Baltic region and eastern Russia, the Rhineland and Switzerland, and into Britain, Ireland and Scandinavia. This cultural metamorphosis is considered one of the largest and most revolutionary transformations ever seen in the prehistory of Europe.

Indeed, recent studies of DNA from ancient skeletal remains from Central Europe show that the foundations of the modern gene pool date to about 4,500 years ago. The research was undertaken by Professor Alan Cooper, formerly of Oxford University and currently at the University of Adelaide, Australia. His work suggests that the genetic legacy of hunter-gatherers and early farmers was all but erased by later migrations during the Middle Neolithic and Bronze Age. At this point, DNA patterns more closely resemble those of people living today, pointing to a major and previously unrecognized population upheaval around 4,000 B.C.E.[63]

This appears to be the first truly pan–European culture, and it was clearly very successful. A significant contribution to the gene pool was made by populations associated with the Bell Beaker archaeological culture. A genetic group known as Haplogroup H dominates mitochondrial DNA variation in Europe and accounts for about 40 percent of European ancestry. The DNA sequenced from ancient skeletons has begun to shed light on the complex prehistoric events that shaped modern European population groups, and it is believed these changes were brought about by the rapid growth and movement of some populations.[64]

In some areas, the new practices seem to have caught on almost immediately while in other regions the process took more time, sometimes even encountering a measure of cultural resistance (especially in regions associated with large ceremonial sites like Stonehenge and Avebury). However in Brittany, where there was a tradition of megalith building, the new innovations were adopted early on. Evidence from Spain and Portugal suggests that peaceful relations took place between established populations and incoming groups, accompanied by the exchange of horses, goods and ideas.[65]

Overall, there is not a great deal of evidence to support the popular theory that these new ways of living spread as a result of violence or oppression. However these developments caught on, radical changes in thoughts and ideas about cultural values, social organization and religious practices had taken place, as well as a new emphasis on different types of material culture. The new way of life seems to reflect the possibility of a more individually focused lifestyle or ethos, which contrasts with the earlier communal emphasis of megalithic cult centers. People were still members of a tribe or community, yet it was a major break from or expansion of previous traditions, one that would form the predominant social and spiritual basis of Europe for millennia to come.[66]

The name usually associated with these incoming population groups and their ideas is "Indo-European." This term is used to refer to people who originally lived somewhere in the region near or between the Caspian Sea and the Black Sea, whose descendants spread their culture, language and cultural identity throughout many parts of the ancient world. The term "Indo-European" was chosen because some of these people migrated south into India, while others traveled north and west into Europe. The language spoken by these people eventually developed into a number of well-known languages, ancient and modern. These include Sanskrit in the south, the Indo-Iranian and Tocharian languages in the east, and most of the languages of modern Europe (with the exception of Hungarian, Estonian, Finnish and Basque).[67]

Early Indo-European people originally settled in major river valleys and their tributaries. Over time, with the introduction of livestock breeding, the domestication of the horse, and the use of wheeled vehicles, they were able to increase their flexibility and range, and moved out into the open steppes. The steppe regions served as an enormous sphere of cross-cultural and intertribal interactions, as evidenced by the almost instantaneous spread of the new burial practices throughout the entire region.[68]

Starting around 4,000 B.C.E., the inhabitants of the steppes, and their distinctive languages and way of life, reached the borders of the Balkan region. The most reasonable avenue for the dissemination of Indo-European language and culture into the rest of Europe seems to be one associated with the spread of Corded Ware (in individual burials that contained ritual vessels, blades and ornaments).[69]

Indo-European root words still form the basis of many words in English and other modern European languages. The ancient word for horse was something like *ek-wo, a reflex of which can be seen in Latin *equus* and Old Irish *ech*, as well as English words like "equine" and "equestrian."[70] The relationship between Indo-European languages is easily seen in the words for the cardinal numbers. The Proto-Indo-European derivative for the number "two" is *duwo*, which we can compare with Latin and Greek *duo*, French *deux*, Welsh *dau* and English *duo*. The word for three was *treyes*, a reflex of which exists in the Spanish and Latin *tres,* French *trois,* Swedish *tre* and Irish and Welsh *tri*. A number of other parallels are evident in words pertaining to animals, the environment and social relationships.[71]

What about Bronze Age religious ideology? What did the Indo-Europeans believe (or, in Indo-European terminology, "to what did they put their hearts"?) Some words associated with religion reflect their Indo-European origins, as in the Proto-Indo-European word for "god" or "deity"—*dyeus*—which compares with Sanskrit *dyaus* and *devas*, Latin *deus*, Lithuanian *dievas* and

Old Irish *dia*. We can piece together other aspects of the beliefs and practices of these ancient people by looking at later Indo-European societies and mythologies, many of which contain a number of fascinating parallels (as well as interesting developments and variations).[72]

As a result of their common Indo-European heritage, certain religious ideas and concepts are seen (in varying forms) in Hindu, Iranian, Roman, Greek, Germanic, Baltic, Scandinavian and Celtic mythology. The in-depth study of Indo-European language, culture and religion constitutes a formal field of research, one which continues to bring to light a great deal of interesting information about the ancient past.

Indo-European pantheons often included a sun-god or sun-goddess (both types are common), a father-deity (sometimes associated with the celestial realms), female divinities associated with the moon and dawn, male thunder-, rain- or storm-gods, and other deities associated with aspects of the natural world. Gods and goddesses were also associated with concepts like wisdom, skill, fertility, healing, battle, prophecy and other social and cultural ideals.[73]

Indo-European mythology frequently includes creation myths, legends of conflicts or interactions between various orders of divine beings, and myths associated with the origins of social structure and religious rites and philosophies. There are often tales of deities associated with the land of the dead and the underworld realms, as well as divine figures who are perceived as the immortal ancestors of human beings.[74]

One common thread that seems to run through many Indo-European belief systems is the significance of the number three. Society was often divided into three main groups or classes: (1) kings and holy persons, (2) warriors and protectors (and possibly craftspersons) and (3) herders and cultivators. There may also be three distinguished classes of holy or learned persons. Sacred figures may have three aspects or titles, and the cosmos was believed to consist of three cosmological realms.[75]

Specific symbolism connected with animals is also widespread in Indo-European mythology. In many traditions, the horse was considered to be one of the most sacred of all creatures. Cattle figure prominently in the myths, frequently as a symbol of wealth and abundance. Birds are a common religious motif, and the serpent plays an interesting role, often associated with the Underworld and the initiatory adventures of heroes. Symbolism associated with the arrangement of sacred space, cyclical patterns of sacred time, the attributes of colors and the cardinal directions, and the ritual significance of sacred objects also display a number of interesting parallels.[76]

In spite of their complex culture and sophisticated religious traditions, the Indo-Europeans have popularly been characterized as a ravaging horde of patriarchal marauders who cut and slashed their way through Europe, decimating peaceful, matriarchal cultures that had survived intact from Paleolithic or Neolithic periods. There are a number of obvious problems with this theory, which previous chapters have already addressed. For one thing, there is little or no evidence of violence associated with the spread of Indo-European traditions.[77] Patriarchal social structures may well have already been in place before they arrived in Europe. In addition, the use of weapons and defenses was already well established in Neolithic Europe prior to their arrival or influence, as we saw in a previous chapter.

In actuality, Indo-European languages, cultures and religions form the basis for many of the indigenous social, cultural and spiritual foundations of Europe, in both the ancient and modern eras. The inhabitants of the steppe regions contributed a number of innovative ideas to our culture which were woven into the myths, legends and practices of European civilization over thousands of years. The figure of a knight or warrior-queen setting out on a journey of personal discovery bearing a magical sword or shield, riding upon a trusty equine companion is an archetypal Indo-European image.

Tales of travelers ranging far from home, using their ingenuity, skill and courage to navigate their way through unfamiliar or supernatural terrain is another facet of the legacy. Social ideals like honor, courage, truth and the glory of a life well lived have passed into modern culture from our Indo-European heritage. The potential of each person to pursue his or her own path, to answer the spiritual call to adventure also hails from this Indo-European inheritance.

The relevance of this wisdom from the past echoes in the words of women's activist Gloria Steinem: "I come from the tribe that has lost its memory.... And the loss of memory is the root of oppression.... We need to take those qualities that existed in most ancient cultures five thousand years ago and bring them into modern times."[78]

Many of the specifics of Indo-European beliefs, rituals and spiritual concepts were not encoded in writing until several thousand years after the initial introduction of steppe-based culture. However, using linguistic and archaeological evidence, as well as social and religious parallels, scholars are able to work backwards in time to retrieve some of the roots of these traditions. The myths and beliefs of the descendants of the earliest Indo-Europeans were eventually preserved in written form and these provide important new vantage points from which to view the wisdom of the past.

Up to this point, much of the cultural and spiritual history of Europe has by necessity been interpreted and reconstructed based almost solely on archaeological evidence: the results of excavations, the mute testimony of set-tlements and burial sites, and the fascinating but difficult-to-interpret artifacts. Fortunately, we have been guided by the expertise of anthropologists and other specialists to help us discern between fact and fiction, probability and possibility, educated theory and rampant speculation.

Now, with the appearance of Indo-European languages, cultures and religious traditions, our window into the ancient past opens into a new world of possibility. From the words of myths, legends and written sources, we will finally know the names and attributes of the goddesses and sacred women of Europe as they step out of the mists of the prehistoric period (prior to the advent of written records) and onto the pages of history itself. And these divine figures and holy women are formidable indeed.

8

Priestess, Goddess and Warrior Woman

Spirit-masters of the Underworld
Sit on your horse, and put on your robe...
Master-spirits of the earth and water...
I burn my juniper and offer water and milk...
Let my people live well...
Let life be without obstacles...

— Excerpt from Tuvan Shaman's Song[1]

You are from the Mother Earth.
What you are doing is as great as warriors do.

— Message of the White Buffalo Calf Woman
to the women of the Lakota nation[2]

A late summer wind blew across the treeless plain, whistling over the green burial mound. Inside lay the bodies of the chieftain and his wife, who had co-ruled in wisdom and honor for many seasons. The chieftain had been elected after years of loyal service to his predecessor, gaining distinction as a horse-rider, orator, counselor, warrior and singer. He was known for his courage, his ability to interpret the stars, and his generosity.

His wife was equally renowned and much loved among the people. She was an expert horsewoman and adept at reading the signs of the natural world. She had trained as a warrior, but after an injury to her shoulder she served the tribe in another capacity. Upon her marriage to the chieftain, she began to follow the vocation of the priestess.

The years passed, and after many seasons the queen left this world for the realm of the gods. After her death, the chieftain seemed to lose his energy and enthusiasm for life. One winter evening, he put on his best garment, one she had embroidered with images of stags and griffins. He walked out of his

117

tent and onto the windswept plains, and there he passed into the world of spirit. The couple lay side by side in a burial mound of exquisite beauty, lined with felt hangings and equipped with gold objects, food and drink, and clothing for the sacred journey that lay ahead.

Much to the people's regret, the couple had no children. Their legacy was cultural and spiritual, for they left behind the blessings of a productive era of peace, prosperity and creativity. They had invested a great deal of effort in training young men and women devoted to the tribe and its ancient traditions, young people who were affectionately known as their "nieces" and "nephews."

One of the queen's "nieces" stood out on the open plain, listening to the voices of her ancestors as they floated in on the wind. She wore a cape decorated with animals who served as her spirit helpers. Small bronze and iron bells were sewn along the edge of her cape, and around her neck was a bronze mirror, used to repel negative energies and gain access to the unseen world. On her head she wore a short, pointed headdress with a light-green veil that covered her face during the most solemn rites of her profession.

It had been over a year since the great funeral procession, and she was now responsible for part of the tribe's spiritual inheritance. She was consecrated to the great horse goddess of the plains, a being so sacred her image was never created by human hands. The blessings of the goddess ensured the fertility of the land and the success of the mortal rulers of the territory.

The young priestess drew her veil before her eyes and turned her thoughts inward. She raised her ritual blade, whose handle was carved in the form of a stag with an elaborate set of antlers. Facing the west, she sang a long epic poem she had practiced in preparation for this moment ever since the funeral rites had ended. Setting a small stone altar on the ground, she lit a mixture of birch bark, artemisia leaves and cannabis seeds. Then, taking a bone ritual spoon from out of her bag, she ladled a mixture of mare's milk and honey around the base of the mound.

After the offering ceremony, she began to drop into an altered state of awareness. Swooning gently with divine connection, she dropped to her knees in front of the burial mound. After a few moments, she lifted her mirror up to her forehead. A low murmur emerged from under her breath, and she repeated an invocation for several minutes. At last, she was ready to look into the mirror.

Holding the mirror in front of her face, she stared intently at its polished surface. At first, she saw only her own reflection and the blue spirals tattooed on her face at the time of her initiation. She adjusted her gaze and looked more deeply inside the oracle. She sensed that her offerings and songs had been well received. The chieftain and his warrior-priestess wife had longed to be remembered since their rite of passage had taken place. The land had also accepted the offerings with gratitude.

Near the end of her vision-state, she caught a fleeting glimpse of the horse-goddess who appeared in equine form, wearing an elaborate mask made of colored felt with the wings of a bird and antlers of a deer. Sitting quietly in reflection, she heard a strange sound, like a gust of wind. Remaining still, she noticed a presence next to the mound. Her heart skipped a beat as she saw a stag with enormous antlers emerge from behind the knoll. Their eyes locked for a long moment and then the stag turned and leapt away. As she followed its path, she became aware of something out of the corner of her eye. A red-and-white hawk spiraled through the open skies just above the mound. The spirits of the land had sent a message through the guardian animals of the chieftain and his wife, the stag and the hawk. They had heard her song. With a sense of joy and humility, she stood in front of the mound and bowed before it. Turning on her heel, she began to walk back towards her tent through the tall grass.

After some time, she saw a rider approaching. As the horseman came nearer, she spotted his distinctive green coat and blue saddle-pad. Unable to believe her eyes, she ran swiftly across the plain. Several years earlier she had betrothed herself to a young man from one of the kindred tribes. The range of his clan extended far to the east, past the great mountain ranges. As a warrior-in-training, he had been called into service and the young priestess sorrowfully felt his return was unlikely. His re-appearance was surely an indication of the spirits' blessings.

In her tribe, the path of the priestess did not require a celibate lifestyle, as it did in other places. Some women involved in spiritual life did choose to remain single in order to focus their energy on their work. This was not her way, for she had been taught that a priestess must fully participate in this world as well as the world of spirit. Her own teacher had been a wife, lover, leader, warrior and priestess. Joyfully, the young warrior lifted her up onto his horse, and she knew if she could live up to half of what her teacher had been, she would be of great service to her people.[3]

As the cycles of time continued, the Bronze Age gave way to the Iron Age. Much like the gradual shift that took place between the Mesolithic and Neolithic eras, this occurred at different times in different places. In the first millennium B.C.E., iron may have originally been produced by accident during the smelting of copper with a high iron content. Over time, it began to replace bronze in the production of tools, weapons and ritual objects. New metal objects made from copper, gold, tin, silver and iron were an important part of the extensive trade systems that existed during the Iron Age. This metal trade was remarked upon by classical authors, and as a result, Europe emerged from prehistory (the era before written records) into the historical period. Two of the most famous of these early accounts are the sixth century B.C.E. *Massaliote Periplus*, a sailor's manual describing travel routes from Iberia northwards into Brittany, Ireland and Britain, and the journeys of the Greek merchant and explorer Pytheas, who sailed to Brittany, Britain and beyond around 330 B.C.E.[4]

Life in Iron Age Europe was varied and diverse, but a number of social patterns are discernable in many regions. Archaeological evidence shows that lavish feasting took place among the noble classes, accompanied by the ritual exchange of gifts between chieftains and their followers. Prestigious objects were buried in noble graves, including gold objects, chariots and funerary carts. These graves also contained mead, drinking horns, and wine drinking equipment from the Mediterranean, attesting to the continued importance of hospitality and ritual drinking ceremonies first seen in the Bronze Age.[5]

The remarkable artwork of this era was created by sophisticated schools of artists, using both native and borrowed artistic motifs. Over time, an entirely new artistic style was created, often referred to as *La Tène* or "Celtic" art. This artwork was used to create and decorate elaborate jewelry, vessels, weapons and ritual objects, and became the first truly pan–European style of artwork.[6]

The Iron Age is a huge, complex period, and to ease our journey of discovery we will explore it in two parts. In this chapter we will learn about the culture and traditions of the eastern part of Europe, and in the next chapter, the western part of the region. Throughout the Iron Age, the Divine Feminine plays an increasingly important role in culture and religion, and these beliefs and practices begin to take on familiar forms, many of which have survived up to the modern age.

Kindred Tribes and Milk of Mares

One of the most fascinating cultures of Iron Age Europe must certainly be that of the Scythians. Numerous tribes of these nomadic herders inhabited a large region that stretched from the banks of the Danube River to the borders of China. They are known for their unique culture and religion, their horsemanship and craftsmanship, and their artwork and animal symbolism (some of which influenced the artwork of great portions of Western Europe). The Scythians had a complex way of life, yet used neither writing nor currency. They were a vital political force during the Iron Age and were described by Classical authors as one of the four great "barbarian" (i.e. non–Classical) cultures of the Age. Scythian beliefs and practices are perceived through archaeological finds, as well as accounts written by the Greeks, Jews, Assyrians and Chinese.[7]

The Scythians were the primary clan of a large group of nomadic peoples who lived in the eastern steppes. Similar and perhaps related clans, sometimes referred to as the "kindred Scythian tribes," also lived in the Altai regions. The Scythians were well established in southern Russia and parts of eastern Europe by the seventh century B.C.E., although their origins may extend back as far as 1700 B.C.E. Around this time, the first Indo-European tribes are believed to have reached the Yenissei, traveling westwards past the Altai Mountains and into the Caucasus area.[8]

As in other periods of European history, the relationship between people and the environment had a profound effect on their cultural and religious traditions. In this respect, the ancient inhabitants of the eastern plains were no exception. The vast Asiatic plains were interrupted by the Pamir, Tien Shan and Ural Mountains, and were extremely cold in winter and hot in summer. This caused the vegetation of the region to be less than luxuriant and the land less adaptable for agriculture. The steppes of Russia, however, were covered with flowers, plants, fruit trees and tree cover (primarily oak, ash, lime and acacia). Lush grasses nourished the herds, and the land produced edible roots and bulbs, coriander for making infusions and cannabis for ritual purposes. Although the Ural Mountains separated the Asian and European steppes, communications and cross-cultural exchange passed between these two areas throughout the centuries.[9]

In the Central Asian plains, elk, bison, wild horses, bears, wolves and leopards roamed the steppes, while in Eastern Europe wild boars, otters, beavers, asses and goats were common. Smaller creatures like hares, minks and ermines existed, as well as eagles, pheasants and other birds, snakes and adders, and bees, valued for their honey. All of these animals are depicted in the artwork of the Scythians, sometimes depicted with realistic features and other times transformed into stylized or mythical creatures.[10]

The Scythians lived in well-organized communities and responded with loyalty and enthusiasm to their tribal chiefs. They are reported to have enjoyed artistry, finery and wealth, as well as feuding and raiding. They built permanent and semi-permanent encampments and roamed throughout the region at will, pasturing their cattle on the rich grasslands and making use of the abundant game of the steppes. They traded with other communities for raw materials like copper and gold, exhibiting great care and artistry in creating beautiful everyday objects and ritual gear.[11]

The distinctive weapons of the Scythian tribes included: long swords; small daggers attached to the left leg with a strap (not unlike the Scottish *sgian dubh*); a double curved bow made of horn (used for both hunting and raiding); and an arrow case which hung from the left hip (Scythian archers shot over their left side). The Scythians were avid horse-riders, and used horses to great advantage in their travels and exploits. Horses were considered so important that they were even buried with the dead.[12]

The daily life of a Scythian was probably quite comfortable. The land was rich in fish and game, as well as plant foods. One staple of the traditional diet was *kumis*, a beverage made from fermented mare's milk still popular in the Caucasus and Mongolia. Scythians ate cheese, onions, garlic and beans, and meat was cooked as a stew in great metal cauldrons or prepared as a sort of haggis, which would have been easier for a semi-nomad people to transport.[13]

Hippocrates reported that the Scythians were well-nourished and enjoyed life to its fullest. They were fond of singing, dancing (to the accompaniment of drums and stringed instruments), drinking wine, and pledging fellowship to each other using individual or communal vessels. They ritually burnt hemp seeds on hot stones placed inside small tents or enclosures, inhaling the vapor in a purification rite or ceremony associated with the attainment of religious ecstasy.[14]

The clothing of the Scythians was often rich and luxuriant. Garments were practical and beautiful in appearance, made from hides, wool and fur and decorated with elaborate appliqué work. Tailored woolen tunics were worn by men and longer garments shaped like a modern tailcoat by women. Other native artwork depicts men wearing comfortable belted tunics and close-fitting trousers with elaborate decoration, as well as soft, high boots and small, peaked hoods tied beneath the chin.[15]

Women's cloaks have been discovered, some of which were made of felt with fur trimmings. These were worn over long, close fitting robes that were highly decorated. Some women wore white stockings attached to leather soles. The stockings were lavishly ornamented on the lower leg or soles so they would be visible when the wearer sat cross-legged on the ground. Belts, bags and satchels were decorated with fur or appliquéd designs, and some women wore square hats or high headdresses covered with a veil.[16]

Archaeological evidence shows that Scythian chieftains were often quite tall, averaging about five feet eight inches in height. Physical prowess, as well as wisdom, courage and skill may have been considered important in a leader (especially when he was an elected ruler). Women were quite a bit shorter, averaging about five feet one inch in height. Some of the Scythians were probably European in appearance; their depiction on metal objects represents them as such. In other regions, Asian features may have been prominent. A number of well preserved bodies attests to the elaborate animal tattoos worn by the Scythians in a number of areas.[17]

Evidence from native artwork shows that the Scythians were quite concerned with personal appearance. Herodotus wrote that after funeral processions, the Scythians washed their heads with water but coated their bodies with an unguent made from pounded cypress and cedar wood pulp. This was mixed with frankincense and water to form a paste. The paste was used as a cleansing compound and kept on the body for an entire day. A pre-occupation with appearance and display is well documented in the rich burial sites of the steppes, where the dead were lavishly dressed in preparation for the journey to the next world.[18]

The Scythians were noted for a number of unusual burial practices. The noble or honored were buried in distinctive mounds. These sites were extremely important to the Scythians, who built no other temples or sanctuaries. Wooden chambers were created inside the mounds, and the walls and ceiling of the chamber were decorated with wicker or rush matting, birch bark, thatch, felt rugs or frescos. Inside the mound, the dead were placed on biers or mattresses or inside elaborate coffins.[19]

Scythian kings, queens and religious persons were buried in their finest clothes and jewelry, and provided with additional clothes for use in the afterlife. They were buried with silver and gold cups and vessels, cauldrons of food or meat, wine and oil, weapons (swords, shields and daggers), mirrors, cauldrons, jewelry, gold and bronze animals, and funerary carts or wagons.[20]

Some of the most impressive of all Scythian burial sites are the royal tombs of southern Russia. At Chertomlyk, a chieftain was buried in a central chamber, facing the east. He wore a bronze torque, a gold-earring and a number of gold finger rings, and within reach of his left hand were an ivory-handled knife, a quiver full of arrowheads, and an ivory-handled riding crop.[21]

In another chamber was a woman on a bronze bier painted with green, yellow and blue designs. She wore gold bracelets, earrings and finger-rings, and on her head was a purple veil decorated with small gold plaques. Nearby were bronze cauldrons, a silver dish, and five swords, and within reach of her hand was a bronze mirror.[22] Ritual blades, vessels and mirrors were discovered at numerous Scythian sites. Like the dagger and the cauldron, the mirror probably served a dual purpose. In addition to practical uses, in many cultures mirrors are used to ward off evil spirits or see into the future.[23]

Animals, Griffins and the Antlered God

Scythian artwork contained a number of interesting motifs, many of which were undoubtedly imbued with spiritual significance. Animals were frequently represented, and would have been of extreme importance in domestic life and in terms of spiritual relationship with the natural environment. The most frequently depicted animals are leopards, bulls, wolves, lions, stags, ibexes, mountain goats, fish, felines, swans and eagles. Overall, the stag seems to have been the favored animal of the Scythians. This is particularly interesting, for in other Eurasian cultures the stag is believed to transport the souls of the dead to the beyond.[24]

Although the horse played an incredibly important role in the daily lives and burial rites of the Scythians, it is rarely depicted in their artwork. There may have been religious significance to this practice, perhaps a sacred taboo associated with not actively portraying certain sacred entities. The horse may have been credited with supernatural powers or elevated to the status of a deity, as it was in other areas.[25]

Composite or mythical animals are very common in Scythian art. One of the most prevalent legendary creatures was the griffin, which had a lion-shaped body and tail, bird-like wings and a large beak. According to the Greeks, these bad-tempered creatures were the guardians of golden treasure located somewhere in the eastern steppes. In the second century C.E., local authors reported that dragons were reputed to live in the land of the Issodonians, a Saka tribe (the Saka were predecessors or early neighbors of the Scythians). The *I Ching* warned of "dragons in the field" and Chinese historians described "heaps of bright white stones like bones" in the Tien Shan mountains.[26]

In 1986, archaeologists working in the territory of the Issodonians discovered the fossilized skeletons of dinosaurs called Psittacosaurus. These unusual looking dinosaurs were about the size of a lion with a great parrot-like beak. Even more remarkably, these fossil remains were found in an area containing gold deposits. Scientists believe that ancient nomads in the region would have frequently come across the skeletons of these beaked dinosaurs, giving rise to the formation of the griffin and its enduring legend.[27]

Many representations of deer, and other composite animals with horns and antlers are found in the artwork of the Eurasian steppes. Some of the most beautiful examples consist of felt pony masks with elaborate decorations, which are topped with antlers also made of felt.[28] Antlers may have played an important role in religious rituals, as carved human and animal figures adorned with antlers were widespread in parts of Asia. Antlers and deer symbolism are also used to decorate the costumes of Siberian shamans.[29]

Years ago, I had the opportunity to meet a group of musicians from central Asia called *Huun Huur Tu*, who come from a horse-herding shamanic culture in Tuva that displays many similarities with other semi-nomadic cultures of the region. They practice a form of singing known as "overtone" or "throat singing." Using a variety of techniques, singers are able to produce more than one note at a time (a technique later adopted by Buddhist monks). This practice developed from their connection with the natural world and the ability to reproduce sounds heard in nature, many of which are rich in overtones.

One year after the group's annual concert in Sanders Theater at Harvard University, my partner and I escorted the group and their manager to a local restaurant for dinner. Afterwards we had the privilege of entertaining them at my home. The members of the group enjoyed playing on various musical instruments in my workspace, and were also very interested in artwork and religious objects. As experienced horse-riders and herders, a photo of a herd of running horses caught their eye. I explained that as a western shamanic practitioner, the horse was my primary spirit ally. The interpreter nodded and said, "Yes, that is your power." Two of the musicians' grandfathers were shamans, and the concept of working with spirit allies in animal form was very familiar to them.

They were particularly interested in the depiction of an antlered deity from a Celtic context, and asked me who this figure was. I said he was a Celtic deity associated with the Underworld, fertility and abundance, as well as animals and the world of nature. My response was translated for the group, who nodded their heads in agreement. The interpreter turned to me and said, "Yeah, we have one of those." It is likely that the antlered god was alive and well in the eastern steppes in earlier times as well.

Magicians, Gold and Goddesses

The ancient Scythians had a group of specialized magical practitioners known as *Enarees*. They came from particular families and were described by Classical authors as androgynes or eunuchs. Their ability to exist in two worlds at once — male and female, mundane and sacred — was believed to enhance their spiritual abilities. The Enarees are said to have practiced divination while braiding and unbraiding strips of bark from the lime tree. As professional soothsayers they were expected to speak only the truth. Those who did not adhere to this high principle were gravely punished, sometimes by death. Hippocrates wrote that the Scythians believed that the unusual condition and powers of the Enarees was caused by a goddess and for this reason they were highly respected.[30]

A Scythian goddess is mentioned in a native origin myth as well. In southern Russia, the Scythians believed that they were descended from the union of Targitaus, the son of a celestial deity, with a goddess who was half-woman and half-serpent, and the daughter of the river Dnieper. This divine couple had three sons. One day a golden cup, golden axe and golden plough fell from the heavens, which the three sons tried to retrieve. However, only the youngest was able to approach the sacred objects, and he later divided the kingdom between his three sons.[31]

These three objects represent the three classes of Indo-European society. The cup symbolizes the first class (rulers and holy persons), the axe symbolizes the second class (warriors and protectors) and the yoke was associated with the third class responsible for working the land. To the Scythians, gold itself was considered sacred because of its connection with this ancient legend. Herodotus wrote that the Royal Scyths guarded the gold with great care, and year after year offered great sacrifices to its honor. If the man who had custody of the gold fell asleep, he was sure not to outlive the year.[32]

Gold was used to make representations of the sacred and mythical animals that populated the Scythian world. These creatures were physical manifestations of divine or invisible forces, bearers of sacred communications, companions and helpers, and spirit allies who were entrusted with carrying out the will of the gods. Some of these animals were tattooed on the bodies of the Scythians as well, as demonstrated by the remarkable preservation of tattooed skin in a number of burials.[33]

In nomadic cultures, wild animals are often associated with the realms of the supernatural. Because they cannot be tamed or controlled, they possess the capacity for benevolence or harm. Spirits take on animal forms in order to interact with human beings, serving as intermediaries between the earthly and otherworldy realms, bearing messages, and even carrying out wishes.[34] Communication and interaction with these spirits was the traditional role of the shaman or shamaness. These religious practitioners worked on behalf of the tribe by performing healing rituals and divination, overseeing religious ceremonies, interpreting omens and serving as elders, seers and guides. The shamanic traditions of Central Asia may include symbols or practices that were also utilized in the nomadic cultures of the eastern steppes of Europe during the Iron Age period.[35]

In addition to antlered gods and deities in animal form, the Scythians also venerated a number of other male and female deities. Historical accounts record that they worshipped Papeus, a god of the air; Thamumasadas, a god of water; and Oetosyrus, a god of crops and herds (and possibly also of the sun), who defended against wild animals and disease. Female deities included Artimpaasa, goddess of the moon; Apia, goddess of the earth; and Argimpasa, the patroness of fertility and marriage.[36]

However, the main devotions of the Scythians were paid to a great goddess known as Tabiti. She is the only deity definitively represented in Scythian artwork and was one of the most ancient figures in their pantheon. Tabiti was considered by the Scythians to be their political guardian, and was often depicted presiding at the taking of oaths, administering a form of communion, and anointing chieftains.[37]

King Idanthyrsos, who reigned around 450 B.C.E., pronounced Tabiti to be the "Queen of the Scythians" and associated her with the ancestral spirits. She was often depicted with animals, and seems to have been associated with fire as well. Oaths made upon her hearth were sacred, and broken vows could cause the chieftain to fall ill (and were punishable by death). The classical author Strabo noted that Tabiti's cult was particularly widespread along the Caucasian coast.[38]

In Scythian art, Tabiti was sometimes depicted as a half-woman, half-serpent figure, likely a reflection of the divine ancestress in the Scythian origin myth. She was also depicted in human form, either standing with an attendant or in conversation with a chieftain. Elsewhere she is shown seated between her sacred beasts, the raven and the dog. A number of objects at Scythian burial sites depict Tabiti seated upon a throne. In these contexts, a chief stands before her — to receive her approval of his election or appointment, or to be invested with powers that would ensure his successful reign.[39]

One particularly impressive version of this archetypal scene was represented on a felt hanging inside a burial mound at Pazirik. The great goddess of the Scythians is shown seated grandly on a throne. In her left hand is a scepter topped with curved or spiraling designs, suggestive of plant or tree symbolism, or the stylized antlers of a deer (similarly represented elsewhere in Scythian art). She wears a long gown, triple gold torque or gold collar, and a square hat or headdress. Part of her head seems to be shaved in a ritual tonsure. She appears strong and confident, with a piercing gaze. In front of her is a mounted warrior who approaches for some sort of sacred or ceremonial encounter.[40]

Tabiti is also depicted on a number of Scythian vases, which may have served as sacred vessels in rites associated with her veneration. Mirrors also appear to have been connected with her rites and observances. A gold plaque from Kul Oba depicts a seated female figure similar to the image found at Pazirik. On the plaque, a woman holds a mirror in her left hand, while a person standing before her drinks from a sacred vessel.[41]

Tabiti may also be depicted on a gold belt ornament that portrays a mythic or sacred scene. Two Scythian warriors dismounted from their horses are resting under a tree. One of the men is seated on the ground and holds the horses' reins in his right hand, while supporting the legs of the other man with his left hand. The second figure rests on the ground, with his left arm in the lap of a female figure wearing a tall headdress. The man may be resting, sleeping, or perhaps even wounded. The woman appears calm and confident, smiling as she gazes stoically ahead of her. Her left hand rests on top of the man's head, perhaps comforting, healing or conferring blessings or power upon the intended ruler, who basks in her presence.[42]

The Amazons of Ancient Europe

The social status of Scythian women has long been a topic of debate. Some scholars think that Scythian women had markedly inferior status to men and were little more than concubines or breeders of children. Others believe that Scythian women would have been respected in their culture. Anthropological studies have shown that mobile societies often afford higher status to women than sedentary societies. Herodotus wrote that among the nomads known as the Issedones, men and women had "equal power."[43]

It is theorized that over time, through contact with the Greeks (whose women had low status), Scythian women's rights began to deteriorate. Once the Scythians began drinking Greek wine (which they apparently took straight, rather than diluted) and began to adopt Greek style stone-built houses and other customs, their native lifestyle became more sedentary and suffered as a result. One particular aspect of native culture that may have deteriorated due to contact with the Greeks was women's social status.[44]

While some Scythian women may have had less political or social status than their husbands, they were probably far from powerless. Indeed, they may have enjoyed the advantages of a nomadic, tribal-based culture, finding personal expression and power in a number of socially approved roles. We have evidence for several roles in which women may have enjoyed high status in Scythian and related steppe cultures during the Iron Age period.

The first of these is horseriding, with the associated use of weapons and participation in armed conflict. In Greek and Roman mythology, tales were told of the Amazons, a nation of warrior women who lived apart from men and were formidable opponents in battle. Herodotus said that the Scythian word for Amazons was *Oiorpata* ('man-slayers') and provides a lively mythical account of the origin of the Amazons.[45]

In his account, Herodotus states that the Amazons were a group of woman warriors who lived among (or had split off from) the Sauromatians. The Sauromations were a tribe of similar origin to the Scythians, who began to encroach on their eastern borders in the fourth century B.C.E. The Scythians and Sauromatians shared a similar language and way of life. However, the Sauromatians invented the metal stirrup, which gave them an advantage in battle.[46]

Herodotus' version of the Amazon legend was based on Greek tales he heard during his travels to the north of the Black Sea. These stories claimed that about a hundred years before his time, a tribe of warrior women rode the steppes of southern Russia. These women were reportedly defeated by the Greeks in a battle at Thermodon, after which the victors set sail with three boatloads of female captives. The women mutinied, took control of the boats and threw their captors overboard.[47]

More skilled at battle than sailing, however, they were eventually shipwrecked on the north coast of the Black Sea — the territory of the Scythians. The women soon found themselves engaged in battle with male warriors of the Scyths. After the battle, while examining the bodies of their slain opponents, the men realized their adversaries had been women. They were very impressed by the women's' courage and military ability, and mused upon the fine children such women might bear them.[48]

The Scythian elders sent a group of their finest young warriors to court the Amazons, and their efforts were largely successful. Although they intermingled with the Scythians to some degree, the Amazon women refused to be assimilated into the main body of Scythian society:

> We could not live with your women. For we and they have not the same customs. We shoot with the bow and throw the javelin and ride horses, but the crafts of women, we have never learned. Your women do none of the things whereof we speak, but abide in their wagons working at women's craft, and never go abroad hunting or for aught else.[49]

The Amazons advised their Scythian husbands to return home and demand their traditional inheritances as married men. The men did as they were instructed, but later rejoined the women for a six-day trek deep into the northeastern steppes, where their progeny became known as the Sauromatians. Ever since then, the story said, the women of the Sauromatae followed their ancient usage, riding, hunting with their men (or without them), going to war, and wearing the same dress as the men.[50]

Herodotus added that none of the women would wed until she had slain a man from an enemy tribe. Apparently some of them grew old and died unmarried because they had not fulfilled this obligation. Hippocrates made a similar observation, saying that Sauromatian women did not "lay down their virginity" until they had killed three of their enemies. As to how the women gained the name "Amazon," he made the dubious claim that these women had no right breasts. Their mothers arrested its growth when they were babies so that all of its strength and bulk were diverted to the right shoulder and right arm, allegedly making wielding the bow easier.[51]

Mounted warriors do require excellent muscle capacity for hurling spears and shooting arrows, and written and archaeological evidence shows that Scythian weapons were shot with the right arm over the left side of the body. Perhaps the Greeks believed a woman's ability to perform these functions would have been hampered by the right breast. However, full-breasted women from steppe cultures in modern-day Mongolia are not impeded by their bosoms when shooting the bow, and they exhibit great expertise.[52]

The legend is apparently a rationalization, based on a spurious interpretation of the word "Amazon," said to derive from a Greek phrase meaning "without a breast." In actuality, the word is believed to come from an Indo-Iranian compound *ha-maz-an*, "(one) fighting together," a phrase that may refer to women fighting together with men.[53]

The Amazons were frequently represented in Greek artwork, in some cases taming horses or bathing, but most often battling with Greek troops or heroes. They are sometimes depicted with both breasts, and at other times with a garment draped over one shoulder to cover the area of the reputed missing breast.[54]

They also featured in Greek legends, including the Twelve Labors of Hercules. Hercules had been commanded to capture the sacred girdle of the Amazon queen Hippolyte. A girdle is a sash made from leather, metal or cloth. In Classical Greece it was a symbol of chastity, and to remove a woman's girdle was to make her defenseless against advances on her virginity. Not surprisingly, Hippolyte refuses to surrender her girdle without a fight. The object had been a gift to her from Ares, the god of war. During the conflict, many of the Amazon women perished in hand-to-hand combat with Hercules. Eventually queen Hippolyte also dies at his hand.[55]

The Amazons were also featured in the Greek epic poem *The Iliad*, where Homer refers to them as "the equals of men." The poem describes their hopeful arrival in Troy, led by their brave and beautiful queen Penthesilea. The Amazons are quite successful in the early stages of the battle, but over time begin to succumb to the Greek forces.[56]

In the final scene, Penthesilea hurls her last two spears at Ajax and Achilles. Achilles walks over to her and impales her on her horse with a single spear thrust. The dying warrior queen removes her helmet so that Achilles can see the face of his enemy. Achilles is so smitten by her beauty that in later legends he kills one of his companions who makes the tactical error of taunting him about his love-struck condition.[57]

Greek poets, historians, philosophers and playwrights all found the Amazonian legend fascinating, and their accounts reflect a conflicted blend of admiration and contempt. Plato praised the Amazons (as well as the Sauromatian women) for their readiness to fight in battle in defense of their people. Classical writers mentioned the Amazon's sexual freedom almost as often as they cite their bravery in battle. Both activities would have been unacceptable for a woman in Greek society. Some of these accounts claimed that the Amazons usually lived apart from men, but united with them once a year (apparently with great enthusiasm) to make sure that their warrior tradition continued on in the form of Amazonian progeny.[58]

In some accounts, the Amazons were said to have worshipped the Greek goddess Artemis, a statement that probably reflects their veneration of a native Scythian or Sauromatian goddess. Classical authors had a tendency to equate foreign divinities with gods or goddesses from their own pantheons based on passing similarity or recognizable attribute. Artemis was a virgin huntress who prized her independence, whose authority did not depend upon the power of men. She was skillful and beautiful, and not shy about dealing out retribution to those who did not show her respect.[59]

The Athenian writer Lysias, writing in the fifth century B.C.E., refers to the Amazons as "daughters of Ares." He says that they were the first in their area to be armed with iron, a comment that may actually reflect an historical connection between the Scythians and the craft of ironworking. Lysias also notes the women's connection with horse riding and horse-culture, even crediting them with the taming and riding of horses:

> They were the first of all to mount horses, with which, owing to the inexperience of their foes, they surprised them and either caught those who fled or outstripped those who pursued. They are accounted as men for their high courage, rather than as women for their sex; so much more did they seem to excel men in their spirit.[60]

Remarkably, there is actual historical evidence for the existence of women warriors in the region mentioned by the Classical authors. Herodotus wrote about a woman called Tomyris who led her tribe to victory against the Persian king Cyrus the Great in 530 B.C.E. She was a member of the Saka, nomadic steppe peoples who existed in the same general territory as the Scythians and Sauromatians from the eighth to third centuries B.C.E. Cyrus had tried to annex Tomyris' territory into the Achaemenid Persian empire, but was vanquished by the warrior queen.[61]

However, before the Saka were able to consolidate their victory, the queen's son was taken prisoner. The young man committed suicide at the first available opportunity, probably as a more honorable alternative to whatever the Persians had in store for him. The queen was distraught over her son's death and in her anger and grief searched the battlefield for King Cyrus' body, whereupon she cut off his head.[62]

Scythian warrior women are mentioned in other sources as well. Herodotus wrote that a group of the Amyrgian Scythians were led into battle once by a woman named Atossa. The Greek historian and physician Ctesias, writing in the fifth century B.C.E., described the adventures of a woman called Zarina, the female ruler of another band of Saka. She was so loved by her people that upon her death they erected an enormous mound in her honor topped with a golden statue.[63]

In addition to historical accounts, archaeological evidence also confirms the existence of female warriors in this region. In early excavations, archaeologists tended to categorize Scythian graves as male or female based solely upon preconceived notions of "appropriate grave goods" (weapons for men, mirrors for women, for example). Insufficient attention was given to anthropological features of the skeletons that could indicate the sex of the body. In recent years, more attention has been paid to the physical details of these burials. As a result, the archaeological evidence now confirms the presence of warrior women in Iron Age Europe.[64]

At one archaeological dig in the Caucasus, a woman was buried with armour, arrowheads, a slate discus and an iron knife, and appears to have been a female warrior. Elsewhere, the grave of a Saka woman included numerous bronze rings that had been used to harness her horse. She was also buried with an animal-headed pole topped with the figure of an ibex, an object usually found only in male burials. An early Sarmation grave contained the skeleton of a young woman who had been buried with an iron dagger, a six-inch-long boar's tusk, and an amulet consisting of a bronze arrowhead in a leather pouch. Another female burial contained a long iron sword over three feet long that could only have been used for fighting on horseback. Other female graves included whetstones used to sharpen weapons.[65]

Additional warrior women were discovered during excavations of the royal Scythian kurgans of Chertomlyk, which revealed that four out of the fifty gravesites were the graves of women. More than forty similar female burials were discovered west of the River Don in the Scythian region. To the east of the Don, in the area corresponding with Herodotus' Sauromatian region, a full twenty percent of the fifth and fourth-century B.C.E. warriors' graves that have been investigated so far have turned out to be the graves of warrior women.[66]

This remarkable convergence of legend, history and archaeology shows that Scythian and Sauromatian cultures traditionally included a socially-approved role for women that involved extremely high status — that of the warrior woman. In the lives of these independent horse-riding and sword-wielding women of the steppes, we have uncovered the historical origin of the legend of the Amazons, in Iron Age Europe.

Priestesses of the Ancient Plains

Another area in which Scythian women may have exercised considerable power is in connection with the realms of the divine. Scholars theorize that some Scythian women, perhaps queens or princesses, may have served as priestesses of the goddess Tabiti. While performing these religious rites they may have worn special garments, for a number of women's burials from southern Russia contain costume plaques which bear depictions of Tabiti. Evidence from other archaeological sites may provide additional information about what the ritual vestments of these women may have been like.[67]

In southern Russia and the Crimea, carved human figures made of stone were placed on top of burial mounds. Many of the stone figures represent women, although male figures are also found. Centuries ago, local people referred to them as *kemenniya babi*, or "stone women." Many of these female figures wear high hats (oddly similar in shape to hats worn by Welsh women in the eighteenth century), although the ritual headgear seems to be covered with a transparent veil. Ritual headdresses with veils were also found inside Scythian burial mounds, and a tall, pointed hat with a veil still forms part of the traditional costume of women among the Kazaks of western Mongolia.[68]

A stone carving from the northern Black Sea region shows a woman wearing a tall pointed headdress and neck ornament, who carries a cup or vessel in her hands. The symbolism of this statue bears a marked resemblance to other carvings located farther to the east, where female figures wear pointed headdresses and are shown carrying or ritually presenting a cup or vessel. These costumes and objects are found in a number of Scythian contexts and may indicate the existence of a specialized priestess class.[69]

The costume and ritual gear of the priestess has been uncovered at several sites. One remarkable burial from Siberia contained the body of a woman whose garments had been preserved by permafrost. She wore an elaborate headdress made from black colt's fur and a fur apron ornamented with leather appliqués. Hundreds of small pyrite beads had been sewn on to her soft leather boots. Her grave goods included objects that are believed to indicate her status as a priestess or seer. These included mirrors, cowry shells, amulets, and locks of hair and fingernail parings tucked inside small leather pouches.[70]

Another possible priestess figure comes from southern Siberia. The mummified remains of a fifth-century B.C.E. Saka woman show that she was buried in a three-foot high conical hat. Her headdress was decorated with images of large felines (probably leopards) as well as birds perched on the branches of a tree. These representations were carved out of wood and covered with gold foil. The woman wore a gold torque decorated with winged snow leopards, and had a tattoo on her left arm depicting a deer whose antlers terminated in the heads of griffins.[71]

A special group of religious artifacts were associated with a number of other women's graves. These unusual sites constitute seven percent of all female steppe burials, and are believed to be the graves of priestesses or female shamans. The burials contained small altars made of stone or clay, as well as bronze mirrors, fossilized seashells, carved bone ritual spoons, and amulets embellished with animal motifs (usually the snow leopard). Several graves also included small chunks of ochre, cinnabar and chalk. These may have been used for tattoos or ritual ornamentation. A number of Saka female graves also contained these special ritual objects, and the faces, arms and hands of the women were painted or tattooed with sacred designs, including spiral patterns.[72]

Some gravesites contained objects that suggest that some women may have served as both warrior and priestess. These burials contained weapons, boar's tusks and arrowhead amulets, as well as shells, white and red pigments, and spindle whorls made of chalk. These spindle whorls would have been too fragile to use for spinning and may therefore have been symbolic of seership or some other oracular function.[73]

The Iron Age priestesses of the eastern European steppes may have undertaken a wide variety of sacred duties. These included performing divination with their mirrors, interpreting omens, and determining auspicious times for various activities. Like many women in the same region today, they may have tended a ritual fire or hearth where they made offerings of *kumiss*, meat or cheese. They probably conducted seasonal ceremonies, served as an oracle for deities, ancestors and animal spirits, and presided over rituals venerating the great Scythian goddess Tabiti.[74]

In the eastern European steppes and adjacent areas, the Iron Age was a time of rich social and religious diversity. Historical sources describe the ritual practices and beliefs of the period, including information about funeral rites, sanctuaries and deities. Through archaeology we can see first hand the sacred garments and objects of the ceremonial life of this era. Sacred vessels, weapons, mirrors and other cult items abound in the archaeological record, displaying in physical form the remarkable spiritual energies of the age. The presence of warrior-women, priestesses and powerful goddess figures in the eastern domains of Iron Age Europe all attest to the presence of the Divine Feminine. As time went on these archetypal powers would take on a number of familiar forms whose sacred authority would influence native beliefs for centuries to come.

PART III: MYTHOLOGY—THE SPIRITUAL ORIGINS OF EUROPE

9

The Cauldron of Immortality

I sing of the Cauldron, a river of wisdom.... An estuary of honour with streamings of lore.... A noble vessel in which is brewed the source of every great knowledge.... An enduring power whose protection does not perish....
— Early Irish Wisdom Text[1]

Although the early morning fog had dissipated, as the tribe walked across the hillocks of grass that dotted the moor they became aware of a gathering mist forming between them and the world beyond. The grey light of this overcast fall day surrounded them like an opaque sanctuary of cloud and dew. The last purple flowers of heather spread across the hills like a cloak, a soft earthtone against the moss and amber leaves.

The tribe moved slowly and diligently through the landscape they knew so well, breathing in air scented with plants and soil and wood-smoke. The bog gave way to a field dotted with hazel trees and winding streams. At the edge was the sacred grove. They waited at the border of the ancient site as the druids, seers and priestesses who led the procession stepped beyond the invisible boundary. Once they had placed a branch of oak on top of the central stone altar, they kindled a small fire in front of it and ushered the people into the grove.

The tribe formed a large circle in front of the oak trees that had served as guardians and doorkeepers for centuries. They were careful not to block the four stone shrines that stood in each of the four directions. In the north and east were shrines for the Goddess of Life, Death and Transformation, and the Goddess of Prosperity, Healing and Poetry. In the south and west were shrines that housed the God of Music, Magic and Fertility, and the God of the Harvest, Wisdom and Skill.

In preparation for the Samain ritual, a group of young druids and priestesses in training walked around the perimeter of the clearing, sprinkling water from a sacred spring on the heads of all those who had come to the assembly. The crowd was hushed as it waited to hear the first sacred song. The chief druid stood in the center, wearing a blue woolen cloak over his long linen tunic. He closed his eyes and began to chant a text in a deep and resounding voice. The words spoke of the sacred meaning of the holiday, which was the end of the old year and start of the new. His ancient liturgy set forth the tribe's myths of creation and transformation, stories that were always recited at the New Year.

A druid-priestess held out her hands and began to sing a haunting melody above the druid's sonorous tones. Her song told of the power of this sacred time and place, a realm that existed between the worlds. She sang about offering respect, gratitude and devotion to the spirits of the three worlds, and rang a small set of bronze bells to honor the gods and other divine beings. The air was filled with a rarified quality that resonated deeply inside the grove. The spirits had come. The Gods and the Ancestors were here.

The druid held up a gold cauldron full of hazelnuts and acorns, while the priestess held up a silver vessel of water in which mistletoe had been sprinkled. The poets stepped forward to recite sacred songs celebrating the creation of the land and the origins of the ancestors. This was followed by a ceremony of thanksgiving. The people approached the altar chanting prayers of gratitude to the gods and spirits. They offered food and drink, jewelry, small replicas of tools or weapons, cauldrons or vessels, and small rods of sacred wood inscribed with prayers.

The priestess drew her veil over her face and the druid pulled his hood up over his head. Standing on either side of the altar they called out to the gods and goddesses of the tribe, invoking their names in a hypnotic chant. As the powerful, resonant words came to an end, they raised the oak branch and poured a cup of mead onto the ground. The veil between the worlds had been parted and gifts of reciprocity received.

A divining priestess stepped forward and knelt in front of the altar. She cast a handful of painted stones onto the ground and covered her face with her palms. The seeress rocked back and forth for several minutes, and then slowly opened her eyes. She carved a series of notches onto a hazel rod and handed it to the druids. The omens were auspicious. When the tribe was apprised of what had been seen, they broke out in an exuberant cry. The winter would not be harsh, the stores of the harvest would last until spring, and no conflict or disease would befall them. This had not been the case every year, and the prophecy came as a welcome respite in the unpredictable cycles of life.

The druid and priestess joined hands over the altar and took a few steps towards the encircled community. They thanked the Gods, the Ancestors and the Spirits of the Land, and after a final prayer announced that the ritual was complete. Blessings were offered to all who had attended the sacred assembly, as was the tradition.

The young priests and priestesses walked around the circle and passed out hazelnuts to any who sought them. The hazel tree symbolized divine wisdom and its nuts were used for fireside divination and making offering cakes. Some were kept year-round, for it was said if you kept a talisman from a sacred place, and held it in the palm of your left hand you could connect with the energies of that time and place. Perhaps it was true, for it was also said that time existed in a circle, as it always had, and always would be.[2]

As the semi-nomadic cultures of the eastern steppes roamed the plains with their flocks and herds, other Iron Age societies flourished in the northern and western parts of Europe. These people also possessed a rich and vibrant culture, one that focused on courage, honor, wisdom and skill. Their society was characterized by powerful and sophisticated religious traditions in which the Divine Feminine played a significant role. Classical authors referred to these people as the Celts, and their unique way of life contrasted with those in the Mediterranean. The Celts made a profound impression on those who encountered them and recorded perceptions about Celtic culture and religion.

What does "Celtic" mean? Celtic culture is defined by the use of a Celtic language, and the presence of certain key elements associated with society, ideology, material culture, lifestyle and religion. Some of the earliest archaeological evidence associated with the Celts dates back almost to the eighth century B.C.E. Celtic speaking people inhabited an enormous territory stretching from Ireland, Britain, France, Spain and Portugal, through most of Continental Europe, including Germany, Austria, Switzerland, northern Italy, the Alps and great Hungarian plains, and as far east as Turkey. It was one of the largest cultural territories in the ancient world.[3]

The artwork of the later Celtic period begins to take on some of the familiar characteristics that typify "Celtic" artwork to the modern mind. This elaborate ornamentation included a variety of stylized human and animal forms, as well as geometrically precise and organically flowing patterns with curving, spiraling and interlocking shapes. Everything from the sheath of a sword to a cooking vessel was decorated with complex symbols and designs.[4]

The Celtic peoples were referred to by a number of different terms in ancient times. The Greeks referred to them as *Keltoi*, although this word does not seem to have been used as a comprehensive term by all the Celts to refer to themselves at that time. The Romans referred to them as *Galli*, a name also widely used by Greek writers. A number of authors (including Diodorus Siculus, Caesar, Strabo and Pausanias) stated that the names *Galli* and *Galatae* were used as equivalent terms for the name *Keltoi,* while Caesar wrote that the *Galli* of his era knew themselves by the name *Celtae.* Diodorus used both words, but seemed to regard *Keltoi* as the more correct form.[5]

The Celts were organized into tribal groups with specific tribal designations. Some of the larger tribes were the *Belgae* in northeast France and southeastern Britain, the *Brigantes* in Britain, and the *Suessiones* in Gaul and Spain. Some of these tribal names still exist in the European landscape. For example, the *Parisii* were associated with an area later associated with Paris, the *Boii* lived in what was later called Bohemia, and the *Aquitani* lived in the region eventually known as the Aquitaine. From a northern British tribal confederation known as the *Caledones* we get a geographic term for Scotland, "Caledonia." Similarly, the name of modern Cornwall comes from a southern British tribe known as the *Cornovii.* As well as tribal names, those of settlements also survived. The place name *Lugdunum* ("The Fortress of the God Lugos") became Lyons in modern France, and *Mediolanum* ("The Sacred Central Field") was later known as Milan.[6] In addition to bequeathing us a great cultural and spiritual legacy, the physical presence of the Celtic ancestors still remains in the names and features of a sacral and numinous landscape.

A People of Skill

Classical authors frequently wrote about the society and culture of the ancient Celtic peoples. The physical traits of the Celts were mentioned by Greek and Roman writers, who remarked in some detail about their unique appearance. To Mediterranean peoples, the Celts were remarkable because of their unusual height, physical build, fair skin, blond or red hair, and blue or green eyes. Of course there would have been many variations in the appearance of the Celts, and the concept of a Celtic "race" would be inauthentic. Certain physical characteristics can be noted in many population groups, and this is what the Classical writers were no doubt remarking upon.[7]

The Celts were also unusual because like the Scythians, they wore trousers, a practical garment quite different from that of their Mediterranean neighbors. They also wore shirts or tunics, although Celtic warriors were reputed to have gone into battle naked, wearing only gold armlets and torcs and a bit of body paint. Traditional Celtic garments included checked or embroidered cloaks of various colors, fastened with a brooch and worn over dyed or embroidered shirts. Celtic attire was augmented with belts bearing gold or silver ornaments, and a wide variety of jewelry and adornments. These included neck rings or *torcs*, armlets, bracelets, finger rings, and even toe rings (for which there is a specific word in Old Irish).[8]

Overall, Celtic society appears to have been characterized by an exuberant love of life. In the late first century B.C.E., Strabo wrote that the Gauls exhibited "general openness and high spirits." Classical sources refer to the importance of hospitality, loyalty, honor and personal bravery and accountability in Celtic society. They also mention the Celts' love of bright colors and elaborate adornment, feasting and feuding, and music and poetry. They were noted for their veneration of wisdom and skill, the preservation of ancestral knowledge, and a sophisticated system of learning focused on oral tradition.[9]

The typical Celtic tribe produced all of its own food through herding, agriculture or both. They raised cattle, sheep and pigs and grew a variety of crops, including wheat, spelt, oats and barley. In some areas the lifestyle was quite rural, while in other regions fortified settlements known as *oppida* were constructed. Houses varied in style and construction, as reflected in the rectangular dwellings of the Halstatt and La Tène regions of the Continent, and the traditional roundhouses of Britain and Ireland.[10]

The early languages of the Celts included Continental Celtic languages like Gaulish, Hispano-Celtic, Galatian and Cisalpine Celtic or Lepontic. The Insular branches would have included various forms of early British Celtic, as well as Primitive and Archaic Irish. Some of these early Celtic languages became extinct, while others went on to become the predecessors of the six modern Celtic languages. The modern languages are Irish, Scottish Gaelic and Manx (known as "Q Celtic") and Welsh, Cornish and Breton (referred to as "P Celtic").[11]

The organization of Celtic society reflected the three traditional Indo-European classifications: (1) rulers and religious persons, (2) warriors and protectors and (3) herders and farmers. There was also a recognition and appreciation of the skilled classes, whose rank was probably akin to that of warriors (or higher, depending upon the profession). This classification was recognized in early Ireland where the people of skill (*aes dána*) contrasted with those who worked the land (*aes trebtha*). Interestingly, this same distinction existed amongst the Irish divinities. The smith was a particularly esteemed member of Celtic society, and frequently had magical associations (a phenomenon prominent in a number of shamanic cultures).[12]

Even the religious class was divided into three groups: druids, bards and seers. The bards sang poems of praise or satire for their noble patrons to the accompaniment of a lyre, while the seers performed divination on behalf of their community. Classical authors wrote extensively about the druids of ancient Gaul, whom they apparently found as fascinating as we do today. Classical commentators like Caesar, Cicero, Strabo, Pomponius Mela and Diodorus Siculus all described the beliefs and practices of the druids in some detail. The druids officiated at religious ceremonies, supervised public and private offering rituals, and expounded upon religious questions. They also provided training for druidic initiates that focused on the use of memory, rather than the written word.[13]

The druids were described as natural philosophers who engaged in a great deal of discussion about the stars and their motion, the size of the earth and the universe, the composition of the world, and the strength and power of the gods. They believed and taught that the soul was immortal, passing after death from one person to another. Written sources indicate that the druids were considered extremely wise and just, and served as judges and arbitrators. They were experts in communicating with the Divine, and their expertise was sought in most religious rites and rituals. One traditional teaching of the Gaulish druids was to show reverence to the gods, do no ill deed, and behave honorably.[14]

One of the primary theological concepts of Celtic religion was the existence of a sacred Otherworld that existed in a parallel realm of time and space. This was the abode of the Celtic gods and goddesses, and was the source of wisdom, skill, healing, fertility, abundance, protection and other blessings. Some deities were associated with cultural concepts like wisdom, poetry, healing, magic, battle, and so forth. Others appear to have been connected with elements of the landscape — hills, plains, groves, water, trees, plants, animals, fish and birds. These were all considered sacred and possessed of a hallowed, numinous quality.[15]

Celtic ritual took place in a variety of settings. In some cases, ceremonies were undertaken in outdoor settings: in sacred woods or groves, on hills or mountaintops, on plains or in clearings, and near bodies of water. Round or rectangular temples were also constructed of wood, stone or earth. Archaeological evidence suggests that bodies of water were extremely popular as ritual sites, and these were used for large tribal events as well as personal rites and devotions. Great quantities of ritual offerings have been found at many ancient sites, a practice that began in the late Bronze Age. These offerings included swords, shields, arrowheads, tools, cauldrons and jewelry. Weapons were frequently offered into rivers, and in ancient Britain swords were offered to the female deities of rivers. Cauldrons filled with jewelry have also been uncovered at many sites.[16]

Both swords and cauldrons played an immensely important role in later Celtic myths and legends. Swords were sometimes given names, or inscribed with the name of their owner. They were reputed to have awareness of happenings or events, and to even speak on occasion. Cauldrons were associated with abundance and nourishment, healing and transformation, and wisdom and inspiration.[17]

In the late first century B.C.E., Diodorus Siculus wrote about the Celts in Britain, contrasting their way of life with urbanized Mediterranean cultures:

> They say that Britain is inhabited by tribes that are aboriginal, and in their lifestyle preserve the old ways.... Their houses are simple, built for the most part of reeds or logs.... Their way of life is frugal and far different from the luxury engendered by wealth. The island has a large population, and the climate is very cold.... It contains many kings and chieftains, who for the most part live in peace with one another.[18]

Around the same time, Dio Cassius mentions two Celtic tribes, the Maeatae and the Caledonii, who lived in the north of Britain (in what is now Scotland). He reflects upon their rural way of life as well as connection with the natural environment:

> Both tribes inhabit wild ... mountains and desolate marshy plains ... they live on their flocks, on game and on certain fruits.... Their form of government is for the most part democratic, and they have a great liking for plunder.... They are very fast runners and very resolute when they stand their ground.... They are able to endure cold, hunger and all kinds of hardship....[19]

Caesar wrote extensively about the Iron Age Celts in Britain and Gaul in his famous work *The Gallic War*:

> The interior of Britain is inhabited by people who claim on the strength of their own tradition to be indigenous to the island ... the population is very large, their homesteads thick upon the ground and very much like those in Gaul, and the cattle numerous.... All the Britons dye themselves with woad, which produces a blue color, and as a result their appearance in battle is all the more daunting...Their customs are in some respects like those of the Celts [of Gaul], in other respects simpler and more barbaric.... They are ruled by chieftains.... The forests are their cities.[20]

In Ireland, the communal group was referred to as a *tuath*, a word that originally meant "the people" but was later used to refer to tribal territory. The tuath was often quite small and usually centered around an area surrounded by natural geographical boundaries. The social structure of the tuath was threefold, and consisted of kings, nobles and free commoners who all had the required *nemed* ("sacred") status to participate in religious ceremonies. Within the tuath were smaller social units known as *fine* ("kin"). Marriages were usually arranged with people from outside of the *fine*, and ownership of land was usually held by the kin-group, rather than by individuals.[21]

In early Irish society, all people of free status had an "honor-price," a physical assessment of one's dignity or status in the community. Honor-price was the amount considered as just compensation for any wrongs directly experienced by the person. It could vary according to one's fortunes and was only recognized within the framework of one's own tuath. Issues of inheritance or social obligation were usually determined by descendants of a common great-grandfather through a group known as *derb-fine*.[22]

The king of an Irish tribe or region was not necessarily the former king's son but was elected from the kin of the former ruler. The king made important decisions regarding all aspects of society, and along with druids or sages presided over ritual assemblies held at certain times of the year. The king could decide whether or not to go to war or establish alliances with other groups. He had a number of religious functions and duties, and his success was believed to rely upon the blessings of powerful goddess figures.[23]

Poets, Heroines and Warrior Queens

Women figure prominently in Old and Middle Irish literature, as well as British sources from a later era. Both mortal and divine women appear in these sources, and their presence reflects a variety of symbolically potent social or religious roles. The vivacity and independence of Celtic women were often remarked upon by Classical writers, as these qualities contrasted with the desired attributes of women in Mediterranean societies. Ammianus Marcellinus wrote about the Celts in Gaul, commenting on the tenacity of Gaulish women:

> Almost all the Gauls are tall, fair and ruddy in complexion, have terrible flashing eyes, love quarreling, and are amazingly insolent. If one of them in a battle calls out for help to his wife, who with her piercing eyes is stronger than him by far, not even a whole troop of foreigners can stand up to them. This is especially true when, swelling her neck, she starts to pound them with her huge white arms and mixes in fierce kicks with her blows, hitting her enemies with the power of a catapult.[24]

Although there is likely a bit of exaggeration in this account, it is possible that Gaulish women sometimes joined in battle with the men. The strength and courage of Celtic women is also demonstrated in a story related by the Greek biographer Plutarch. The story concerns a remarkable woman called Chiomara who lived in the Celtic territory of Galatia (in modern-day Turkey) in the early second century B.C.E. She was the wife of Ortiagon, and when the Romans conquered the Celtic tribes in Galatia she was captured along with other Galatian women. Chiomara was raped by a Roman centurion, who then had the audacity to demand a large ransom for her return.[25]

The Galatians agreed to the culprit's terms, but after giving him the sum he had asked for they slew him and cut off his head. Chiomara returned home to her husband and threw the head down at his feet. Ortiagon was much amazed and said to her, "Wife, it is important to deal honourably." She replied, "Yes, but it is more important that only one man who has slept with me should remain alive." Polybius himself claimed to have met Chiomara, and was struck by her intelligence and unquenchable spirit.[26]

Classical sources also mention the existence of female political and military leaders during the Iron Age period. One account, possibly written as early as the fifth century B.C.E., mentions a Galatian woman named Onomaris, who was held in high honor and esteem by her people. When the tribe was threatened by famine, they sought a leader willing to lead them to another region to improve their fortunes. None of the men wished to do it, so Onomaris stepped in. She put all of their property into a common pool for the use of the tribe as a whole. She helped her people cross the Danube, conquered any opposition they encountered in battle, and ruled over the new territory as queen.[27]

The most famous warrior-queen from the historical Celtic record is Boudicca (or Boadicea), an early British queen whose name comes from a root meaning "Victory." In 48 C.E., a British tribe known as the Iceni revolted against the Roman invaders. The Romans crushed the rebellion and appointed a man named Praesutagus to rule over them as a loyal client king. Boudicca was the wife of Praesutagus and queen of the Iceni. When the king died, he bequeathed his kingdom to the Roman Emperor as a way of securing his legacy. However, instead of honoring their agreement the Romans mistreated members of the royal family, beat Boudicca, and raped her two daughters.[28]

The Iceni once again took up arms, this time led by Boudicca. She encouraged other tribes to join the revolt, pointing out that if the Romans had treated her people in this way, there was no reason they would not do the same to them. As her growing army moved through southern Britain, they sacked and burned several Roman cities, including *Londinium* (later known as London). She also vanquished a number of Roman legions. Eventually Boudicca and her army were surrounded, and she took poison rather than submit to Roman authority. The writer Tacitus described the arrival of Boudicca on the battlefield at the height of her campaign:

> Boudicca rode in a chariot with her daughters before her, and as she approached each tribe, she declared that the Britons were accustomed to engage in warfare under the leadership of women. On that occasion, however, she spoke not as someone descended from great ancestors avenging her kingdom and wealth, but

as an ordinary woman avenging the freedom she had lost, her body worn out with flogging, and the violated chastity of her daughters.[29]

Dio Cassius remarked on the great devastation suffered by the Romans "at the hands of a woman," something that caused them "the greatest of shame." He describes the striking appearance of the warrior-queen, the details of her campaign, and the words of a speech she was reported to have made to her native Britons:

> In stature she was very tall and grim in appearance, with a piercing gaze and a harsh voice. She had a mass of very fair hair which she grew down to her hips, and wore a great gold torque and a multi-colored tunic folded round her, over which was a thick cloak fastened with a brooch.... And now, taking a spear in her hand so as to present an impressive sight to everyone, she spoke as follows:
>
> "You have learned from actual experience what a difference there is between freedom and slavery ... though some of you were previously deceived by the Romans' tempting promises ... you now understand how great a mistake you made in preferring an imported tyranny to your ancestral way of life...what great dishonor, what extremes of grief have we not suffered from the moment these Romans arrived in Britain?
>
> But if we have not done so in the past, let us do our duty now, my countrymen, friends and kinsmen. Now, while we still remember freedom, so that we may bequeath it to our children both as a term and a reality. This I say ... in order to praise you, because of your own accord you choose the necessary path of action, and to thank you for being ready to unite with myself and with one another...."[30]

After her speech, Boudicca performed a type of divination by releasing a hare from the folds of her garment. The hare ran on the side that was considered lucky or auspicious by the Britons, which caused them to shout with joy. Boudicca raised her hands to the skies and invoked a Celtic goddess known as Andraste:

> I thank you, Andraste, and I call upon you woman to woman ... as one who rules over Britons [whose] women too possess the same valour as the men. As queen, then, of such men and women I pray to you and ask for victory, safety and freedom from those who are insolent, unjust, insatiable and impious.... For us ... may you alone, Lady, be forever our leader.[31]

In addition to serving as rulers and battle-leaders, women also enjoyed enhanced power and prestige in the roles of physicians, smiths, wrights and poets.[32] Poets underwent rigorous and lengthy training, and composed and recited poems either honoring (or satirizing) their king or patrons. Their words were believed to be so potent that they had the power to harm the physical body, as well as to damage a person's reputation. Satire could be legally used by poets to pressure a wrong-doer into obeying the law. For this reason, poets were both honored and feared.[33]

The poets' supernatural powers could also be used for positive purposes, like establishing justice or protecting the king from malicious magic. Poets were widely credited with the power of prophecy, an ancient connection that was part of the Indo-European cultural legacy. As late as the sixteenth century, the powers of the poet-seers or *Filid* were well-attested in native writings.[34] In the year 934, one Irish text recorded the death of *Uallach,* a woman described as *banfili Érenn,* "a woman poet of Ireland."[35]

A woman's status as a poet would likely have given her legal rights above and beyond those of ordinary women. Although women's position was not equal with that of men, their status and their rights are clearly enumerated in Irish law texts. Women could own and inherit certain types of property, and had the right to own items of personal property, which they could independently sell, pledge, or make a gift of in accordance with their rank. In most marriages a woman could disagree with and "disturb" any disadvantageous contract her husband tried to make. A disadvantageous agreement affected both the man and the woman, and therefore a woman was allowed to voice her opinion or interrupt the arrangement if it was not advantageous to her.[36]

Polygamy was practiced in Ireland long after the introduction of Christianity. The church was opposed to the practice of having more than one wife, but opposition met with limited success. In early Ireland there were two grades of wife, the chief wife and the *adaltrach* (concubine). The sons of both types of unions had rights of inheritance.

Marriages were formalized when the husband-to-be gave a "bride-price"to the woman's father. If the marriage broke up due to the fault of the husband, the brideprice was kept. However, if the fault was with the woman, the brideprice was returned to the husband.[37]

Interestingly, the law texts do not seem to refer to the consequences of non-virginity in a bride. The harsh taboos and social ostracizing associated with virginity (or the lack thereof) in the later Christian era do not seem to have played a large role in early Irish society. Some law sources maintained that children born out of wedlock were to be reared by the family without prejudice. Under the law, women themselves were well protected against abuse or violation of honor. Full honor-price had to be paid if a woman was kissed against her will.[38]

In general, a woman was entitled to a share of her deceased father's personal valuables (but not his land). However, if he had no sons, she could become a female heir, and possessed more legal rights than other women. In this case, she could inherit a life-interest in a piece of land and would have had a number of rights associated with that arrangement. If a woman married a man who had no land (or who was a "stranger" from another *tuath*), the usual roles of husband and wife were reversed. In this instance, the woman made the decisions, and also paid any fines or debts.[39]

In early Ireland, divorce was allowed for many reasons. If a husband repudiated a wife for another woman, she was free to leave him (although she had the right to stay in the house if she wished). A woman could also leave her husband if he did not support her, spread a false story about her, or tricked her into marriage through means of sorcery. A woman could formally divorce a man if he was sterile, too overweight to have sex, practiced homosexuality, or was impotent (because, as the text states, "an impotent man is not easy for a wife"). If either the man or the woman was infertile, the other partner was permitted to go away "to seek a child." This was a useful practice so that they did not have to leave an otherwise harmonious partnership. If a women left to become pregnant by another man, the child was treated as if it were her husband's own child.[40]

As members of society, women and men were both expected to obey the laws. There were seven types of women who were not entitled to payment or honor-price: a women who steals; a woman who wounds another; a woman who betrays; a woman who refuses hospitality to law-abiding persons; a "prostitute of the bushes"; a "chantress of tales" (whose kin "pay for her lying stories"); and a woman who "satirizes every class of person." Honor was an important concept and reality in Celtic culture, something that had to be respected and also had to be earned.[41]

Most of the laws mentioned above applied to ordinary women. There were also special categories of Celtic women who had independent legal capacity and did not consider themselves as dependent on a husband. If they won a legal case of illegal injury, the award was based solely on the basis of the woman's possessions and personal dignity (rather than her male protector). One source also listed categories of women who were considered to be particularly important to the tribe. These included: female physicians, female wrights (carpenters and professional craftswomen), women who "turned back the streams of war," women who could negotiate in hostage situations, women who performed miracles, and women who were "revered by the *tuath*."[42]

Druidess, Seer and Priestess

The legends of Ireland and Britain abound in accounts of druids, poets, seers and magicians. Many of these practitioners were male, although a number of legendary or divine women in Celtic tradition also possessed these skills. The goddesses *Macha*, *Bríg* and the *Mórrígan* were all credited with the gift of prophecy. The mythical warrioress and martial arts teacher *Scáthach* made prophecies to the hero *Cú Chulainn* about his destiny using a potent oracular power. This power was known as *imbas forosnai* ("Great Knowledge of Illumination") and is one of the most important aspects of the Celtic spiritual wisdom tradition. The prophetess *Fedelm* also used this power to provide prophetic counsel to the legendary warrior-queen *Medb* (whose name was anglicized as Maeve). Fedelm was said to have studied poetry and prophesy in Britain and held a gold weaving-rod in her hand (symbolic of her oracular powers). She rode armed in a chariot, had three "tresses" or braids, and triple irises in her eyes (probably reflecting her ability to see into all three cosmic realms).[43]

Female seers are mentioned in historical sources as well as myths and legends. One of the most well known historical seers of the Iron Age period was *Veleda*, a virgin of the tribe known as the Bructeri (who are believed to have been ethno-linguistically Celtic). Her name contains a root word meaning "to see," and according to Tacitus she possessed great power. The Bructeri maintained that many of their women had the gift of prophecy. Veleda performed her divination secluded in a tower, while one of her relatives delivered her responses. Her fame apparently reached its apex when she foretold the triumph of the tribes in her region and the overthrow of the Roman forces.[44]

The question of whether there is historical evidence for the existence of female druids is somewhat difficult to answer. Druidesses are mentioned in a number of myths, but this does not constitute proof of the historical existence of female druids. Early Irish legends mention that Finn mac Cumhaill was raised by two women, a druidess and a wise woman, who guarded and advised him, and taught him the arts of warcraft, hunting and fishing. In a collection of Irish place-name lore known as *The Dindshenchas*, several legendary women are described as female druids. A woman named *Dreco* ("Dragon") was referred to as a druid and a poet, although she appears to have been associated with the darker aspects of the magical arts. However, a woman by the name of *Duiblind* ("Dark Pool") was depicted as an honored and esteemed figure. In the text she is called a druid (*druí*), as well as a poetess (*ban-fili*) and seer (*fáith*).[45]

Historical sources mention a number of women in the ancient Celtic world who also may have been druidesses. The Roman leader Aurelian was said to have consulted a group of druid priestesses in Gaul regarding the fate of his descendants. Another classical author relates a story in which Diocletian consulted a woman described as a *dryadas* ("a woman druid") from the Belgic Tongri. In the fourth or fifth centuries C.E., Lampridius mentioned a woman he calls a *mulier dryadas* (a term that must mean "woman druid"). The account mentions that the woman spoke in *Gallico sermone,* which likely means that she spoke in a Celtic language. While these women are referred to by terms that appear to mean "female druid," in these anecdotes the only act they perform is prophecy. They may have been female seers, rather than official druidic figures. However, it is also possible that they were female druids and that the Romans' interest in them focused on their prophetic abilities.[46]

A famous written account pertaining to women and druids was recorded by Tacitus in the first century C.E. During Boudicca's revolt, a large number of Roman troops were in the western region of Britain pursuing a group of British druids because of their social and political power. While the Romans were generally tolerant of native spiritual practices, it was official Roman policy to break up any organized complexes of religious or aristocratic influence that might develop into resistance or rebellion.[47]

After a lengthy pursuit, the Romans caught up with the British druids in the northwest corner of Wales on the island of Mona (modern day Anglesey). It was from this place that the druids were attempting to escape to the safe haven of Ireland. The troops encountered a close-packed array of armed men interspersed with women who were "dressed like Furies in funereal black, with streaming hair and brandishing torches." All around the women were the Druids, with their hands raised to the skies uttering curses against their attackers. The Roman troops were so astonished at this sight that they stopped in their tracks and were unable to move. Their commanders urged them not to be afraid of "a mass of fanatical women" and they regained their composure. The Roman troops killed all they encountered on the Isle of Mona that day, and then cut down their druidic groves.[48]

This particular episode has generated a great deal of commentary and speculation. Who were the women dressed in black? Were they female druids, or the wives of the druids mentioned in the account? One of the most curious aspects of the story is that all of the women were dressed in the same way. No other account mentions a group of Celts (or a group of women) dressed in black, or garbed in uniform fashion. Their attire may have been an emblem of a specialized role or position, perhaps even that of the female druid. For this reason, it is sometimes theorized that the women on Anglesey were female druids who were also fleeing the persecution of the Romans.

Another exalted position in which women served was the role of priestess. In some instances, Celtic priestesses appear to have lived apart from society in sacred communities. In other cases they lived and worked among their people. Some of these women may have served as the priestess of a particular deity. An inscription from Celtic Spain describes a woman as a *flaminica sac-*

erdos ("priestess of a particular deity") of the Celti-Iberian goddess *Thucolis.* The warrior-queen Boudicca may have enacted the role of a priestess of the goddess Andraste during her rebellion against Rome.[49]

Classical authors described communities of Celtic women who lived on offshore islands where they served as priestesses. In the late first century B.C.E., Strabo mentioned a group of women from the Samnitae who lived on an island off the coast of Gaul (near the mouth of the Loire River). He states that these holy women were possessed by a god whose name he gives as "Dionysus," a divine being they propitiated with initiations and other sacred rites. This of course refers to a native Celtic deity whom the author equated with Dionysus. Once a year the priestesses removed the thatched roof from their temple and replaced it with a new one. Dire consequences befell any woman who let her portion of the temple roof fall to the ground. Apparently the priestesses did not allow men on the island, but traveled to the mainland to have sex whenever they wished.[50]

Strabo also mentions an island near Britain on which sac-

Celt-Iberian priestess figure, carved stone image showing headdress with rayed sun symbol and traditional offering cup or vessel. First century C.E., Spain. Artist: James Möbius.

rificial rituals "having to do with Demeter and Core" were performed. Once again, this refers to Celtic deities who were symbolically equated with familiar Mediterranean gods. A somewhat later account, dating to the early first century C.E., mentions the holy inhabitants of Sena, one of a group of islands off the coast of Gaul. On the island was an oracle attended by a group of nine priestesses who could predict the future, cure disease and control the elements.[51]

In addition to written sources, the archaeological record also provides evidence of women who may have been druidesses or priestesses. Several wooden statues of women wearing hoods and torcs were found at healing springs in France. These are believed to be representations of priestesses (or perhaps even goddesses) associated with these sacred sites. A bronze figurine from Britain, dating to the Roman period, depicts a priestess holding an offering plate with her head draped in preparation for an offering ceremony.[52]

Two unequivocal representations of priestesses come from Celtic Spain. These consist of large stone statues whose detailed features provide us with information about the costume and presentation of these sacred women. The first statue depicts a priestess wearing an elaborate head-dress decorated with the image of a rayed sun figure. She wears a long veil and her hair is tied up in short, looped braids. Around her neck is a torc or neck ornament and in her hands she holds a ritual cup or vessel.[53]

The second statue comes from Albacete and is referred to as "The Dama of El Cerro de los Santos." The dress and posture of the statue are typical of Iberian sculptures from the fourth and third centuries B.C.E. The woman is believed to be a priestess officiating in a religious ceremony. She wears a headdress with a veil and her hair is arranged in long braids or ringlets. She wears a carefully folded cloak on top of a gown whose hem is trimmed with fringe. The face of the priestess has a calm and noble demeanor,

Carved wooden statue of woman wearing head-dress or cloak and neck torque, possibly a Celtic priestess (or goddess figure). Healing spring of La Chamalières, Puy-de-Dôme, France, early first century C.E. Artist: Donna Martinez.

and in her hands is the ubiquitous offering cup.[54] As we have seen, ritual presentation of a sacred vessel by holy or divine female figures was also part of the spiritual iconography of Iron Age cultures in the east. It would remain an important spiritual and cultural icon for centuries to come.

Goddess of the Grove

One of the most important aspects of the Celtic spiritual tradition was the belief in the existence of a sacred Otherworld. While the Otherworld existed near or around our world at all times, it could most easily be accessed at certain places and times. These sacred realms were frequently associated with, located near, or accessed through earthly portals that led to the Lower world realms of earth and water.[55]

The Otherworld was inhabited by a variety of divine figures. The early Irish referred to these sacred denizens as the *Aes Síde*— "People of the *Síd*" or "Fairy mounds." These are actually the burial mounds of the earlier Neolithic inhabitants of Ireland, whose sanctity was apparently recognized and woven into the

La Dama of El Cerro de Los Santos (front view). Limestone statue (originally painted), 1.35 m. tall. Celt-Iberian priestess figure, Albacete, Spain, 4th–3rd c. B.C.E. Artist: Donna Martinez.

mythology of Celtic-speaking Gaels whose culture arrived in Ireland around the fifth century B.C.E.[56]

In later sources these divine beings were referred to as the *Tuatha Dé Danann* ("People of the Goddess Danu"). In Britain they were known as the *Plant Annwn* ("The Children of the Unworld") or *Tylwyth Teg* ("Fair Folk" or "Family"). In later folk traditions, these realms and the supernatural beings who inhabited them became associated with what are popularly known as the fairies. Originally, these terms and concepts referred to the gods and goddesses of the Celts and their Otherworld dwellings.[57]

The Celts venerated a number of male and female deities. Some appear to have been local in nature while others were more widely worshipped. One of the most popular pan–Celtic deities was *Epona*, whose name means "Divine Horse Goddess." Venerated in Britain, Gaul, Bulgaria and the Rhineland, her cult traveled through Roman channels to North Africa and even to Rome itself. Epona was often portrayed riding sidesaddle in the presence of a foal, bird or dog. She seems to be a benevolent goddess associated with horses, fertility and abundance. As a goddess of stables and horsebreeding, she was venerated as a protectress of horse-riders and their mounts. In this guise, Epona was popular with the Roman cavalry, and as a result she was given a feast day in the Roman calendar (December 18th).[58]

La Dama of El Cerro de los Santos (side view). Limestone statue (originally painted), 1.35 m. tall. Celt-Iberian priestess figure, Albacete, Spain, 4th–3rd c. B.C.E. Artist: Donna Martinez.

Horses were symbols of wealth, beauty, strength and speed, and associated with passages to the Otherworld. At one Gaulish cemetery, Epona was depicted riding a mare, followed by a human being she may be leading to the afterlife. A funerary plaque from south-western Gaul depicts the goddess on horseback accompanied by supernatural sea creatures and celestial symbols, perhaps reflecting passages between the three cosmic realms. In later Irish and British myths and legends, goddesses with a pronounced connection to horses are often associated with the land, sovereignty and prophecy. These include the Irish goddess Macha and the medieval Welsh figure of Rhiannon. Horses also appear to carry people over the boundary between this world and the Otherworld.[59]

Another popular goddess was *Brigantia*, the patron goddess of a large and powerful tribe known as the Brigantes in north central Britain. In addition to attributes like abundance, protection and sovereignty, she was also associated with sacred rivers and springs. Brigantia may be related (at least in name or title) to the Gaulish goddess *Brigindo* and the Irish goddess *Bríg* or Brigid.[60]

Nemetona was widely worshipped in both Britain and Gaul. Her name, which means "Goddess of the Sacred Place (or Grove)," appears in many inscriptions. She was associated with sacred springs and healing waters, including the thermal springs of Aquae Sulis (modern day Bath in England). The primary goddess of the warm healing springs at Bath was *Sulis,* a British god-

Stone relief of British tribal goddess Brigantia, Romano-Celtic style, Birrens, Dumfriesshire. Iron Age period. Artist: Donna Martinez.

dess of healing and protection (whom the Romans equated with Minerva). Metal vessels were found at the spring, and some may have been offerings to Sulis. Other votive offerings included coins, jewelry, spindle whorls and small solar wheels. In addition to serving as a goddess of healing, Sulis was invoked as an avenging goddess who could be petitioned to assist those who had been wronged. More than one hundred curse-tablets were found inside the spring asking the goddess for justice or revenge (usually in cases of theft).[61]

Sirona, whose name means "Divine Star Goddess," was another popular goddess who was worshipped in Gaul, the Rhineland, Austria and Hungary. She was associated with healing springs where supplicants offered her coins, figurines and other gifts. She was frequently depicted with a lapdog (symbolic of healing), bowls of fruit or eggs (fertility or abundance) and a snake (healing and transformation). Her name may suggest a symbolic association with the

Image of Celtic goddess figure with Celtic-style tonsure. She is surrounded by birds, animals, a seated priestess or smaller deity, a male figure near her breast, and attendants who braid her hair. Outer plate from silver Gundestrup Cauldron, Denmark, second or first century B.C.E. Artist: James Möbius.

moon and the nighttime sky, perhaps indicating that she had some connection with women's cycles or childbirth.[62]

There were numerous river goddesses throughout the Celtic world. These deities included *Verbeia* (the goddess of the river Wharfe), *Tawa* (goddess of the river Tay) and *Sequana* (goddess of the river Seine). The tradition of honoring river goddesses was also prevalent in Ireland, where *Boand* was revered as the goddess of the River Boyne and *Sinand* as the goddess of the River Shannon.[63]

In addition to rivers, springs and groves, Celtic goddesses were also connected with other aspects of the natural world. The goddess *Arduinna* was associated with the Ardennes forest and depicted riding a boar. The name of *Artio*, a goddess associated with bears, contains a root word (*Art-*) which means "bear." This root word is also seen in the name of the famed figure of King Arthur and the legendary Irish king Cormac mac Art. Representations of these deities suggest they may have been associated with the wilderness and its creatures, both as protector and as patroness of hunters. The goddesses themselves decided the destiny of the animals and the land under their protection.[64]

Several Celtic goddesses were associated with deer imagery. A model of a ritual cart was buried in a warrior's grave in Austria that depicts a ritual stag hunt presided over by a goddess figure. She stands in the center of the cart, holding a large bowl above her head. At either end of the cart are women who hold the antlers of a stag. They are flanked by groups of mounted warriors.[65] A bronze chariot mount from a fourth-century B.C.E. burial in Germany depicts a horned figure with hands upraised in a magico-religious posture. This figure has often been interpreted as a horned god, but the two circular forms on the chest of the figure may indicate that the divinity is female.[66]

The horned or antlered god is a very ancient deity archetype in Europe, seen in many Celtic contexts. Early Celtic art also depicts several antlered goddesses, although their names are not known. Some are shown with vessels of fruit or food, suggesting that one of their attributes was fertility or abundance. These divinities may be similar to the Irish goddess *Flidais*, an independent deity associated with fertility, feasting, female sexuality and potency, as well as the forest and its creatures.[67]

The Goddesses of Ireland

In Irish mythology, the land of Ireland was associated with three eponymous goddesses, Ériu, Banba and Fódla. One myth relates how the Gaels gained admittance into Ireland by promising each of these goddesses in turn that her name would forever be upon the land. While the names Banba and Fódla were used by poets as allegorical terms for Ireland, it was the name of the goddess Ériu that forever clung to the land.[68]

In Ireland, as in Britain and elsewhere, river goddesses were widely worshipped. In one legend the goddess *Boand* approaches the Well of *Segais*, the source of the sacred River Boyne. She walks around it counter-sunwise, an inauspicious direction in Indo-European tradition. However, only her husband *Nechtan* (whose name is the linguistic equivalent of Neptune) and his three cupbearers were allowed to approach the well. The waters rose up and she was drowned, becoming the goddess of the river itself.[69]

A similar tale is told of the goddess Sinand. In this legend, it states that the woman possessed every type of knowledge and power except "the mystic art" (*imbas*). In order to obtain this special power, she approaches the well of wisdom. In one version of the tale she approached the Well of Segais, while in another it is called Connla's Well. In both cases the well was located beneath the ocean and was surrounded by nine hazel trees that magically bore leaves, flowers and nuts at the same time. The trees dropped their nuts into the water where they were eaten by the salmon of wisdom. From the juice of these nuts came "mystic bubbles" which floated down the stream. Sinand pursued them and was drowned, thereby being transformed into the goddess of the river Shannon.[70]

Another well-known female divinity was the Irish goddess *Bríg* (commonly known as Brigid). She was the daughter of a well-known deity known as the Dagda, and was described as a triple goddess of healing, smithcraft and poetry. Brigid was especially beloved by the Irish poets. She was the wife of *Bres*, an unfit king, with whom she gives birth to a son, *Rúadan*. When her son is killed, in her grief she lets forth the first mourning chant or "keening"ever heard in Ireland. In later times, the goddess Bríg appears to have been transmuted into the figure of the Christian saint Brigid.[71]

The daughter of a slave woman (or secondary wife), she was reared in the house of a druid and credited with performing many miracles. These included many acts of generosity and abundance, as well as the copious brewing of ale and the performing of love magic. Many legends are associated with Saint Brigid that reflect her connections with fertility and abundance. In the twelfth century, Gerald of Wales wrote that a company of nuns tended an inextinguishable flame in Bridget's honor at Kildare (*Cill Dara*, "Cell of the Oak"). Brigid is one of the three patron saints of Ireland (along with Patrick and Columba) and is extremely popular. Her feast day is February 1st, the Feast of Imbolc.[72]

Another powerful Irish goddess was *Anu*, whose name means "wealth or plenty." Her name was given to two hills in the southwest of Ireland, which are still known as the "Paps (Breasts) of Anu." Associated with prosperity and abundance, in some texts Anu was referred to as *Daghmáthair* ("good [best] mother"). She was an esteemed divinity who served as a caretaker of warriors, as well as the gods themselves. Anu was the seventh daughter of *Ernmas,* whose name means "Death by Iron."[73]

Another deity with whom Anu is sometimes confused is *Danu.* In my academic research, I demonstrated that Anu was the same figure as Danu, the deity who lent her name to the Irish god-tribe (the *Tuatha Dé Danann*). Her name comes from a root word meaning "earth," and is cognate with that of a Welsh divine ancestress called *Dôn.*

Many popular sources claim that Danu's name is connected with the Old Irish word *dán,* meaning "gift or skill," although this is not etymologically correct. Like Anu, Danu was associated with place names connected with fertility and abundance, including a site known as the "Breasts of Danu." She was said to be a female druid and a witch, and in one text is called the "Mother of the Gods" (a title also used to describe Anu).[74]

In my research, I eventually discovered a third divine connection. In a medieval Irish text known as *Lebor Gabála Érenn* (often referred to as the Book of Invasions), Anu is explicitly stated to be identical with yet another divine figure, a powerful Irish goddess known as the *Mórrígan.* Her name means either "Great Queen" or "Nightmare Queen," (depending on the spelling of its earliest form). The Mórrígan appears more frequently than any other goddess in the Irish sources. She is often described as a battle goddess associated with war, sexuality and magic, yet she has many other attributes as well.[75]

The Mórrígan had two sisters, *Macha* and *Nemain,* and all three goddesses were referred to as *Badb* ("Raven or Scald-crow"). These three daughters of the witch Ernmas — Macha, the Mórrígan and Nemain — were collectively referred to as *na Morrigna* ("The Great Queens"). Nemain was associated with conflict and battle, while Macha was associated with the land, abundance, sovereignty and prophecy, as well as horses and ravens. In one story she is referred to as *Macha Mongruad* ("Macha of the Red Mane"), said to have been queen of Ireland around 325 B.C.E. The legend recounts how she became heir to the throne of Ulster when her father *Aéd Ruad* ("Red Fire") drowns at Essa Ruaid ("Red [or Noble] Waterfall"). Other male claimants to the throne refused her claim, but with magic and ingenuity she overcame their denial of her rights and became queen of Ireland. She also forced her previous opponents to build a great fortress in her honor, the ritual site of Emain Macha (modern-day Navan Fort).[76]

The Mórrígan features prominently in a number of myths and sagas, and can appear in the form of a beautiful young woman, a battle goddess, or a raven. In one story she also fights with Cú Chulainn in the form of a wolf, an eel and a heifer. She also has a number of other attributes, including fertility and abundance. The Mórrigan was the mother of 52 warrior-children (26 male and 26 female), as well as an ill-fated son Meche and a daughter Adair (whom she has with The Dagda). Her name is associated with a variety of sacred sites throughout the Irish landscape, including the "Breasts of the Mórrigan," located near the famous Neolithic site at Newgrange.[77]

In a remarkable passage from *Lebor Gabála Érenn*, the text demonstrates that The Mórrigan, Anu and Danu were all names for the same divine figure:

> *In Mor-rigu ... is dia forainm Danand o builead Da Chich Anann ... ocus o builead Tuatha De Danann...*

> "The Morrigan ... it is from her other name 'Danann' that the Paps of Anu are called ... as well as the Tuatha Dé Danann...."[78]

The entire Irish pantheon was known by the name Tuatha De Danann and headed by a female deity. The linguistic connection with a Welsh legendary ancestress suggests that Danu (in its earliest attested form *Donu*) may have been the original form of her name. Other sources support Anu as the original form, with Danu as a secondary development. The term *In Mórrígan* — The "Great Queen" or "Nightmare Queen" — is likely a title or epithet. This powerful goddess was associated with the powers of life and death, fertility and abundance, wealth and prosperity, healing and magic, prophecy and skill, the land and the waters, druidism and witchcraft, and many other attributes. It was she who ultimately headed the Irish pantheon of gods and goddesses.[79]

The Mórrígan, Macha and other goddesses reflect a divine archetype that is very widespread in Celtic tradition: the Goddess of Sovereignty. This sacred figure has a wide variety of attributes and was frequently associated with horses, warfare, kingship, fertility and abundance. She was the personification of the sovereignty of the land and associated with its fertility and well being.[80]

The Goddess of Sovereignty had the power to bestow or withhold her blessings from the mortal ruler of the land. She is often involved in selecting the rightful king, testing or challenging him to see if he is worthy. The Goddess of Sovereignty may appear as a young woman or an old hag, and part of the candidate's test is the ability to recognize her divine presence and respect her authority. If he passes the test, the two may engage in a sexual union.[81]

In some sources, the Goddess of Sovereignty prophetically offers a cup of red ale to the rightful king. Once he has obtained her blessings, the king, the land and the people prosper. This archetypal scenario may be similar to representations of the Scythian goddess Tabiti, where a mounted warrior approaches the goddess in anticipation of her acceptance or blessings. Sovereignty goddesses are also prevalent in other Indo-European mythologies. This powerful goddess archetype had an especially enduring power, and as our journey continues we will meet other Sovereignty goddesses in the centuries to come.

The rich spiritual traditions of the Celtic people are enticing and mysterious, and yet strangely familiar. They evoke a deep memory of ancestral wisdom, a sense of eternal connection with sacral landscapes, and knowledge of symbols and practices not yet entirely forgotten. In classes and training programs, when students first hear the sounds of an Old Irish poem or Middle Welsh wisdom text, a folk prayer from the Highlands of Scotland or early Irish hymn, they often report "having once known those words," a sense of "having come home." These traditions resonate in our core, and in reconnecting with this ancient wisdom, we can more fully become who we are, and who we are meant to be.

While history books have long taught us that our culture is derived from that of Greece and Rome, during much of the ancient history of Europe its inhabitants developed their own indigenous cultures. The vast majority of Europeans did not have contact with the Mediterranean nor could they read their written accounts. After the introduction of "Bell-Beaker" culture — the cultural and spiritual traditions inherited from the Indo-Europeans — an enormous part of Europe's cultural heritage had its foundation in (or was heavily influenced by) the culture and religion of Celtic-speaking people.

In these and other traditional cultures, respecting and preserving the wisdom of the past was extremely important.[82] Honoring the knowledge of the elders and ancestors creates a powerful social and spiritual foundation, and also provides a bridge between past and future. In one early Irish poem, the poet chants: "Chant to me the lore of my people. It is sweet for my heart to hear it."[83]

Writer and anthropologist Joan Halifax speaks about the importance of connecting with the ancestors and their wisdom:

> Just as our mothers, fathers, and grandparents live inside of us, so do generations upon generations of mothers and fathers before them. Part of our task is to discover how all our ancestors continue to inform our lives, and the same holds true for all forms of life. For we have been shaped not only by our human ancestors but also by the environment in which they lived...
>
> The veneration of the ancestors confirms the continuity of existence in time and space or place. The world is brought back into balance through the renewal of ceremonial life that confirms that continuity.... By venerating the dead we can

experience the fullness of our own souls. Losing touch with these ancestors, we lose touch with the soul, both theirs and ours.[84]

In this day and age, we are moving away from our cultural roots and spiritual origins at lightning speed, egged on by the illusory marvels of technology and promise of material wealth. Our connection with the wisdom of the past and the Earth, with community and tradition, is sacrificed for temporary satisfactions that exist only in an unbalanced and unsustainable cycle of consumption and destruction.

If we shift our focus back in time and space and move into our center, slowing down and breathing deeply of the natural world around us, we can embark upon a journey of reconnection with the things that really matter. These are sacred things that can truly sustain and nourish us and have the power to transcend the cycles of time. One step towards this place of centered existence and connection is to listen for the voices of the ancestors: "We are here, we are here, we are here...." In truth, the ancestors and their wisdom never left us. We can open our souls and remember.

10

The Tribes of the Goddess

You are not just here for yourself ... you represent our tribe, our people.
So when you go somewhere, that's who you are — our representative...
— Mona Polacca, Hopi–Havasupai–Tewa[1]

The prince heard the speech of the Valkyries,
Noble women, sitting on their steeds,
They sat helmeted, in deep thought,
Holding their shields before them...
—10th Norse poem Hákonarmál[2]

A light snow floated to the ground as a small band of families walked across the barren winter fields. The women gathered heavy woolen shawls around their heads, enveloping small children in the folds of their homespun garments. The older children ran ahead in excitement, tipping their heads back to catch snowflakes on their tongues. They had left their homes before the sun was up, and now a gentle rose colored glow began to illuminate the winter's morning.

A few lonely birds sat on the branches of an ancient oak tree that had been there as long as anyone could remember. Next to the oak tree was a small stone shrine. The people walked over to the shrine and dipped their hands in a spring that flowed ceaselessly, regardless of the season or weather. The shrine contained a stone shelf covered with the fragments of beeswax candles. Several candles had already been lit, and a few carefully chosen stones and shells placed lovingly next to them.

This was the old shrine of the local Goddess of the land, the hearth and the harvest, the divine protectress of warriors and patroness of seers. It had once been housed in a beautiful wooden temple carved with intertwining animals and symbols of her many powers. After the new priests arrived, the building had been taken down. For some reason, however, the shrine had been allowed to stand.

161

A new building had been constructed several fields away from the oak tree. The church was dedicated to a female saint who appeared to possess many of the same attributes as the local goddess. In front of the church was a stone walkway that led to a polished marble basin set into the ground. Inside the vessel was a sacred flame that was kept lit in honor of the holy woman. Above the doorway was an equal-armed cross whose arms turned sunwise in the traditional manner.

The families quietly entered the precincts of the small church. They were glad to arrive early and find seats near a small fire lit in an iron grating near the front. They could hear the monks talking in the back of the room, and noticed several nuns from a nearby convent who were there to assist with the ceremony. Several other families arrived and sat down. Most weeks the church was only about a third full. However, on feast days more people made the long journey from outlying villages to partake of extra libations. Today the church was more than half full, and the villagers rubbed their hands together to keep warm. A bell tolled and the thick wooden doors were closed to keep out the cold.

For some reason, the new ceremonies were conducted in a language the people could not understand. They sat quietly, however, thinking that eventually the ritual would be explained or translated for them. After the main ritual, the priest often spoke to them in their own tongue and read passages from his book of religious legends. Today he spoke about the Saint and her life of generous deeds. He stressed the importance of offering hospitality to anyone who came to the door, for a stranger could be Christ in disguise. This was a familiar concept to the assembly, though it was usually said one should treat a stranger with respect, for it could be one of the elves visiting our world.

The young priest also recited a prayer in the vernacular on this special day, for it was the Feast Day of the Saint herself. The sentiment of the prayer was also familiar to the people, who had recited a more ancient version of it the previous evening during household ceremonies:

> May the blessing of the holy one be upon you
> Before you, behind you,
> Above you and below you
> Her blessings upon the hearth and household all
>
> She is the flame of compassion
> And the sacred spring of healing
> She is the star of each night
> And the fiery gladness of morning.

After the prayer, the priest blessed each person with holy water from the spring. This was a custom the people were completely familiar with, for the holy men and women of the old temple had performed the very same ritual in the past. After the blessing, the nuns walked up and down the aisles with wooden buckets of ale symbolizing the generosity of their patroness and her miraculous ability to create vats of ale from a small sack of malt. Each person was given a measure of the liquid to take with them, depending upon their age and status. The bell tolled once again and the small congregation emerged into the bright morning light.

As they began the long walk home, several of the women began to sing old songs about the end of winter and the warmth of springtime to come. The morning promised to be a fine one as the group returned to the shrine of the well. There they poured a libation of ale at the foot of the oak tree. More stones and shells were placed on the ledge as ancient prayers were intoned in voices hardly above a whisper. One old woman took out a small straw figure from beneath her shawl. She kissed it and placed it in front of the shrine. With tears of joyful devotion in their eyes, and remembrance of their ancient goddess in their hearts, the group turned to the pathway home.[3]

During the later Iron Age and early medieval eras, a number of events profoundly influenced the lives of native European peoples. The latter part of this era is sometimes referred to as "The Dark Ages," a term that is more and more falling out of use. "Dark Ages" referred to the paucity of written records for many of the cultures of the time period, as well as the alleged disintegration of "civilization" in Europe after the downfall of the Roman Empire. As we will see, no dark clouds obscured the sun, plunging the people of Europe into utter darkness after the retreat of Rome. In addition, there were many vibrant societies throughout Europe, whose cultures and traditions are revealing themselves to us through archaeology, ethnography, and many other sources.

Stepping back to the time period when Rome was still expanding, its military exploits profoundly affected traditional cultures in almost every part of Europe. Some societies were subsumed into the dominant Roman culture, while others maintained aspects of their native beliefs and practices in spite of the invasion. Ireland, the north of Britain, and other parts of northern Europe were never conquered by the Romans and were able to preserve a great deal of their cultural integrity during this time of upheaval and discontinuity. People in other regions, however, were not so fortunate.[4]

Roman aggression and atrocities were numerous. In 56 C.E., a Gaulish tribe known as the Veneti rebelled against the Roman occupation of their land. Caesar had all of the tribe's elders put to death and sold the rest of the tribe into slavery. The Aduatuci also resisted the Roman occupation. When the Romans laid siege to their fortress, 4,000 men from this Gaulish tribe were killed. The rest of the tribe — some 53,000 people — were sold into slavery as a single lot.[5]

The Carnutes killed Roman traders as a sign of their rebellion and were even more harshly treated. All but 800 of the 40,000 men, women and children of that tribe were killed. The Carnutes had lived in a central part of Gaul where the druids of Gaul gathered each year in sacred assembly. Elsewhere, the Nervii in northern Belgica rebelled and were also nearly wiped out. From a tribe originally numbering 60,000, only 500 men survived. Their Council of Elders, originally numbering 600, was reduced to only three people.[6]

We have been taught to think of Greek and Roman cultures as paragons of "civilization." While the societies of ancient Greece and Rome did have many positive things to offer, they also impacted the lives of people around them in a variety of ways. Some regions profited from increased commerce and trade, while the effects in other areas ranged from disruption to devastation. In some places, native peoples allied themselves with the Romans to avoid danger and bloodshed. However, this was not always possible, nor were their alliances always successful.[7]

Because the Greeks and Romans recorded a great deal of their social, historical and religious beliefs in written form, we know a great deal more about them than we do about other ancient cultures. However, the practice of writing alone does not mean that they were culturally superior, nor does it justify the unbalanced historical bias that has been promoted in Western society for millennia.

For the vast majority of time that people have lived in Europe, most members of society did not participate in Greek or Roman based culture or value systems. There are two reasons for this. First of all, numerous indigenous cultures existed in Europe both before and after the Roman invasions. These societies and their traditions constituted the predominant cultural paradigms in Europe. In addition, most people in Europe could not read until relatively recent times. The average European peasant would not have known (or cared) about Roman emperors or Greek heroes. The influence of Classical culture has been over-emphasized by the upper classes of society, but this influence did not trickle down into the lives of the common people who made up the majority of the populace and had their own cultural and spiritual heritage.

Knowledge of Mediterranean cultures was minimal until fairly recent discoveries like the Rosetta Stone, the decipherment of Linear B, and the rediscovery and distribution of Classical texts. The writings of Caesar, Tacitus and other Classical authors were not rediscovered, translated, edited and available in print until the fifteenth and sixteenth centuries. The subsequent interest in the Celts and other early Europeans as "noble savages," the Druids and Germanic holy people as "priests of nature," and other antiquarian notions, was fuelled by the discovery of native peoples in the New World.[8]

Ancient monuments in the landscape like Stonehenge and Avebury, whose actual origins had been forgotten, could now be "explained" as "temples of the druids" (a notion which persists to this day). Ancient Europeans — and ancient Britons in particular — were re-envisioned as "Children of Nature." By the late eighteenth century the druids were re-invented and their imagined rites practiced by male upper-class nobles in white robes and regalia, celebrating the fabricated mystic rites of the past. Secret societies were formed, resulting in "druid orders" that still exist to this day.[9]

While it would be easy to scoff at these ceremonies and the people who developed them, their motivation derives from an understandable human impulse: the need for connection with native traditions and indigenous roots. These are things that the people of Renaissance and Early Modern Europe were increasingly disconnected from. In their fantasies, they sought to replace the ceremonies and elders they had lost. While their efforts may seem misguided, we know that the people of Europe did have ancestral cultures and native wisdom traditions. Since most of these cultures did not create written records, it is an ironic twist that through Classical texts we are able to shed some light on the past. Greek and Roman writers recorded valuable information about the native cultures of ancient Europe, and this is a fortuitous event for which we are grateful.

The Intertwining Tree of Faith

Another influence that affected the people of ancient Europe was the gradual introduction of Christianity. Originally Christianity was a small, obscure Judaic cult whose members were not in agreement about the teachings of Jesus, or their doctrine or theology, even in the years immediately following his demise. Modern discoveries of non-canonical texts like the Gospel of Thomas, the Gospel of Mary Magdalene, and the Gospel of Judas paint a very different picture of the beliefs and practices of early Christianity than the canonical version that has been promoted for many centuries.[10]

In early times, Christianity was just one of many religious movements in the Near East. Early Christian enthusiasts had to compete with the vibrant spiritual traditions of the powerful cultures of Greece, Rome and Egypt (among others), as well as a number of extremely popular mystery religions. The three most influential mystery religions of the time were the veneration of Isis (which had spread from Egypt), the worship of the *Magna Mater* or

"Great Mother" (a tradition from Asia Minor), and the immensely popular cult of the god Mithras (which originated in Persia).[11]

A number of theological elements from these religions may have found their way into the beliefs of the competing Christian cult (or were at least familiar to its members).

The cult of the Great Mother was the oldest of the mystery traditions, and Her ceremonies focused on the natural cycles of death and rebirth. This symbolism extended to the lives of mortal beings, as initiates of the cult were promised a second birth. The cult of Isis, a highly revered mother goddess figure, also involved symbolism of life and rebirth. This religious tradition was extremely popular among women, and likewise promised its devotees the possibility of immortal life.[12]

The cult of Mithras was based on a dualistic notion of the universe and the soul engaged in a struggle between light and dark, or good and evil. As a god of light and the sun, Mithras fought against the powers of darkness and evil and assisted human beings in their struggle to avoid temptation and pursue a virtuous life. As a result of right actions, they would be rewarded with a happy existence after death.[13]

The early Christian movement was not immune to the events of its time. Early Christians experienced disapproval and persecution because of their refusal to pay homage to the Roman gods and the deified Emperor. This veneration, as well as the acknowledgment of Rome's political and military authority, was required of all citizens in the Roman Empire. Eventually the movement got the boost it needed when Emperor Constantine gave imperial sponsorship to the new religion in 313 C.E., fusing Rome's wealth and power with the structure of Church hierarchy, and setting in motion a new power that would affect people around the globe in many unforeseeable ways.[14]

Regardless of Rome's support, the introduction of Christianity was a gradual process that took more than a thousand years in various parts of Europe. Early clerics and monks traveled to Britain by the fifth to seventh centuries, arrived in Ireland in the sixth century, and reached parts of Scotland during the seventh and eighth centuries. In more remote regions, particularly in the north, people continued their traditional practices for many more centuries to come. For example, Christianity was not adopted in Scandinavia until sometime between the tenth and twelfth centuries. The Lithuainians did not convert until the fourteenth or fifteenth centuries, and ecclesiastical authorities in eastern Prussia had their hands full trying to eradicate pagan practices as late as the end of the sixteenth century. The Saami of Finland did not begin the practice of Christianity until just a few centuries ago, and still maintain many shamanic beliefs and practices.[15]

There are still places in Europe where native religions have not entirely died out, or where they survive as a blend or hybrid with Christian practices. The Udmurts and Besermians, two of the ancient agrarian peoples of Eastern Europe, were not Christianized until the end of the eighteenth and early nineteenth centuries, and have preserved many traditional cultural elements up to the present time.[16] The Mari are a Finno-Ugric people who live in Central Russia. The "Hill Maris" are Orthodox Christians, while the "Meadow Maris" practice their own traditional religion, which is often referred to as "natural religion," with a focus on manifesting the animation of nature.[17]

Written records from various church authorities frequently mention difficulties encountered while trying to eradicate the traditional beliefs and practices of Europe's native inhabitants. In the twelfth century, a visitor to Ireland claimed to have met two men who had never heard of Christianity. In the late thirteenth century, a Scottish priest was chastised for allowing his parishioners to engage in an ancient fertility rite in which a large phallic symbol was carried in a procession. It was eventually decided that the priest could not be held personally responsible because the practice was so ingrained in local tradition. Christian churches were frequently built on or near ancient pagan holy sites, and well veneration and other traditions were incorporated into local Christian practices. What the church couldn't get rid of, it wisely chose to incorporate.[18]

As the Roman-sponsored Christian cult began to spread throughout Europe, it came in contact with countless other religions, many of which were far older than Christianity. From what we can ascertain, most of these religions had a healthy respect for the natural world and believed the sacred was numinous (present in all that exists). These religions venerated powerful spiritual beings associated with the natural world, as well as with culture and knowledge; they also included many beliefs and practices associated with the Divine Feminine.

The Ancient Tribes of Europe

During the Iron Age and early medieval periods, a number of indigenous populations and tribal groups occupied the great European landmass. We have seen that the Celtic peoples inhabited large parts of Europe, especially before the expansion of the Roman Empire. Many other groups of native people lived in Europe during this time as well. In addition to writing about the culture and religion of the Celts, Caesar also wrote about Germanic tribes living to the north and south of the River Rhine.[19]

In his account, Caesar wrote that in these regions the land was held in common by the tribe and was divided up amongst individual clans in a system that required annual re-distribution. This prevented any group from having constant access to the best (or worst) farmland. Young men received formal martial training, and acts of bravery and good leadership were encouraged. Public assemblies were held at which Germanic chiefs announced upcoming raids. Those who promised to participate in these activities were expected to show up at the actual event. If they did not, they were ridiculed by their tribe and lost all honor. Noble classes had a great deal of authority, and leaders were measured by the size of their loyal entourage and their ability to bestow wealth on their followers.[20]

A population group known as the Alamanni inhabited a territory between the upper reaches of the Elbe and the border of the Roman frontier. Their name meant "All Men" or "Everybody," which suggests they were a confederation of local tribes. When the Roman frontier was abandoned in 260 C.E., Alammani settlers moved into the region between the Black Forest and the upper Danube. They advanced upon other population groups living in the upper Rhine valley and eastern Gaul. Later, the Alamanni and their neighbors the Franks moved into a number of adjacent territories.[21]

The Franks appear in the historical record in the third century. Like the Alamanni, the Franks may have been an amalgamation of tribes who gathered together to oppose the Romans (particularly once the empire's strength had begun to diminish). They lived in a large area that included major parts of the Rhineland, Belgium and Gaul, and eventually gave their name to modern-day France.[22]

The grave goods of the Franks show they had made a cultural break from the influences of Rome. A number of rich Frankish warrior graves have been discovered dating to the late fourth century. Many of these burials included elaborate weapons, vessels and personal ornaments. The earliest royal burial was that of Childeric, who died around 482 C.E. His grave was filled with gold, silver and garnets, as well as swords, ornaments, coins, and a crossbow. He was buried with a rich brocade cloak on which were sewn three hundred ornaments in the shape of bees. Childeric was pagan, but his son Clovis, who succeeded him, became a Christian. Even after Frankish kings and nobles made the transition to the new faith, warriors were still buried with elaborate grave goods for many centuries, according to the old ways.[23]

Rich female burials have also been found from this period. The grave of a Frankish noblewoman was found near Paris that contained a number of interesting items. She was buried in a stone sarcophagus and wore magnificent garments, including a red silk cloak and splendid ornaments. Her gold signet ring was inscribed with the words *Arnegundis Regine,* which tells us that the woman in the grave was Arnegunde, the second wife of Clothar (who died around 570). Like the Frankish warriors, Frankish women were buried with fine grave goods long after the introduction of Christianity.[24]

In Eastern Europe, just above the Black Sea, was a group of people who the Romans referred to as Goths. This term was probably used to refer to a number of ethnic groups in the area, and would have included eastern nomads, Germans, and people living in and around old Greek and Roman cities near the shores of the Black Sea. These allied groups posed a military threat to other groups in the region, including the Romans. By the 4th century, the Goths were known by two different names: the Ostrogoths (who lived in the East) and the Visigoths (who lived near the lower Danube). Both cultures seem to have been relatively stable, making good use of the productive land in their region and developing relationships with others living near the Black Sea (especially in the western steppes).[25]

However, around 370 C.E., the peace that had once existed in the region was disrupted when a group of steppe nomads known as the Huns rode into Eastern Europe. They overran the Visigoths almost immediately and ruled over them for eighty years. Large numbers of Goths begged to be permitted to cross the Danube to re-settle in the northern Balkans. Although they were permitted to leave, they did not fare terribly well there. The Goths moved around Europe for some time, and took possession of Rome in 410 C.E. (an act which changed the history of Europe forever). Gothic leaders established a kingdom in southern France that lasted for about a century, and from this stronghold they helped defeat the Huns in 451 (who had progressed as far as Gaul). Later, the Visigoths established a kingdom in what is now Spain, and the Ostrogoths did the same in northern Italy.[26]

During the Iron Age, southeastern Europe was a region of varying alliances and shifting population groups. Many of the people in the area were nomadic or semi-nomadic. A group of people now referred to as the *Przeworsk* culture lived in an enormous territory and flourished for more than four hundred years. They appear to have been influenced by Germans and Celts, as well as people living on the eastern steppes.[27]

Another prominent society in the area is referred to as the *Cjernjakhov* culture, whose people inhabited the region between the Danube and Dniepr rivers. The roots of this culture are believed to have originated in the Scythian and Sauromatian steppe cultures. By the fourth century these people had expanded southwards as far as the Danube. Archaeological evidence shows this society to have been a very dynamic and innovative one, producing excellent ironwork, metalwork and pottery.[28]

Another population group, known as the *Sclaveni*, was probably a confederation of cultural groups that engaged in contact with both the Baltic and Germanic peoples. Over time the Sclaveni moved into Bohemia, Poland, eastern Germany, Bulgaria and the Balkans. These diverse and widespread groups eventually produced a number of Slav states, which contrasted with the more unified powers of Germanic Europe at this time. The Sclaveni are believed to be the ancestors of the Slavs.[29]

Farther to the west, in the lower Elbe and Weser regions, was a group of people known as the Saxons. In Classical sources, the word "Saxon" seems to refer to a specific culture, but it may actually denote any raider or immigrant who crossed the northern seas. The Saxons moved towards Holland and into central Germany where they had contact with the Franks and Thuringians. They were a powerful force in Europe for some time, especially during the sixth and seventh centuries. Their exploits in Britain were legendary, as we will see in the next chapter. The Saxons finally succumbed to the Franks, and were subjugated by Charlemagne in the latter part of the eighth century.[30]

Far to the north, in what is now Scandinavia, were other native peoples. The most powerful of these population groups were the Sviar of central Sweden and the Gotar of southern Sweden. A number of graves excavated at Gamla Uppsala may represent noble burials from the ruling dynasty of the Sviar. These nobles were known as the Ynglingas and are well documented in both Norse and English saga traditions. Three large mounds were discovered dating to the sixth century, surrounded by hundreds of smaller mounds, and a large group of ship burials found next to a medieval church. These noble gravesites contained swords, shields, helmets, horsegear and personal ornaments.[31]

Many other cultures lived in Europe at this time, in a wide range of territories that included much of modern-day Spain, Italy, the Rhineland, the Balkans, the Baltic region, Germany, the Danube regions, Holland, Denmark, Scandinavia and the British Isles. These cultures included the Bavarians, the Danes, the Lombards, the Angles, the Frisians, the Avars, the Gepids, and a number of tribal groups from Jutland. Villages and farming communities existed throughout the region, and people raised barley, wheat, spelt, oats, millet and rye. Legumes and vegetables were also grown, as well as a plant known as woad that produces a rich blue dye for textiles.[32]

People also raised cattle, pigs, sheep and goats, though these would have been much smaller than farm animals of today. Horses were also raised, but were of such value that they were much rarer than other animals. Domestic dogs were kept for herding and guarding, but do not seem to have been used much for hunting. Evidence for hunting is quite rare at this time, and even fishing and the gathering of shellfish does not seem to have played an important role in many local economies. Craftsmen and women produced a number of sophisticated goods including pottery and textiles. Metalworking flourished and had developed to include the use of semi-precious stones (especially garnets).[33]

History books promote the idea that the origins of medieval Europe (and consequently, of modern Europe) are to be found in the cultures of Greece and Rome, and that our civilization derives from these traditions. The Roman invasion did have a monumental impact on parts of Europe, but certainly not all of it. Roman military and political power reached an apex after several centuries, and eventually began to decline. Historians, archaeologists, anthropologists and religious scholars are now realizing that the contributions of the many non–Classical cultures of Europe have been underestimated. The formation of European culture was the product of a number of social and historical forces, and the result of the cultures and traditions of many different kinds of people. The myths, legends and religious beliefs of the native people of Europe greatly contributed to the rich tapestry of European culture. Therefore, it is to these indigenous traditions that we should look when seeking the roots of our way of life.

Earth Mother and Boar Goddess

The religious traditions of ancient Europe contain many interesting beliefs and practices that attest to the widespread veneration of the natural world and the importance of the Divine Feminine. Descriptions of the religious practices of early Germanic tribes indicate that they frequently worshipped their deities in an outdoor setting (particularly in sacred groves). Divinities were not typically represented in physical form. Instead their presence was invoked and felt by worshippers as they visited sacred places.[34] Tacitus refers to this practice in his work entitled *The Germania*: "They do not ... deem it consistent with the divine majesty to imprison their Gods within walls or represent them with anything like human features. Their holy places are the woods and groves, and they call by the name of a God that hidden presence which is only seen by the eye of reverence."[35]

Over time, these animistic beliefs and ceremonies were augmented by the construction of pagan Germanic temples that did contain representations of Germanic deities. The divine pantheon of the Anglo-Saxons was described in later written sources, and included a number of powerful male and female divinities. One of the most well-known of these ancient deities was *Woden* (known as *Odin* in Norse tradition). His name is preserved in the word "Wednesday" (Woden's Day) and he was associated with battle and warriors, as well as healing and magic.[36]

Another popular Germanic deity was *Thunor* (*Thor* in Norse mythology), a son of Woden. Thunor was worshipped in sacred groves or meadows, and was a god of strength and thunder. His primary symbol was the hammer, a talisman that had the power of life and death. Thor's name is commemorated in the word "Thursday." The Germanic god *Tiw* was a god of battle, law and order, and his name exists in the word "Tuesday."[37]

The Anglo-Saxons also worshipped a number of powerful female deities. The most prominent was Woden's consort *Frigg* or *Friga*. She was a goddess of marriage and childbirth, and a respected divine matriarchal figure. Her name is remembered in the word for "Friday."[38]

The Anglo-Saxons also acknowledged an "Earth Mother" who was venerated in a number of regions. Germanic tribes known as the *Aestii* who lived near the Prussian coast worshipped a figure whom Tacitus refers to as the "Mother of the Gods." In honor of this goddess, people wore the symbol of the boar as an emblem of their religious devotion to her.[39] Some Germanic tribes worshipped an Earth Mother goddess known as *Nerthus*. The rites associated with her worship in Denmark were recorded by Tacitus:

> In an island ... stands a sacred grove, and in the grove is a wagon draped with a cloth which none but the priest may touch. The priest can feel the presence of the goddess in this holy of holies, and attends her, in deepest reverence, as her wagon is drawn along by oxen. Days of rejoicing and merry-making ensue in every place that she honors with her presence. None participates in war, no one takes up weapons, and all iron objects are locked away. Then ... peace and quiet are known ... until the goddess is once again restored to her temple by the priest, when she has had her fill of the company of men. Afterwards, the wagon, the cloth and the goddess herself are washed clean in a secluded lake.[40]

The worship of this indigenous Earth Mother goddess continued well into the Christian era. Both the Earth and the Christian god are invoked in an Anglo-Saxon charm intended to bring prosperity and fertility to the land:

> I stand facing the East and pray for favour
> I pray to the Great Lord, to the Almighty Ruler
> I Pray to the sacred Guardian of Heaven
> I pray to the Earth and to the High Heavens.[41]

After this recitation, a ritual honoring the Earth Mother took place. Incense, fennel, soap and salt were rubbed on the wooden handle of a plough. Afterwards, seed that had been obtained from a beggar was placed upon the plough and a chant recited to the Goddess. The word *Erce* may be name of the goddess herself:

> Erce, Erce, Erce, Earth Mother,
> May the All-Ruler, the Eternal Lord

Grant your fields increase and growth,
Strength and fruitfulness
A shining harvest of fruits and millet,
Broad blades of corn and barley
Hail to you, Earth, Mother of men!
May you bring forth, in the Lord's embrace,
And be filled with food and goodness
for the use of mortal men.[42]

Mother goddesses appear to have played an important part in the seasonal calendar of the Germanic tribes. The Christian scholar Bede wrote that in earlier times the Germanic ritual year began on the 25th of December and that this night was called *Modranect* ("Mothers' Night"). This was a pagan festival that was absorbed into the celebrations associated with Christmas. The same is true of *Giuli* (or "Yule"), the English name for the season that ran from December to January. As a mid-winter festival, Mothers' Night may have acknowledged the Earth Mother in order to ensure abundance in the upcoming spring season. Traditional Yule festivities included the gathering and hanging of evergreen boughs and the burning of a Yule log. The Yuletide feast also involved a ritual procession with a boar's head, which was the symbol of the Earth Mother among some of the Germanic tribes.[43]

In this annual ritual cycle, Christmas (or "Mother's Night") was associated with a group of female divine figures. The plural reference to the divine "mothers" may be similar to the *Matronae* (Mother Goddesses) who were depicted during Roman times and venerated in the later Celtic and Germanic worlds. Stone sculptures of these figures portray them in single, double and triple form. They are often shown holding babies or baskets of fruit, and were probably associated with fertility, abundance and childbirth.[44]

In addition to Frigg and the Mother goddesses, Bede mentions two other Anglo-Saxon goddesses, *Hreda* and *Eostre*, also associated with the ritual year. Hreda's name may mean "glory" or "fame," and she was associated with *Hred-monath* ("Hreda's Month"), which took place in March. Eostre's name is connected with the word for "east," and may have been associated with the dawn. She was venerated in *Eosturmonath*, the month of April. In later times, French and Italian-speaking Christians adopted names for Easter that were derived though Latin and Greek from the Hebrew word for Passover (like the French word *Pasques*). However, the English word "Easter" and the German term "Ostern" both derive from the name of Eostre, an Anglo-Saxon goddess of Spring.[45]

There are a number of interesting parallels between Germanic and Norse mythology and religion. Medieval texts provide us with a great deal of detailed information about the beliefs of the Scandinavian people. The Norse are sometimes depicted as little more than ruthless marauders. In actuality they were skilled craftsmen and bold traders who produced sophisticated metalwork and ships that were marvels of technology by the standards of any era.[46]

The Vikings colonized Greenland and Iceland, although their presence in the fragile ecosystem of Iceland eventually decimated the forests of that island. This once again underscores the impact of ancient farming and herding on the natural environment. The Vikings reached North America long before Christopher Columbus, landing in Newfoundland and New Brunswick where they established a temporary settlement. Viking traders and adventurers even traveled as far as Bagdad and Constantinople, and the Norse kings of what would be Kiev helped found the nation of Russia (whose name may possibly derive from *Rus*, a term for the Norsemen). In fact, the Norse traveled farther from their homelands than the Greeks or Romans ever did.[47]

Norse mythology describes three cosmic realms that were connected by a world tree known as *Ygdrassil*. Beyond the heavens was *Asgard*, the realm of the gods. The Norse deities were classified in two groups, the *Vanir* and the *Aesir*.[48] Odin was the head of the Aesir, and was known as the All-Father. In the Old Norse poem *Hávamal*, Odin is described as having sacrificed himself on the World Tree for nine days and nights, pierced with a spear. During his ordeal, he looks down from the tree and takes up the runes, which symbolize divine wisdom and sacred lore.[49] During his initiatory ordeal, Odin uttered the following words:

> I know I hung on the windswept Tree,
> Through nine days and nights
> I was stuck with a spear and given to Odin,
> Myself given to myself
> They helped me neither with meat nor drink...
> I peered downward,
> I took up the runes,
> Screaming, I took them
> And then I fell back.[50]

It was initially believed that this image of a suffering god hanging on a tree and pierced by a spear was influenced by the story of Jesus' crucifixion. However, scholars now understand that this pagan god's self-sacrifice formed part of the indigenous beliefs of the Norse, and probably reflected a shamanic death-and-rebirth scenario.[51]

Odin's eldest son was the god Thor, whose divine mother was *Fjorgynn*, a poetic name for the Earth. His other son was *Balder*, who was exceedingly wise, merciful, and possessed of great beauty. The god *Tyr* was revered for his ability to provide victory in battle. In one tale, he binds a monstrous wolf known as *Fenrir*, a supernatural conflict that cost him his hand.[52]

The gods *Freyr* and *Njord* also dwelt in Asgard, but they were of the Vanir. Njord controlled the winds and the sea, assisted with fishing and sea voyages, and brought wealth and abundance. His son Freyr was a god of fertility and plenty. He owned a magical boar with golden bristles, and possessed a ship large enough to hold all the gods but small enough to fold into a pouch. The god *Bragi* was extremely skilled with words and poetry. *Loki*, the divine trickster, helped and hindered the gods in their activities. He gave birth to the wolf *Fenrir* and the World Serpent, as well as the goddess *Hel* who ruled over the land of death.[53]

Heimdall, the "White (or Holy) God," was said to be the son of nine maidens. He lived beside a rainbow bridge where he served as divine guardian, protecting the realm of the gods from the frost-giants. He could see things far in the distance and his sense of hearing was extremely acute. Heimdall owned a horn called *Gjallarhorn* whose blast could be heard throughout the three cosmic realms.[54]

The Norse also venerated a number of goddesses, many of whom figure prominently in the myths. *Frigg* was the wife of Odin. Like her husband, she could foresee the future of gods and men. She was the mother of Balder, and along with the goddess *Freyja* she was invoked by women in childbirth. Frigg was a highly revered wife and mother. Although she was the esteemed consort of the primary male deity, she was also considered to be the divine queen of the heavens in her own right.[55]

A number of other goddess figures are mentioned in Norse myths and legends. The goddess *Skadi* was the wife of Njord. She came down from her mountain home in order to marry the sea god. However, their marriage was not successful because neither was willing to live away from their home. Eventually Skadi returned to the hills where she went about on skis and hunted with a bow. Bragi had a divine wife called *Idun*, and this goddess was responsible for guarding the apples of immortality, the food on which the gods feasted in order to maintain their eternal youth.[56]

Gefion was a Norse goddess to whom unmarried girls went after their death. Once she was sent by Odin to look for land in the mortal realms, and King Gylfi of Sweden offered her as much land as she could plough. She visited a giant with whom she had four sons, and transformed them into a team of powerful oxen. Gefion ploughed around the edges of Zealand (the island on which Copenhagen now stands) and separated it from the rest of Sweden. After this supernatural feat, Gefion went to live with *Skiold*, a divine son of Odin.[57]

Another important group of divine women in Norse tradition were the

Valkyries. They formed a link between Odin and the slain, and also between the worlds of the living and the dead. The Valkyries wore amour and rode on horseback, flying swiftly over both land and sea. They carried out Odin's will during battles and conflicts, either awarding victory or leading the dead to Valhalla. In some texts, human princesses are said to "become" Valkyries, which may suggest that they were priestesses of the Valkyries' cult. The word "valkyrie"means "chooser of the slain," and in the eleventh century the Anglo-Saxon Bishop Wulfstan listed "choosers of the slain" in a list that included witches and other "sinners and evil-doers."[58]

Norse mythology includes a sacred Well of Wisdom that existed among the roots of the world tree Ygdrasil. The well was guarded by the god Mimir, who was said to be the wisest of the Aesir. In another Lower World region was the Well of Urd, a sacred spring of Fate or Destiny. Every day the gods assembled there to hold a court of law, settle disputes, and discuss their common challenges and concerns. Near the spring of fate lived three divine maidens called the Norns, who ruled over the destinies of men. Their names were *Urðr* ("Fate"), *Verðandi* ("Being") and *Skuld* ("Necessity"). Every day the Norns nourished the World Tree with pure water and whitened it with clay from inside the spring, preserving its eternal life and maintaining the connection between the three sacred realms.[59]

One of the most popular and widely venerated of the Norse goddesses was *Freyja*, the twin sister of Freyr. She rode about in a chariot drawn by cats and was called to assist in matters of love. Freyja also had some power over the dead. One text stated that she received half of those who died in battle, while the other half went to Odin. Freyja is sometimes depicted as a weeping goddess, (perhaps weeping for the slain). Elsewhere it was said that she had a husband called *Od* who left her, causing her to weep tears of gold and silver in his absence.[60]

Like her twin brother Freyr, Freyja owned a magical boar (the symbol of other Germanic goddesses). She possessed a magical necklace called *Brosingamene*, which was her most cherished possession. The name of this necklace may derive from the rare Norse word *brísingr* meaning "fire," perhaps referring to an amber necklace of some kind. Another of Freyja's attributes was that she possessed a "feather" or "falcon" shape. This referred to her ability to change into the form of a bird, in which shape she could travel vast distances (a power also attributed to Odin and Loki).[61]

Freyja was associated with a special form of magic known as *seiðr*. A priestess of the Vanir, she was said to be the deity who first taught this knowledge to the Aesir. In this practice, a high platform or seat was constructed on which the magical practitioner sat. In most cases, this was a woman. The *seiðr* priestess sang or chanted certain spells, after which she fell into an ecstatic trance state. At the end of the ceremony, the person working the *seiðr* was able to answer questions in an oracular fashion.[62]

A number of written sources indicate that the goddess Freyja was still worshipped long after the introduction of Christianity. In the twelfth century, an Icelandic scholar named Snorri Sturluson decided to write down the myths and beliefs of his ancestors before they were lost. In his work, he states that Freyja was the most renowned of all the goddesses, and that of all the Norse gods, she alone still lived.[63]

Snake Worshippers and Sun Goddesses

A number of other religious traditions also flourished in late Iron Age and early medieval Europe. In the Baltic regions, the reports of a Bohemian monk stated that there were a number of tribes in the area who practiced their own brand of spirituality. Some of these groups he describes as "snake worshippers." Other groups maintained a perpetual sacred flame that formed part of the oracular ceremonies of a sacred priesthood. Deeper in the Baltic interior, people were said to worship the sun and "with extraordinary veneration" adore an enormous iron hammer (perhaps a symbol of the thunder god). Other Baltic tribes worshipped sacred groves, particularly venerating an ancient oak that was held to be extremely holy, above all other trees.[64]

Less than a century later, a Polish chronicler wrote that the Lithuanians worshipped the same elements as in earlier accounts (fire, lightning, groves, and snakes). He also stated that they made offerings to the dead. The persistence of native Baltic religious practices was noted by later Christian authorities as well. They referred to a "savage race of men" living under the northern star, who worshipped blue-colored snakes as deities and performed "improper sacrifices."[65]

Other texts provide us with details about the early gods of the Baltic regions, including a thunder-god called *Perkunus* (whose name means "Striker"). Groups of holy women known as *Waidlotten* maintained the god's perpetual flame, and paid with their lives if it were ever extinguished. Perkunus was worshipped along with two other gods, *Patrollo* and *Patrimpo*, and their idols were said to have stood together in an oak tree.[66]

In some accounts, the three gods appear to represent the three ages of man. Patrimpo was sometimes described as a young, unbearded man, a joyful god of crops who was crowned with ears of grain. He had a snake that was kept in a jar covered with sheaves of grain. Sacred priestesses guarded and fed the snake with libations of milk. Perkunus was sometimes represented as an angry middle-aged man with a curly black beard and a face like fire. He was associated with a divine flame and its female guardians. Patrollo was said to be an old man with a long green beard and a deathlike complexion. He wore a white cloth wound around his head like a turban and looked up at the others from below. His sacred symbols were the skulls of men, horses and cows.[67]

Other early Baltic deities included *Diviriks*, whose name means something akin to "Ruler of the Gods" and *Teljavel* the divine smith, who was said to have created the sun. Once a year the Prussians fashioned an idol of a god named *Curcho* who they venerated by offering him the first fruits of the harvest. Another deity called *Wurschayto* (or *Borsskayto*) was worshipped in Baltic villages wherever there was an oak tree. He provided good health and luck in fishing, and was offered gifts of young fish or fowl.[68]

In another source, native Baltic deities were said to include: *Occopirmus* (a sky- or star-god), *Suaixtix* (a sun-god), *Auschauts* (a healer deity), *Autrimpus* or *Antrimpus* (a sea-god), *Potrimpus* (god of rivers and springs), *Perdoytus* (a seafarer's god), *Pergrubrius* (god of the spring), *Percunus* (thunder- and rain-god) and *Pecullos* or *Patollos* (an Underworld god). There was also *Piluitis*, who was either a god or a goddess associated with a rich harvest. For some reason, early texts do not provide much information about Baltic goddesses. However, they do mention veneration of a woodland goddess named *Mejdejn*, and a deity called *Veliuona* ("Ancestral Goddess").[69]

In Latvia, which is part of the Baltic region, a number of goddess figures were widely venerated. One of these was *Laima*, a very important female deity. She did not reside in the sky like other Latvian gods, but was frequently encountered in the bathhouse where she helped women in childbirth. She determined the fate of the newborn, and her name became synonymous with the concept of "fate." Laima was invoked prior to and during childbirth, and also received offerings after the birth of the child. Chastity and marriage were the concerns of this goddess, and even men were ruled by her powerful decisions.[70]

As a goddess of fate, Laima was sometimes revered and other times cursed. She was so important that she maintained her power long after the memory of the other gods faded in the centuries after the introduction of Christianity. In many cases, Laima was depicted standing next to the Virgin Mary, with whose cult her own was sometimes intertwined. In recent times, songs addressed to Laima are believed to represent the expressions of a living faith.[71]

In Latvian tradition, there were a number of divine women known as *mate* or "mother" (a term that appears to be synonymous by usage with the word "goddess"). *Dahrsemate* was invoked when working in the garden. *Lauke-*

mate was called upon while working in the fields and thanked for a bountiful harvest. Hunters invoked *Meschemate,* the mother or goddess of the forest, asking her to grant them luck.[72]

There were goddesses associated with the natural world: *Zemes mate* ("Mother Earth"), *Juras mate* ("Mother Ocean") and *Meza mate* ("Mother Forest"). In Latvia, brandy was poured into the ocean as an offering for the Ocean Mother, and bread and milk were sometimes offered. The term *mate* was also used in connection with man-made places, domestic activities, and even abstract concepts. *Pirts mate* was "Mother of the Bathhouse," *Risu mate* was "Mother of Spinning" and *Gausa mate* the "Mother of Blessing."[73]

Another important Latvian goddess was *Saules mate*—"Mother Sun." She was a celestial divinity who had the ability to see all things. Her daughters were called *Saules meitas* ("Daughters or Young Women of the Sun"). A number of folksongs describe Saule wearing red or golden garments and a silver crown or wreath. She is sometimes depicted spinning silken threads amongst the leaves of an apple tree, gathering hay with a silver rake, or playing a harp in the eastern wind.[74]

Traditional lyrics frequently refer to Saule's journey through the heavens. One song described three yellow horses that drew her carriage, a vehicle she rode over land and sea. When the sun dipped beneath the waves, Saule's carriage had taken her into the waters where she either "drowned" or resided in an unknown place. In one song, when the goddess is asked where she spends the night, she weeps and says she is not permitted to sleep, but steers her golden boat upon the waves all night long.[75]

Native songs tell how Saule married off her daughters and offered them rich wedding presents. She cried piteously after the departure of a newly married daughter. She was also said to cry because her boat had sunk in the waters of the western seas, because the leaves had blown from the birch trees, or because an apple had fallen to the ground. Her divine compassion was so great that she sent warming rays to orphaned children. Saule showed great tenderness towards humans, but sometimes argued with the other gods. In one tale, she was reported to have torn the moon-god to pieces because he had stolen someone else's bride. She herself was said to have been a bride, in the early days when the world was new.[76]

In the eastern parts of Europe, certain elements of the mythological and religious traditions of the Scythians may have been preserved in folk traditions and legends. This is especially prevalent among the Osset from the Caucausus region, who preserved certain mythological elements in their *Nart* Saga. Here, the deceased are believed to cross a bridge as narrow as a hair while attempting to pass to the Otherworld. Myths tell of a Cosmic Tree whose branches reach towards the sky and in whose roots is a magical spring. Diviners, seers and psychopomps played an important role in these spiritual traditions. The most important of these magical practitioners were the *Messulethe,* who consisted primarily of women and girls. Their primary function was to escort the souls of the dead to the afterlife. They were also said to be able to enter a trance state and allow the dead to speak through them.[77]

In certain parts of Russia, a Great Goddess was venerated with great enthusiasm and devotion. This divine figure may be derived in part from Tabiti, the great goddess of the Scythians. The veneration of this deity was especially strong in heavily wooded areas of Russia, where the goddess was venerated in sacred groves and at sacred springs.[78]

Remnants of these traditions were still practiced in remote areas until the first few decades of the twentieth century. When a lone birch tree was encountered in a clearing, it was said to be the personification of the great goddess. The tree was clothed in a woman's dress and on its branches was placed a special towel embroidered with sacred emblems. The design consisted of a female figure with her arms on her hips. On either side of her were two horsemen, who sometimes bear offerings. This imagery is reminiscent of depictions of Tabiti and the horsemen who attended her.[79]

The grove ceremony existed in an even more evocative form. When a lone birch could not be found, a young girl was placed in the center of the clearing and birch branches were entwined in her hair. The embroidered towel was placed on the bough of a convenient tree. In the ceremony of the birch-maiden, the assembled company gathered and formed a ring around the representative of the goddess. A circle dance was enacted which involved the stamping of feet to simulate the sound of running horses (perhaps invoking the presence of the horsemen of the goddess).[80]

A similar ritual took place among the Northern Udmurts and Besermians until very recent times. There were still special female sacred places where rituals were performed until the middle of the twentieth century. Female "priestesses" ("prayers," i.e. "one who prays") organized rituals at a sanctuary where there was a birch tree and a fireplace in a clearing in the forest. Women tied fabric and towels to the birch trunk and prayed for fertility for themselves and health for their children, burying coins at the roots of the tree to reinforce their requests.[81]

A number of goddess figures were also venerated by the *Saami* of Finland (a population group of non–Indo-European origin known as Lapps outside their own culture). Their primary source of sustenance was reindeer herding, and to this day they have shamans and preserve shamanic traditions in their culture.[82]

For the Saami, the goddess *Bieve* was the personification of the sun. In some Saami cultures she was considered to be the mother of all living creatures, particularly the reindeer (who were a gift from the goddess to the Saami). The Saami living in Norway venerated a female creation spirit named *Madder-Akka* ("Origin-Grandmother"). This creator-goddess had three daughters: *Sar-Akka* ("Birth-Grandmother"), *Juks-Akka* ("Bow-Grandmother") and *Uks-Akka* ("Door-Grandmother"). These three divinities gave life to all creatures, including human beings, and were sometimes associated with determining the gender and destiny of the young.[83]

The Saami who lived in Russia venerated *Pots-Husjik* ("Reindeer Mistress") and *Luot-Hosjik*, both of whom were connected with the herding and raising of reindeer. A female spirit known as *Jabmi-Akka* ("Death-Grandmother") was the counterpart of *Madder-Akka*, for death was perceived as a natural and important part of the life cycle. The Saami have been nominally Christian for only about two hundred years. Several of their native goddesses were transmuted to adapt and survive within the new belief system. *Bieve* the sun-goddess is sometimes associated with Anna, the mother of Mary. The figures of *Madder-Akka* and *Sar-Akka* also merged or linked with the Virgin Mary, allowing their veneration to continue under a new guise.[84]

The tribes of ancient Europe possessed rich cultural and spiritual traditions, most of which included powerful and highly respected goddesses. From the survival of the Great Goddess of the Scythians in the east, to the powerful cults of the Earth Mother in the west, these indigenous traditions connected people with the powers inherent in nature, and with the wisdom of the past. The religions of Europe venerated goddesses of nature (the sun, the land, groves and springs) as well as goddesses of destiny, magic, and fate.

These native traditions were sometimes interwoven with the incoming faith, as in the case of Mother's Night (originally held on December 25th,) and the invocation of the Earth Goddess along with the Christian God in ceremonies honoring the earth. Some goddesses became associated with the Virgin Mary in order for their veneration to continue. Others were transformed into Christian saints, and their rites continued in a new guise. Still others, like the goddess Freyja, were so powerful in their own right that they continued to be worshipped, never stepping under the veil of the new religion at all. For in all their power and wisdom, and all their authority and complexity, they simply *were*.

11

The Once and Future Goddess

My first word was spoken about the cauldron,
Kindled by the breath of nine maidens.
The Cauldron of the Chief of Annwfn,
What is its virtue, with its edge of dark pearls?
— Medieval Welsh poem

The Grail is being in perfect accord with the abundance of nature,
the highest spiritual realization, the inexhaustible vessel
from which you get everything you want...
— Joseph Campbell[1]

The great hill rose from the plain like a temple, its towering presence looming over the countryside. Its contours seemed to evoke the shape of a woman's body, its sides terraced by farmers long ago when the hill was surrounded by water. As the years went by, the water turned to marshland and was transformed into rich and fertile soil, now covered by a blanket of grass and wildflowers.

A line of pilgrims walked along the path that led to the holy site, sometimes called the Isle of Glass. This was the festival that heralded the start of the bright half of the year. People came from miles around to behold the *Tor* or sacred hill, which was said to be a portal to *Inis Afallon*, the Sacred Island of Apple Trees. All along the pathway the fruit trees were in full bloom, the clouds of blossoms creating a dream-like atmosphere.

Further to the north in Scotland, another procession was taking place, for there was a sister-hill like the *Tor* near the Firth of Forth. It was rumored that a similar gathering was held in Ireland, for the Irish also knew of a sacred realm called *Emain Ablach* ("The Twins of the Apple Trees"). At the bottom of the Tor, food and drink were provided for those who had come to pay homage to the Gods and Goddesses. In addition to being the home of the goddesses of Avalon, this was also the dwelling of *Gwynn ap Nudd*, a deity who battled for the hand of a beautiful maiden every year at May Day.

After pausing to rest and take refreshment, the pilgrims picked up their staffs and began the trek up the hill. They walked along a walkway formed by the ancient terraces, an almost labyrinthine path that wound its way up the flanks of the hill. The sun had reached its mid-point, and a ceremonial horn was sounded three times. On top of the hill were two large stacks of firewood that had been collected at dawn. The horn sounded again and the druids and priestesses struck stones together to kindle the sacred flame.

The bonfires crackled slowly at first, but soon were blazing with a great roar. The hermits led two white oxen between the fires to protect the herds and flocks. They walked around the fires with a vessel full of grain and a basket laden with flowers and fruits, symbolizing the bounty of the land. Finally the pilgrims processed between the fires, purifying themselves and asking for blessings and protection in the months to come.

Next, four men stepped forward to enact a ceremony that had been performed in this land since time immemorial. They wore headdresses made from deer's antlers and linen tunics embroidered with symbols of four sacred creatures: the dragon, boar, raven and bear. They stood in each of the four directions, waiting in silence in the middle of the assembly. At last, the faint sound of small bells began to drift up onto the hillside from a pathway on the far side of the grounds. The assembly bent their heads as a group of nine women processed towards the center of the site. These were the priestesses of Avalon, holy women who lived on a sacred island off the coast. Several times a year they traveled to the mainland on a sacred barge to perform a series of ancient rites. They served the gods and goddesses of Avalon, a spiritual realm that existed inside the Tor as well as in the hearts of the people.

The priestesses walked around the circle, sprinkling water from two local holy wells to consecrate the ground beneath their feet. Holy water from the White Spring was offered to the gods and goddesses, and water from the Red Spring to the spirits of the land. The high priestess held up a silver vessel and poured in the water from the two springs, mixing it with an elixir made from apple blossoms, meadowsweet and violets.

Four priestesses dipped wooden cups into the vessel and poured the water on the ground in front of the four men. The other four priestesses processed forward with a large object hidden under a white cloth. They set it on a large flat stone and lifted the covering. There was a statue of the great Goddess of Avalon. Her robe was emblazoned with her sacred symbols, the horse and the bird, and as always, she carried a sacred vessel. Holy water was sprinkled on the statue, and the people came forward to make offerings and prayers. In no time, she was covered in a proliferation of white, pink and yellow flowers.

The priestesses stood facing the statue with their palms held up, and fell into a trance state as they chanted a hymn in their ancient tongue. The sound of their voices and the ringing bells, along with the smell of the elixir and freshly picked blossoms, created a hypnotic atmosphere that seemed to open a portal into the realms of Avalon itself.

The crowd stood back to witness a ritual that took place only when one leader had passed over and a new leader was to be chosen. He was selected by the high priestess, the representative of the Goddess on earth. Only with her blessing could the leader rule successfully and honorably, and with her power the land and the people would prosper.

The four men engaged in a ritual battle to win the favor of the goddess. Using only pairs of deer antlers held in their hands, their movements created a resonant, rhythmic sound that echoed in the silence of the ceremonial grounds. No one dared speak, for this was a sacred ceremony and not a mere contest of sport. Each man had been chosen as a potential candidate on the basis of his many honorable qualities, his virtuous character, and dedication to the traditional ways.

The contestants stalked and swirled in a display of skill that had to be enacted according to strict rules. Two of the men rose above the others, but one began to display anger towards his opponent. This dissipated his focus and tainted his honour. The other man remained grounded in the earth and gained a strong advantage. The head priestess cried out and the action was stopped in its tracks.

She stepped forward and pulled out a silver sword from beneath her cloak. Brandishing the sword, she called out an ancient proclamation. The victorious man fell to his knees and lowered his head in the presence of the goddess incarnate. The crowd was hushed. Would the man be accepted by the goddess? If he was accepted, it was an auspicious omen. If rejected, the priestess would enact a ritual beheading and receive no further supplicants that year, which did not bode well for the land or the people.

There was no sound except for the cry of a raven that flew above their heads. At last, the sword of the priestess began to fall, cutting swiftly through the air. It came to an abrupt halt on the man's shoulder, and the crowd sighed audibly in relief. She carefully placed the flat side of her sword on the candidate's right shoulder, and then his left. He had been chosen as leader of the people.

The man stood up in front of the priestess. As he raised his face towards her, she placed a silver branch decorated with apple blossoms in his hand. This was a symbol of passage between the worlds and indicated that he would be invited to take part in an ancient rite later that night. No one had ever witnessed this rite, nor were they meant to.

The ritual took place at midnight in the center of an apple grove, lit only by the light of the moon. There the priestess would test the candidate, challenging him physically, mentally, emotionally and spiritually. No one who had experienced the challenge ever spoke of it, though many went on to become great leaders or holy people. The prophet Merlin was said to have undergone this ritual many years ago, and was gifted with the power of foresight as well as the ability to change his shape.

The priestess sat in a wooden chair decorated with knotwork and sacred symbols. She held up a gold chalice decorated with running horses, symbols of the Goddess of Sovereignty. In the bottom of the chalice was the image of a dragon that symbolized the power of the land. The priestess filled the cup with red-colored mead and held it out towards the sky, the earth and underworld realms. She poured some of the mead in front of the statue of the goddess as a sacred libation. She then turned and ritually presented the cup to the candidate — another test. The red mead of Avalon was legendary and contained ingredients so intoxicating that the candidate might forget himself and all he knew before.

The man was dedicated to his faith and paused only for a moment before taking the cup from her hand. It was important to empty the chalice with a single draught; any hesitation was a sign that the candidate lacked courage and perseverance. He completed his task admirably and handed the chalice back into the priestess' waiting hands.

Once the ale-feat had been completed, the priestesses chanted an eerie hymn. Four of the priestesses carried the image of the goddess back towards its sacred enclosure, a place sometimes sought by the unwary, whose exact location was a mystery. The other priestesses began to chant a familiar song, throwing flowers and offerings after their sisters as they went. The new initiate stood mutely at the edge of the grove, unsure of what would follow.

After a few minutes, the mead began to take effect. The man's eyelids grew heavy and his feet felt rooted to the ground. He called upon his ancestors for guidance, and as others had done before him, he found the strength and courage to walk into the depths of the grove. There he would undergo a powerful initiatory experience, a spiritual union with the Goddess of Sovereignty. This was the greatest blessing a leader could hope to receive. For was it not said that from Her all things came, and to Her all things returned? He had received the sword blessing, and partaken of the indescribable contents of the cup. Whatever now came to pass were the ways of the Goddess of Avalon. The pursuit of these mysteries constituted the most important focus of one's personal and spiritual path. By drinking from the Cup of Truth, as the new initiate was beginning to understand, his connection with the wisdom of the Otherworld and all that was important in life would be revealed.[2]

The story of the Divine Feminine in Europe would not be complete without one final tale. This legend has been told for more than fifteen hundred years and is so ingrained in our cultural framework, that it has become far more than myth or saga. In many ways, it could be described as a foundation myth of our secular theology. Its symbolism resonates so deeply that even the names of its characters and hallowed sites evoke a powerful response. This is the archetypal legend of a mysterious woman who empowers the rightful leader to restore the land and its people to a harmonious state of existence. It is a story so powerful that it connects us with some of the most fundamental aspects of our cultural and spiritual inheritance. This is the story of King Arthur, a leader of the British Celts whose mythic fame spread throughout Europe and still forms part of our spiritual core and cultural mythos.

The Arthurian legend has a special place in my own life experience. While researching my family tree, I came across a number of intriguing references to my early British ancestors. I followed these references back through medieval annals and other early sources, which confirmed a most remarkable thing. According to traditional Welsh genealogies, through the female line of descent I was a descendant of King Arthur's father, Uther Pendragon, through his daughter (and King Arthur's sister), Anna Morgawse. How was this possible? Certainly the legend of King Arthur was just a myth? But what if it wasn't? What if Arthur really existed? Thousands of other people, whether they were aware of it or not, could also claim this same ancestry.[3]

I knew that in traditional cultures, genealogies were carefully preserved over many centuries. In some cases, these genealogies stretched so far back that they included mythical or divine ancestors. This was precisely what I saw in my own lineage. Beyond the names of Uther and Anna were figures from earlier legends, including the god *Beli Mawr* and the British goddess *Dôn*. Needless to say, this discovery inspired me to re-visit the Arthurian corpus to gain a deeper understanding of its relevance and symbolism. In that quest, I have never looked back.

The Wisdom of the Past

The most well known version of the Arthurian legend is one many of us heard as children. King Arthur, a young man of humble lineage and personal integrity, removes a magical sword from a stone. In doing so, he is recognized as the rightful king. Under his beneficent and divinely inspired leadership, the land prospers and a heaven on earth is created. Arthur is guided by the wizard Merlin who teaches him about leadership, right living, and the mysteries of kingship. Arthur marries the lady Guinevere, but she falls in love with one of his chief knights, Lancelot. Their adulterous affair (as well as the scheming of the king's nephew Mordred) result in Arthur's downfall and the destruction of his kingdom and the dream it inspired.

This late version of the Arthurian story is the one most familiar to us, and it does contain some seeds of the original myth. The earliest versions of Arthur's story, however, are in many ways quite different from this legend. Some of the same characters appear in earlier sources, but the original story and its significance have become obscured under a veneer of medieval accretions. Some innovations appeared in the first few centuries after Arthur's lifetime, but many others followed after the publication of the first secular best-seller in Europe. These innovations would change the Arthurian story forever.[4]

In the year 1138, a well-educated Welshman named Geoffrey of Monmouth published a book called *The History of the Kings of Britain*. It claimed to be a complete history of the island of Britain, a monumental task that had never before been attempted. Its historical authenticity is far from accurate, but the book was immensely popular at the time. Geoffrey claimed to have gotten his information from "an ancient book written in the British language" that recounted the names of the kings of Britain and their famous deeds. In spite of this dubious claim, no such book has ever come to light, nor is it mentioned in any other medieval source. Scholars now realize that much of what Geoffrey wrote was the result of his own creative efforts. It was, however, a very cleverly contrived composition, and did include some isolated elements of Celtic lore.[5]

In spite of these contradictions, Geoffrey's work did much to popularize the story of King Arthur, and as a result the Arthurian legend spread throughout Europe. In the hands of courtly storytellers and entertainers, Arthur's story began to take on new elements and characters. These storytellers were concerned with providing entertainment for patrons and their court audiences, rather than preserving the legends of the past. Their courtly creations are the Arthurian tales people are most familiar with — the works of Chrétien de Troyes, the later Merlin legends, and the most well-known variant of all, *The Death of Arthur*, written in the late fifteenth century by Sir Thomas Mallory.[6]

In many popular modern sources, these late medieval creations are claimed to be ancient repositories of spiritual lore, which, if explored deeply enough, will reveal the inner workings of the past. Although some parts of the medieval Arthurian repertoire do contain isolated elements that reflect their roots, the vast majority of these stories are clever fabrications produced by professional writers and entertainers. The real origins of the myth, however, are to be found much farther back in time.[7]

In order to pick up the original threads of the story, we must set aside most of what we think we know about King Arthur and travel back to the late Iron Age and the expansion and decline of the Roman empire. After the Romans conquered Gaul, they set their sights on the island of Britain in the first century C.E. Although they succeeded in taking over most of the south of Britain, they were never successful in conquering the northern regions (nor did they conquer Ireland). Parts of south Britain became Romanized (to varying degrees), although some Celtic tribes in the north and west retained their independence and preserved their traditional cultural identity.[8]

During the fourth century, the Roman Empire found itself weakened by increasing rebellions and military attacks along its eastern frontiers, as well as internal civil wars. In 410 C.E., the Romans abruptly left Britain. During the three and half centuries they had occupied the southern part of the island, they had secured the security of the region. When they left, the native Britons found themselves relatively unprotected, with no army and no central leadership. In order to defend themselves, native leaders invited Saxon mercenaries into Britain to help protect their borders until they could re-organize.[9]

When the Saxons arrived, legend has it, they exploited the vulnerability of their hosts and attacked the very people they had agreed to help. Thousands of Celts were said to have been murdered, while thousands more fled into Wales and Cornwall. Many also escaped by sea over the English Channel into northern France where they founded the Celtic nation of Brittany. After having survived the Roman invasion and occupation, these native peoples found themselves persecuted. Their culture and traditions, as well as their very existence were in a precarious position. Things seemed nigh to hopeless.[10]

This is the point at which Arthur steps onto the scene. He is described as a courageous leader who turns the tide of war (at least for a time), and who works tirelessly to preserve the ways of his people and return the land into their care. His legend grows with each passing year, and his remarkable courage and heroic deeds are supported by a cast of heroes, as well as a number of supernatural figures who assist him in his cause.

The Roots of Ancient Legend

The first surviving record to mention the Saxon invasion was written by a monk named Gildas in the year 547, more than a century after the events in question took place. He describes the persecution of the Britons and mentions a person called *Ambrosius Aurelianus*, who challenged the Saxons in battle. His name seems to be a title ("Divine Excellent One") rather than a personal name. Gildas says that at the Battle of Mount Badon the Celts achieved a great victory over their former oppressors. The story seems to end happily, yet we know that the Anglo-Saxons became the dominant cultural force in south Britain. If this were not so, we would be speaking Welsh, rather than English.[11]

The next scribe to mention the Saxon invasion was Bede, writing in 731 C.E.. He mainly repeats what Gildas set forth, but states that a leader of the Britons named *Vortigern* (a title meaning "Overlord") invited the Saxon mercenaries into the island.[12]

Around the year 800, a Welshman by the name of Nennius wrote a famous chronicle called *Historia Brittonum* ("The History of the Britons"). Although written in Latin, scholars believe that some details were derived from native Welsh sources. Here we find the first written mention of Arthur, who is described as an important battle leader (but not yet a king). He is credited with twelve victories in various regions where native Celts were still living, as well as with other supernatural marvels (showing that his fame had already passed into the realm of legend). Nennius mentions the death of a son of Arthur's, contradicting the later belief that he had no children.[13]

More than a century later, Arthur is mentioned in a document called *The Annals of Cambria*. The annals state that in the year 518 Arthur fought in the Battle of Badon (something previously credited to Ambrosius). He also fought in the Battle of Camlann where he and his nephew *Medraut* (one of the original spellings of Mordred's name) fell. It is not indicated whether Arthur and his nephew were enemies or allies. As the son of the king's sister, Medraut would have been a candidate for the throne.[14]

The next source to mention Arthur is the Life of the Breton saint Goeznovius, dated 1019. Here Vortigern is depicted as an unjust king who invited the Saxons to become his allies. This situation was held in check for many years by the efforts of "the great Arthur, King of the Britons." This is the first time Arthur is referred to as a king.[15]

A century later, in 1125, an Englishman named William of Malmesbury wrote a book called *The Deeds of the English Kings*. He states that Ambrosius ruled after Vortigern and that the Saxon menace was halted with "exemplary assistance of the heroic Arthur."[16] He then goes on to make a rather remarkable observation about the hero:

> This is that Arthur who is raved about even today in the trifles of the Bretons—
> a man who is surely worthy of being described in true histories rather than

dreamed about in fallacious myths — for he truly sustained his sinking homeland for a long time and aroused the drooping spirits of his fellow citizens to battle.[17]

This account describes Arthur as a man "whose second coming has been hymned in the dirges of old," and says that his grave is "nowhere to be found." This is the first reference to a continuing tradition that Arthur was not dead, an allusion which led to the belief that Arthur would return one day. More than six hundred years after the Saxon invasions, Arthur was still being raved about by the descendants of the British Celts for whom he was apparently both an historical and a legendary hero.[18]

Arthur's courage was also mentioned by the twelfth-century Welsh poet *Llywarch ap Llywelyn* who described him as a paragon of strength, valor and generosity. Other Welsh poems referred to Arthur's noble qualities, as well as the fact that he had a noble and esteemed son named *Llachau*, who did not survive. *Medrawd* appears several times in these sources, and it is interesting to note that these native references to Arthur's nephew are all favorable (and may predate Geoffrey's depiction of him as a traitor).[19]

Arthur makes a brief appearance in a thirteenth-century Welsh poem known as *Englynion Y Beddau*, "The Stanzas of the Graves." The poem lists a number of landmarks in Wales that were believed to be the graves of ancient heroes. Arthur's grave is said to be *anoeth*, a word which means "a wonder" or "a thing difficult to find," possibly referring to the belief that Arthur's grave was unknown (and his return therefore possible).[20]

Arthur and his company appear several times in a Welsh text called *The Triads of Britain*, a collection of traditional Welsh lore arranged in groups of three. While the manuscript itself dates to between the twelfth and fourteenth centuries, the information contained in many of the triads is believed to be much older. In the Triads, Arthur is listed as a Chief Ruler in Wales, Cornwall and southern Scotland, places where Celtic culture survived after the Saxon onslaught.[21]

What can we deduce from all of this? Was Arthur actually an historical person? For a long time, scholars maintained that his story was merely a legend. However, in more recent times many scholars believe that there was a real person named Arthur. None of the events described in the chronicles are out of line with what is known about the era. Historical sources from other parts of Europe mention a person known as *Riothamus* (a title meaning "Supreme King") who was a leader of the British Celts. In addition, after the time of Arthur's purported existence, people began to name their children "Arthur." This had been a rare name before his time, but afterwards became much more common.[22]

One of the most intriguing clues about Arthur's historicity comes from an epic Welsh poem known as *The Gododdin* (whose name refers to a British Celtic tribe called the *Votadini*). It was preserved in a manuscript dating to the thirteenth century, but refers to a battle that took place around the year 600, not long after the events associated with the Saxon invasions. Around this time, a group of Welsh-speaking Celts were living in what is now southern Scotland. These tribes, in alliance with other Celts from all over Britain, made a series of heroic attacks against a much larger English force. Tragically, all of the Celtic warriors perished in the conflict except one man, the poet Aneirin, who was said to have written the poem.[23]

It is unclear if the poet credited as Aneirin is actually the historical sixth century poet, or a later poet writing in his name. The historical Aneirin would have been born during Arthur's lifetime, which is a fact of great consequence. In the poem, Arthur is compared with one of the warriors who fought in the battle. It states that although the warrior achieved great deeds, "he was no Arthur." There is no way to know if this statement was part of the original poem or if it was added after the legend of Arthur had grown. Many elements of the poem appear to be quite old, and it does mention other historical rulers of the same time period as Arthur. If the reference to Arthur is original, this Welsh text may be the earliest written record of his name.[24]

In both the Latin and Welsh sources, Arthur is depicted as a brave and generous leader who made wise judgments, freed those who were oppressed, and performed many extraordinary deeds against impossible odds. However, his success was not solely the product of his own skill and integrity, but was inspired and supported by a number of important figures. In addition to brave warriors and cunning advisors, Arthur was guided, assisted and empowered by a number of divine women who played an enormous role in the formation of the Arthurian mythos.

The Abducted Goddess

Many of the mysterious female figures in the Arthurian legends seem to exist somewhere between the world of humans and the realms of the divine. Arthur is associated with a variety of divine women in a number of medieval Welsh sources, including the 12th–13th century mythic poem *Preideu Annwn*, "The Spoils of Annwn." The poem was said to be the creation of the legendary poet-seer Taliesin, and mentions a journey undertaken by Arthur and his men to *Annwn*, the Welsh Otherworld. There they hoped to obtain a magical cauldron that was kindled by the breath of nine maidens, who may have been goddesses or priestesses.[25]

Other divine women are mentioned in the Welsh tale "How Culhwch won Olwen" which is believed to date from before the publication of Geoffrey of Monmouth's work. In the story, Arthur and his men are asked to assist the king's nephew *Culhwch* in winning the hand of *Olwen* ("White [or Holy] Track"), the daughter of a most disagreeable giant named *Ysbaddaden* ("Hawthorn"). The giant imposes a number of impossible tasks on the young man, and Arthur and company set forth to help him achieve his goals.[26]

In the course of their adventures, Arthur and his entourage are required to obtain a magical cauldron from *Annwn* (as in the poem *Preideu Annwn*), as well as a flock of magical singing birds that belong to *Rhiannon*, a Welsh goddess of Sovereignty. They are also to free *Mabon* ("Divine Son") son of *Modron* ("Divine Mother"). Modron was a goddess who was later venerated in southern Scotland, Wales and Cornwall in the guise of Saint Madrun. In Welsh tradition she was said to be the daughter of Vortigern.[27]

The most famous woman associated with Arthur was his queen, Guinevere. Her beauty was legendary, and in early written sources she was depicted as a wise and generous consort. However, her alleged affair with Lancelot (a story which only circulated in the later medieval era) seems to have eclipsed all other knowledge of her.

In Geoffrey of Monmouth, Guinevere was abducted by Mordred, not Lancelot. Some time later, the two were reported to have engaged in an adulterous union.[28] The tradition that Arthur's nephew betrayed him (rather than his best knight) is also seen in the Welsh triads. There it was said that Medrawd came to Arthur's court and ate and drank everything inside his uncle's fortress. He then pulled the queen off her throne and struck her. Arthur's nephew challenges the king by destroying the abundance of his resources and dethroning his queen in order to force him to retaliate.[29]

The theme of the abducted woman also appears in the twelfth-century life of Saint Gildas. The saint was asked to help adjudicate in a matter concerning Arthur and Guinevere. In the tale, Arthur's wife was abducted by King Melwas who ruled over Somerset (the area in which Glastonbury is now located). After a year of searching, Arthur found the queen in captivity in Glastonbury and laid siege to Melwas' stronghold with an army of warriors from Cornwall and Devon. The abbot of Glastonbury, accompanied by Saint Gildas, advised Melwas to release Arthur's rightful queen.[30]

The theme of the competing suitor and the abducted woman also appeared in an earlier native source. In the tale of Culwch and Olwen, Arthur must make a judgment concerning the maiden *Creiddylad*. Although attached to another suitor, she had been abducted by the god *Gwynn ap Nudd*. Arthur decreed that the two suitors must battle every May Day for the hand of the maiden (perhaps reflecting a seasonal myth or ritual enactment). Gwynn ap Nudd was said to live inside the sacred hill of Glastonbury Tor.[31]

What do these stories represent, and how did Guinevere change from Arthur's noble and rightful queen into a disloyal adulteress? The answer may be found in the identity of a divine figure that Guinevere represents. Guinevere's name is a variant of the Welsh name *Gwenhwyfar*. The first part of the name, *"gwen,"* means "white" and is cognate with the Old Irish word *find*, "white, bright, or blessed." The second part of her name is cognate with the Old Irish word *síabair*, "a supernatural being." Therefore, the name *Gwenhwyfar* means a "Blessed Supernatural Being."[32]

In the stories of the abduction, a noble or royal woman is pursued by several male parties and stolen away from her chosen partner. She herself appears to be blameless, and it is the abductor (Gwynn, Melwas, Medrawd, etc.) who behaves dishonorably. Their actions are predicated on the concept that whoever obtains the woman has the potential to be king. Seen in this light, Guinevere is an earthly manifestation of the Goddess of Sovereignty, with whom the king must unite in order for his reign to be successful.

What the abductors fail to realize is that the power belonged to the woman herself (or the Goddess she represented) to choose the man she would support and bless with her presence. She cannot be obtained by force, and the only way to win her favor is through honorable intention and right action. It is not the men who choose the woman, but the Sovereignty Goddess who chooses them.

Far from the disloyal queen of later medieval tales, Guinevere was actually the cornerstone of Arthur's successful reign. Her reputation seems to have become tarnished in the later period as people began to forget who and what she originally symbolized. In *The Triads of Britain* Guinevere is mentioned in several references, which likely date to different parts of the medieval era. In one case she is referred to as one of the "Three Faithless Wives of the Island of Britain." However, in another reference (which may be earlier), Arthur was said to have three queens, all named Gwenhwyfar. The most well-known of these queens was referred to as one of "The Three Great Queens of Arthur."[33]

As we have seen, in Indo-European tradition, divine figures sometimes have three names or aspects. The goddess Bridget was said to have had two sisters also named Bridget. Irish tradition preserves the legends of another trio of divine sisters, the Mórrigan, Macha and Nemain. Like the "Three Great Queens of Britain," these divine women were collectively known as *Na Mórrígna*, "The Great Queens."[34] They display attributes of the Goddess of Sovereignty, challenging heroes and leaders to test their worthiness and bestowing blessings and power upon them.[35] This is undoubtedly the mythic ideal behind the original character of Gwenhwyfar, a "Blessed Supernatural Being" who helped manifest an idealized kingdom on earth which could only exist because of her innate divine power.[36]

The Dragon and the Star

The legend of Arthur was also shaped by the presence of other divine women. In Book Eight of Geoffrey's work, he describes a supernatural portent that signaled the coming reign of Arthur. A huge, bright star appeared in the eastern sky that emitted a single ray, ending in a fiery ball shaped like a dragon. It then emitted two other beams, one that shone towards Gaul, and another beam (which consisted of seven smaller rays) that shone towards the Irish Sea.[37]

The star appeared three times. It was seen by Uther Pendragon, who summoned the wizard Merlin to interpret the omen for him. Merlin tells him that his brother Ambrosius is dead and that the star and the fiery dragon represent Uther. The beam that shone towards Gaul represented a future son, who would control all the kingdoms that the beam illuminated. The second beam, with seven rays, represented a daughter, whose sons and grandsons would, in succession, obtain the kingship of Britain.[38]

Uther fights bravely against the Saxons and is eventually crowned king of Britain. The following spring he holds a great feast. Gorlois, the Duke of Cornwall, attends the gathering, along with his wife Igerna. Her beauty was said to surpass that of all the other women in Britain. Uther falls in love with Igerna and sends her many gifts. Gorlois is angered by the king's attentions towards his wife and the two end up in a bitter conflict.[39]

Gorlois places Igerna in the impenetrable stronghold of Tintagel Castle, located in Cornwall at the edge of the sea. Uther is undeterred and engages the magical assistance of Merlin. The wizard transforms Uther into the likeness of Gorlois and in this guise he is able to enter the castle and sleep with the queen. Gorlois is slain in battle, an event that grieved Uther greatly. Nevertheless, he marries Igerna and they "dwelt together thereafter as equals" at Tintagel, bound by a great love. Together they have a son Arthur and a daughter Anna (also known as Anna Morgawse).[40]

The magical star heralded the birth of a legendary man and woman, both of whom would have a tremendous impact on the future of their people. Anna would marry King Loth (whose name derives from Lothian, a region in southern Scotland near Edinburgh where the early Welsh resided at that time). She gave birth to two sons, Gawain and Modred, who were both portrayed as positive figures in the earliest tales. While many aspects of Geoffrey's work are known to be creative interpretations or fabrications, it is also apparent that he had some access to authentic native lore.[41]

After the publication of Geoffrey's work, other writers began to mention the legend of Arthur. In the late twelfth century, Gerald of Wales published a work called "On the Instruction of Princes" in which we find the first mention of a famous figure from Arthurian legend, Morgan Le Fey. Gerald refers to her as "the noble matron and lady-ruler" of *Inis Avallon*, and a person who was closely related to Arthur by ties of blood. He says that Morgan transported Arthur to the Isle of Avalon after the Battle of Camlann, in order to heal his wounds. Her name, which means "Sea-Born" (and is not related to the name of the Mórrígan) refers to her connection with sacred waters or islands.[42]

Ten years after the immense success of his first book, Geoffrey of Monmouth published another book, the "Life of Merlin." In this work, he credits Morgan with many powerful attributes, including healing, herbal medicine and shapeshifting. She was said to dwell in a place known as "The Fortunate Isle" (probably *Inis Avallon*) where she lived with eight of her sisters who she exceeded in beauty and in the healing arts.[43]

The healing power of Otherworld women was also mentioned in the *Brut* of Layamon (c. 1200 C.E.), a parish priest from the upper reaches of the Severn River in Worcestershire. This was a poetic adaptation of the earlier work of Wace, as well as the first full account of the Arthurian story in English. Layamon describes the journey of the wounded Arthur into the realms of mist. Here, however, the woman who ferries the king to the sacred realms is called *Argante*. This word means "The Silver One" and appears to be a title rather than a proper name.

Argante is described as "a queen," "the fairest of maidens," and "the comeliest of fays." Arthur declares that Argante will heal him by preparing health-promoting potions for him and make him whole. After this healing, he will be able to come once again into his kingdom and reside with his people "in joyous bliss." Layamon concludes his story by saying that the Britons still believe Arthur is alive, lingering in Avalon with "the loveliest of fays" [Morgan Le Fay] and that they await the time when he will return.[44]

Also around the year 1200, a cleric named Robert de Boron wrote a work known as the Prose *Merlin*, a narrative describing Merlin's life and deeds. Although in Geoffrey's earlier work, Uther and Igerna were said to have only two sons, Gawain and Mordred, in Robert's work they have five, with the addition of Agravain, Gareth and Gaheris. In addition, while in Geoffrey's story they have only one daughter, Anna, they now have three. One of the daughters married King Lot, who now resides in Orkney, rather than Lothian.

Another daughter, who was said to have been a bastard, was married to King Neutre of Sorhaut. The first daughter, Morgan, was sent for schooling at a convent, one of the best places to get an education at the time. She was very gifted and able to learn the "seven arts," including a remarkable knowledge of astronomy which she frequently utilized. Morgan also studied nature and medicine, and through this study she came to be known as Morgan the Fay.[45]

Here again we see the theme of the three divine or supernatural sisters. In Welsh and Irish sources, the "Three Great Queens" were sisters. As in Welsh tradition, the first or primary sister (Morgan le Fay — the Mórrígan) is described as having many skills and powers. The second or next most well known sister (Macha or Morgawse in the earliest tales) gives birth to two children. The third sister (Nemhain — the unnamed Welsh sister) is only briefly mentioned.

Anna Morgawse followed her sacred destiny and produced offspring who would continue the line of Uther Pendragon. Macha gave birth to divine twins, who in Indo-European mythology are often said to be the divine ancestors of the human race. The three sisters together embody the attributes of the Goddess of Sovereignty, a powerful manifestation of the Divine Feminine on earth.

The Lady of the Sword

Another influential female character in the Arthurian tradition is an enigmatic figure known as the Lady of the Lake. She is most well known from her appearance in the *Prose Lancelot*. This was one of a series of works known as the *Vulgate Cycle*, believed to have been written by a monk (or monks) living in Champagne or Burgundy in the early thirteenth century. The original identity of the Lady of the Lake, however, is far more ancient than this medieval manuscript attests.[46]

In the story, the infant Lancelot is stolen by a "fay" and taken to her underwater realm beneath a lake. She raises him to be a paragon of manhood, yet is distressed when he expresses his desire to become a knight. Nevertheless, she provides him with a horse and arms, and takes him to Britain where she introduces him to Arthur. Lancelot is knighted and pledges himself to Arthur's service. However, he soon falls in love with Guinevere, who accepts him as her knight. With the help of the Lady of the Lake, and magical shields she provides, Lancelot accomplishes a number of remarkable deeds.[47]

The theme of the Otherworld woman who arises from a body of water to interact with mortal beings is well known in European myth and folklore.

In an early medieval Irish tale known as *The Voyage of Bran*, a woman from the Otherworld appears to Bran. She describes the world from which she comes, an underwater realm of exquisite beauty.[48] This concept was also known in Welsh tradition, and expressed in a famous folktale known as the Lady of *Llyn y Fan Fach*.

A mortal youth falls in love with a divine woman who appears from beneath the surface of a lake. After passing a series of tests, the young man is accepted and the two are married. The years pass and the couple live happily together, producing three fine sons. However, on three occasions the husband inadvertently offends the Welsh Lady of the Lake and she returns to her underwater realm.[49]

Before leaving, she bestowed upon her three sons the knowledge of healing and herbal medicine. The eldest son *Rhiwallon*, and his three sons, became physicians to *Rhys Gryg*, Lord of *Dinefwr*, who lived in the thirteenth century. The grandsons went on to found a long line of famous physicians known as the "Physicians of *Myddfai*." Their remedies were recorded in medieval manuscripts that still exist to this day. As late as the nineteenth century, people still gathered at the edge of a mountain lake called *Llyn y Fan Fach*, near Llandeusant, on the first Sunday in August. There they waited to observe the "boiling" waters, a sign that the "Lady of the Lake" was about to appear. Photographs of the Lady's modern descendants can still be seen in the local area.[50]

In Celtic tradition, bodies of water (particularly rivers and lakes) were associated with female divinities. The names of goddesses associated with these sites have been recorded since the Iron Age period. People all over Europe made offerings into bodies of water, including swords, shields, vessels and jewelry. As the Bronze Age progressed, swords were increasingly given as offerings to the water spirits, and the votive offering of swords into rivers and lakes was especially common in Britain during this time.

If rivers and lakes were the abode of female spirits or goddesses, then it stands to reason that the swords and other objects that were offered were gifts to the goddesses that lived in the waters. In return, these powerful deities bestowed blessings upon the people, including abundance, healing, skill, wisdom and protection. This ancient belief in the reciprocity between the worlds found expression in many myths and legends.

Lancelot was trained and guided by the Lady of the Lake, who also provided him with magical shields of protection. The Lady of *Lynn Y Fan Fach* gave her descendants the power and knowledge of healing herbs. My Scottish Clan, Clan MacLeod, was given a magical banner by a fairy woman who married an early MacLeod king. It had the power to provide magical assistance on three occasions, and has been used several times with success. The "Fairy Flag" is still on display in Dunvegan Castle on the Isle of Skye.[51]

Arthur's own sword, Excalibur, was also a gift from the Otherworld realms. Geoffrey is the first person to have mentioned the sword (in written form). He refers to it as *Caliburn* and says that it was forged on the Isle of Avalon itself.[52] This belief was also mentioned in Wace's *Roman de Brut*, written in 1155. Here the sword is called *Excalibur,* a name believed to derive from a phrase meaning "Great Sword" (*Cleddyf Mawr* in Welsh, or *Claideb Mór* in Old Irish).[53]

This powerful symbol is a physical manifestation of the reciprocal relationship between the rightful leader and the Otherworld goddess. Since the late Bronze Age, swords were offered to goddesses who lived in rivers and lakes, the original "Ladies of the Lake." In return they bestowed blessings, power, skill and even magical talismans upon those who showed them honour and respect. The goddesses of Avalon present the divine sword of kingship to Arthur, supporting him as steward of the land.

In the later Arthurian tales, Excalibur is returned to the Land beneath the Waves. With this act, the sword comes back to the Lady of the Lake, the divine being to whom it had been offered centuries before. Now it is returned to her for safekeeping, until such time as she sees fit to offer it to another who will return the land to its former glory. With the promise of this golden age comes the understanding that peace and bounty are created when we honour the earth and the powers that dwell within it. This harmonious balance can only be preserved when we develop a right and respectful relationship with the land.

The Goddess of the Grail

Another powerful symbol connected with the divine women of Arthurian legend is the Grail, a sacred cup or vessel. Many of the later Grail stories recount the adventures of Arthur's knights as they journey to places where the vessel was kept (much like the earlier journey of Arthur and his men to the Welsh Otherworld to obtain a magical cauldron). In some legends medieval authors attempted to connect the Grail with Christ. Although it has been popularly interpreted as a vessel that received the blood of Christ at the time of the Crucifixion, its origins stretch back much farther in time.

The concept of a sacred cup or vessel with divine or supernatural properties is well documented in the European mythic tradition. Irish and Welsh legends abound with accounts of magical cups and cauldrons that provide nourishment and abundance, healing and transformation, or wisdom and inspiration. In some Arthurian Romances, the Grail was similarly said to provide abundant food or drink. The common description of the Grail (or *graal*) as a "wide and slightly deep dish" was very similar to a type of serving dish commonly used in medieval Wales. Although the Grail later became equated with a platter containing the consecrated wafer of Christian tradition, this association was the result of confusion in translation.[54]

In a medieval French text called the *Conte de Graal*, the Grail is referred to by the Old French word *cors*. This word had two meanings, "horn," and "body" (both of which are used in the text). In one episode the word *cors* is used to refer to a magic horn called *Beneiz* or *Beneoiz* (a word meaning "blessed"). As stories were copied and recopied, confusion ensued between the use of *cors* meaning "horn" (and referred to as a "blessed" object) and the use of *cors* meaning "body" (as in the connection with the communion wafer). This resulted in the interpretation of the object as the body of Christ.[55]

In actuality, the sacred object in question was a "blessed horn" of plenty, a talisman that was well known in Welsh tradition. A British god or supernatural figure named Bran ("Raven"), sometimes referred to as "Bran the Blessed" (*Bendigeidfran*), was said to dispense great hospitality at legendary feasts. He also possessed a magical horn of plenty. This was one of the traditional functions of the Celtic symbol of the cauldron.[56]

This traditional myth was still half-remembered in the later medieval period. In the story of Perceval, a figure called the Fisher King owned a great hall in which he sumptuously entertained his guests. In several texts, the Fisher King is referred to by the name *Bron*. In the twelfth-century work of Chrétien de Troyes, the Fisher King was wounded in the leg or thigh with a spear. Likewise, in early Welsh sources the god Bran was wounded in the thigh (or in some cases, in the foot) with a spear. These stories led to the association of the *graal* with the spear that pierced Christ's side.[57] The god Bran was also associated with a ruined castle called *Dinas Brân* above the River Dee (a river name meaning "Goddess"). It is located in an area well known for its plentiful fishing. The Fisher King, then, is a later incarnation of the Welsh god Bran, and the Grail was originally his sacred vessel of plenty.[58]

Other supernatural women were also associated with the Grail legend, as in the medieval story of Perceval. When the young man enters the hall of the Fisher King, he is welcomed warmly by his host. A squire enters with a remarkable sword he says has been sent to the Fisher King by his niece. The king's niece had sent word that only three of the swords existed. She wished her uncle to bestow it upon someone who would use it well. The sword was given to Perceval, who was very pleased.[59]

Later, a mysterious procession passes through the hall. A beautiful maiden walks into the room holding a grail (or *graal*) between her hands. It was made of gold and set with precious stones. As she entered the hall with the grail in her hands, the room was filled with a brilliant light. Many courses of food appear before the guests as the grail passes by the table. In the morning, Perceval awakens to find that his host and the other guests have all disappeared, a common occurrence in Otherworld encounters.[60]

In this story, a woman, who is the relative of a deity, sends the gift of a sword to be presented to a worthy candidate. Later, another woman enters the hall bearing a vessel with magical properties. This episode reflects a widespread mythic motif in which the Goddess of Sovereignty offers a cup of ale to the rightful hero or leader.

One of the most famous descriptions of this ritual is in the early Irish tale *Baile an Scáil*. In the tale, a legendary king called *Conn Cétchathach* is brought to an Otherworld location where he encounters two beings, one female and one male. The male figure is the god Lug, who says he has come to prophesy the length of Conn's kingship and the destiny of his descendants. The woman is seated upon a crystal throne, and ritually hands a golden cup of red ale to Conn, after which she reveals that she is Sovereignty.[61]

The ritual presentation of a cup by an esteemed female figure also had its parallel in the earthly realms. In a number of ancient stories mortal women offer a cup to the man they favor as a partner. One of the very earliest examples of this tradition actually dates to the Iron Age period. A noble marriage was being arranged in the household of a king in Massilia (a Greek trading port in the south of Gaul). The king's daughter stood before a group of suitors, and offered a bowl of drink to the one man she preferred as husband. He was from a different culture, suggestive of the Earthly / Otherworld union of the Sovereignty Goddess and the King, and her choice surprised her family. However, her father concluded that she had "acted in accordance with divine will," indicating that this ritual was associated with sacred providence. The woman's name was *Petta*, which is related to a word meaning "land / portion of land."[62]

A similar ritual was also performed among the Germanic peoples in early times, and may have been traditional in other parts of Europe as well. The presentation of a cup was a symbolic part of ceremonies associated with the selection of leaders. Women played a significant role in these rituals, and the noble bearing of the female cupbearer was a feature of the rite. Some of the women had the power of prophecy or foresight, and their divinely inspired support of the candidate was considered extremely important.[63]

In early Ireland, the selection of a king was associated with a ceremony known as "The Sacred Marriage." The king assumed power during a rite known as the *banais rígi* ("wedding feast of kingship"), which comes from the word *ban* ("woman or wife") and *feis*, a word associated with feasting and dispensing drink, as well as with sexual union.[64]

How far back do these myths and symbols originate? The vessel has been a sacral object in Europe for more than six thousand years, when the cultural and religious traditions of the Indo-Europeans spread throughout the region. This process, which began around 4,000 B.C.E., was marked by the widespread use of pottery vessels in noble burials. These vessels are believed to have been associated with ceremonies, as archaeologists have discovered the remains of herbs and beverages once contained inside them.[65]

These vessels were often found in connection with other significant objects, including jewelry, tools and blades. The ritualized combination of the vessel and the blade seems to have first manifested in a very early period, when flint daggers were placed in burials along pottery vessels. Over time, this sacred assemblage of talismans took on new forms, finally manifesting in the swords and cauldrons of later eras.[66]

Magical swords and vessels appear throughout the mythological traditions of Europe. These objects are frequently represented in stories from the medieval and early modern periods as well. In legends and historical accounts, the worthy candidate is chosen or invested through the bestowal of a sword, and empowered by the presentation of a sacred vessel. The rightful ruler is charged with preserving the land and the traditions of the people, and is assisted by an Otherworld woman who consecrates her chosen candidate with a sacred cup and blesses the upcoming reign with the gift of a sword.

These sacred gifts of the Sovereignty Goddess may extend back to the cultural legacy of the Indo-European peoples, as represented in the Bronze and Iron Age offerings of Europe and the legends of goddesses of Sovereignty and the Land. The origins of this spiritual and symbolic heritage extend farther in time than we realized. Through our deeper understanding of the tales of Excalibur and the Grail, these ancient gifts of the Goddess have come home.

The Mysteries of Avalon

In this exploration, we have come to understand that the sacred vessel was an instrument presented by the goddesses to consecrate the rightful ruler of the land, a figure she herself had chosen as consort, and one who would support the spiritual and cultural traditions of the people. One of the most enduring legends associated with the sacred vessel is the pursuit of the object itself. Journeys of a physical or spiritual nature were undertaken to distant or divine locations to obtain these vessels and the powers they possessed. In *Prei-*

deu Annwn, Arthur travels to the Otherworld to obtain a magical cauldron kindled by the breath of nine maidens. This group of women brings to mind the Iron Age account of nine priestesses who lived on an offshore island, as well as the medieval legend of nine sacred women of Avalon (Morgan le Fay and her eight sisters).

The quest to obtain the wonders of the cauldron is symbolic of the quest for spiritual illumination, as well as reconnection with the wisdom of the past. The Grail symbolizes the spiritual potential of human existence, and the quest for the vessel is a personal quest that can take each person to the center of his or her being. On the journey, we encounter many challenges and obstacles — physical, emotional, mental and spiritual — that can deter or delay us from achieving the highest level of spiritual fulfillment.

Joseph Campbell refers to this as the hero (or heroine's) journey. It almost always begins with what he refers to as the "the call." A spiritual guide or teacher appears (often in an unexpected form) and encourages us to arise from the half-awakened state in which we have been living. We must answer this call or forever exist in what Campbell calls the "wasteland," a self-created world of complacency and emptiness.

Answering the call means leaving the known world behind and entering the realm of the unknown. This can be challenging for the ego-based parts of our psyche, which self-identify with and cling to old habits, beliefs, jobs, relationships, possessions, and so forth. The spiritual quest is often undertaken because we realize that something is missing. By setting out on the hero's journey, we seek to find those things that have been lost and retrieve their power. In doing so, we reclaim our own power and wholeness.[67]

It is important to realize that we do not undertake this journey alone. All along the way, heroes and heroines encounter spiritual teachers and guides. One aspect of the quest is to recognize sacred messengers and omens, which are manifestations of the divine. They may appear in dreams or visions, during prayer or meditation, as a series of coincidences or synchronicities, or as an intuitive or felt presence inside us. The wisdom traditions of many cultures maintain that spiritual teachers come in many shapes: human, animal, plant, stone, wind, water and so forth. They can also appear in human-like forms that manifest in our world the spiritual power of gods and goddesses, as well as the sages and ancestral spirits of our inherited spiritual traditions.[68]

In many of these ancient stories, many powerful guides and spiritual catalysts appear in the guise of the ever-present Divine Feminine beings. These sacred figures have access to the powers of life and death, and can bestow blessings upon us or present us with tests that encourage us to rise to our highest potential. Seeking the grail is a metaphor for the personal quest to develop a true and rightful relationship with the powers of the Divine. As Joseph Campbell has written: "What the Holy Grail symbolizes is the highest spiritual fulfillment of a human life. Each life has some kind of high fulfillment, and each has its own gift from the Grail."[69]

In every moment, the goddess stands before us and offers us a sword of spiritual power. How many of us will be ready to wield it? When the Goddess of Sovereignty appears before us in the dreamtime, what will we do? She calls to us and offers us a luminous cup filled with a powerful elixir. "Drink," she says, "and forget what you thought you knew. Drink, and remember that which you have always known." It is up to us whether we answer the call.

12

She Who Dwells Within Us

How shall you know your nation? You shall know your nation through the women. They will be carrying the line. Because the earth is female the women will be working with the earth. The earth will belong to them...
— Haudenosaunee Leader Connasetaga[1]

The Ancient Ones are speaking through our voices.... Every one of us has been called.... We have been brought from the four corners of the world for this work.
— Agnes Baker Pilgrim, Takelma Siletz Elder, Oregon[2]

Aboriginal people are real. They are translators. They remember. We forget or ignore what they know at our peril.
— Robin Ridington, Canadian Anthropologist[3]

All across the country, people rush home to watch a popular innovative news program called "N.E.T."— New Earth Television. The show carries news stories about positive change and documentaries exploring progress in green living and conservation, creating new communities, and preserving the wisdom of traditional cultures:

"Welcome to New Earth Television, where we report on new trends in ecology, balance, and revitalizing our world. Tonight's program will feature four of the most highly rated stories we've brought you over the last year...."

"Our first story is about a remarkable archaeological find dating back more than 2,600 years. In the Baden-Wuerttenberg region of Germany, archaeologists discovered the grave of a Celtic princess. A subterranean chamber was fitted with massive oak beams and preserved by the water of a local stream. Inside were the remains of a Celtic noblewoman and her child, accompanied by objects made of gold, amber, jet and bronze.

"The entire burial chamber was removed from the ground intact and transported to a laboratory near Stuttgart where it will be examined in painstaking detail. 'In dry ground, the wood wouldn't have had a chance to survive over so many centuries,' said Nicole Ebenger-Rest, head of the Stuttgart research team.

"The grave was near Heuneberg, an early settlement and center of Celtic culture in southwest Germany that housed as many as 10,000 people. Although we usually think of Celtic countries on the western edge of Europe — Ireland, Scotland, Wales and Brittany — the original Celtic heartland was in the region of the upper reaches of the Danube, from where the Celts traveled throughout Europe to trade.

"'It is the oldest princely female grave yet from the Celtic world,' said Dr. Kirk Krausse, who is in charge of the dig. 'The oak trees used to create the burial chamber were felled 2,620 years ago, meaning that our lady died in 609 B.C.E.'

"Roman writers often described the Celts as barbaric, excelling only in violence and war. 'That's a distorted view,' Krausse points out. 'There's a bit of propaganda involved, since the Celts conquered Rome in the year 387 B.C.E., so they couldn't have been so primitive.... Celtic art and culture have their origins in south-western Germany, eastern France and Switzerland, and spread from there to other parts of Europe.'

"From this remarkable find, researchers are hoping to gain a new understanding of Celtic culture, a result that could change our view of the Celts and our history.

"Our second story [continues New Earth Television] takes us to Athens, where Greek pagans made a comeback by adding their voices to protests against the removal of statues and other antiquities from ancient temple sites. With arms held skyward, a group called Ellinais, who are reviving their native religion, chanted Orphic hymns invoking Athena, the goddess of wisdom, asking her to protect the sculptures taken from the temples.

"The proposed project would house the objects in a modern glass and concrete structure to be called The New Acropolis Museum. Supporters claim the new building will offer better protection for the antiquities and an improved viewing space for spectators. Opponents argue that the new museum insults Greece's native heritage, that it is too large in scale and in the wrong location.

"Ellinais spokeswoman Doretta Peppa and other members of the group are campaigning to revive ancient religion, and have defied Culture Ministry bans to hold prayers at several temples, including this protest near the Parthenon. Roman Emperor Theodosius wiped out the last vestiges of veneration of the Olympian gods when he abolished the Olympian games in 394

C.E. The Parthenon was converted into a Christian church in the fifth century C.E.

"Efforts to revive native Greek religion have been described by the Orthodox church as a 'miserable resuscitation of a degenerate dead religion.' Peppa told members of the press, 'We will just sing three hymns ... I don't know how many of us will be there. People are afraid. The fact is that we are subject to religious persecution.'

"The ceremony represents a major coup for Greek polytheists whose faith has long been banned by the country that gave birth to the gods of Mount Olympus. It is the first time in nearly 2,000 years that pagans have held a religious ceremony on the site.

"Next we travel to the Hill of Tara, an ancient site seen by many as the spiritual and historic heart of Ireland. An economic boom in Ireland in the last decade resulted in many projects designed to improve local infrastructure. As a result, the government approved construction of a new four-lane tollway, the M3, which would cut through the Tara complex.

"Proponents of the M3 say the road will improve life for tens of thousands of commuters living northwest of Dublin who spend hours each day on traffic-clogged two-lane roads into the capitol. Others say the highway will disturb farms and private homes, and although almost a mile from the actual Hill of Tara, would cut through the large archaeological complex which contains a number of ancient sites.

"George Eogan, the archaeologist who excavated the site in the 1960s, points out that although the road doesn't go directly through the hill, it does damage the sacred complex. 'The Hill of Tara is only the core of a much larger archaeological and cultural landscape.' Tara was the site of the inauguration of Irish kings. Ceremonies of sacral kingship involved the king's symbolic union with the Goddess of Sovereignty, whose blessings ensured the success of his reign and the prosperity of the land and the people.

"Since the project began, 38 new archaeological sites have been unearthed by construction teams along the section of the motorway closest to Tara. Heavy equipment shaved off the top of a cremation urn, leaving the ashes exposed, and desecrated the body of a child unearthed in one of the trenches. The Green Party, Irish Labour, and Sinn Fein, as well as many Irish citizens and worldwide supporters, were among those protesting the project. As a result of the protests and media attention, construction teams and archaeology and heritage groups are attempting to work together to preserve the finds, and the site is under consideration to become a UNESCO World Heritage Site.

"Finally [N.E.T. continues], we travel to Norway, where shamanism has been officially recognized as a religion in that country. Shamanism has long been practiced by the Saami people, whose traditional culture focuses on reindeer herding and veneration of the natural world. Many Saami were Christianized in the 16th and 17th centuries, but others still follow their traditional faith and practice their ancient religion.

"In Norway, a shaman is known as a *Noaide*, and shamanic traditions are passed down within families. Elder shamans train a relative to take their place after their death. Training continues as long as the Noaide lives, but the student must prove his or her skills before a group of Noaide before becoming a fully-fledged shaman.

"This is the first time that shamanism has been officially recognized as a religion in Norway. Members of the press spoke with Lone Ebeltoft, director of the newly founded Shamanic Federation. Ebeltoft said she welcomed the decision and expressed her wish to preserve and continue shamanic traditions and practices in Norway.

"'It is about understanding and respecting nature,' said Ebeltoft. 'Shamanism is a world religion. Where we are up here in the North, we are committed to preserving Saami and Norse (Arctic) traditions.'

"The Saami pantheon consists of four primary gods: The Mother, The Father, The Son and the Daughter, as well as a god of fertility, fire and thunder; a goddess of death; and the Sun Goddess. Like many pagan religions, the Saami view life as a circular process of life, death and rebirth.

"That's it for tonight, thanks for tuning in. Your positive focus and support helps bring change into the world. As always, that change depends on our dedication and participation. Join us next week for another edition of New Earth Television, where we bring you news stories about how to protect, balance and inspire our world."[4]

All of the news stories you have just read are true. Most traditional cultures, whether they existed in the past or live in the world today, acknowledge the sacredness of all life and the interconnection between this world and the world of the divine. They also acknowledge the existence and importance of the Divine Feminine, which is an integral part of the Sacred. The Divine Feminine may be perceived as Mother Earth, spirits of nature, guiding ancestors or powerful goddesses. This must have been true for our ancestors as well, and it is vital that we begin to remember this ancient wisdom.

In this quest for knowledge, we have undertaken an epic journey through time and space, learning about our origins and the role the Divine Feminine played in making us who we are. The first human inhabitants of Europe survived the ice ages of the Paleolithic Era and did so with enthusiasm and

208   Part III: Mythology — The Spiritual Origins of Europe

confidence. Around 40,000 years ago, they began to perform elaborate burial rites to honour the dead, and created the first artwork and ritual as well. For several thousand years, people created female images in different shapes and forms that were used for many purposes. Instead of symbolizing one intention or one deity, these powerful images represented the complex ways human beings interacted with the realms of the divine, in ritual and in their daily lives.

The earth and the climate began to change, and people's lives changed dramatically. The innovative artwork and female imagery of the Paleolithic era disappeared, never to return again in the same form. More than twenty thousand years would pass before female figurines were once again created, in a very different world. They symbolized a wide array of spiritual purposes, and these new objects and the sanctuaries created to house them attest to the sophistication of Neolithic people and their diverse religious traditions.

It was during this period that the concept of land ownership, rather than land stewardship, likely first came into being. This was probably not a pleasing concept to the spirits of the land, who are independent and sovereign beings much like ourselves. In spite of their veneration of female imagery, early farmers unwittingly depleted, overworked, and exhausted the land. In doing so, they created bogs and wastelands, as well as increased social tension and competition for territory. Violence came to play a role in the societies of the Neolithic, an era that has been popularly characterized as a time of peaceful matriarchal societies.

For more than ninety-five percent of the time that we have inhabited the planet human beings have lived in hunter-gatherer societies and existed in a harmonious relationship with the earth. As we turned away from our hunter-gatherer origins, situations were created in which people had to compete for land and resources, changing our cultural patterns and the landscape forever. In spite of these self-created challenges, the people of ancient Europe continued to adapt and thrive. The remarkable stone carvings and monuments of northwest Europe, and the shrines of the southeast, attest to the highly developed religious traditions during this era.

As time went on, some of the most important cultural and religious tradition bearers of Europe moved onto center stage. These were not Greeks or Romans, nor the cultures of Biblical tradition. Starting around 4,000 B.C.E., small bands of semi-nomadic people came riding across the plains, and their innovative social and religious traditions spread throughout Europe. Far from being patriarchal destroyers of peaceful societies, their culture and religion were widely (and in many cases enthusiastically) adopted across the region, serving as the basis for much of what was to follow.

The descendants of these people developed into a number of well-known cultures, including those of Greece and Rome, as well as Germanic, Baltic and Slavic societies, each with their own rich cultural and spiritual traditions. Some of the most influential descendants were the Celts, who inhabited a vast territory stretching from Turkey through eastern and central Europe, Austria, Switzerland, Spain, Portugal, France, Britain and Ireland. Their unique social and religious traditions constitute some of the most important elements of our cultural and spiritual inheritance.[5]

The Divine Feminine has taken on many shapes and forms during the prehistoric and early historic eras. In the earliest periods, we do not have direct knowledge of names or titles, or precise information about powers and attributes. In order to understand the role of the Divine Feminine in early prehistory, we can look to modern hunter-gatherer societies to see how they perceive and interact with these sacred entities. We can also examine written records that have chronicled how female divinities were venerated around the world. In this way, we can work towards a deeper understanding of the complex ways the Divine Feminine has manifested in our culture of origin. One thing is clear from looking at ancient and modern traditional cultures: the Divine Feminine is a powerful and integral part of the Sacred, and without her, any tradition is incomplete.

The Wisdom of the Elders

In our exploration of the ancient past, we have come to understand that the Divine Feminine encompasses many powerful archetypes. The goddesses of Europe (as well as other regions) possess a tremendous number of powers and attributes, many of which reflect specific cultural and spiritual environments. In other words, the faces of the goddesses you perceive and venerate may reflect the time and place in which you live. The origins of these spiritual entities are not to be found in one single archetypal being, but in the diversity of the religious and cultural traditions of the world.

Rather than theorizing or envisioning a single goddess religion that existed in an unbroken lineage since the dawn of time, we can see that there were actually many goddess-based or goddess-encompassing religions. This is an exciting realization, for it shows that the worship of the Divine Feminine was actually much more widespread and influential than many popular or historical sources have suggested.[6]

It also shows that the rituals and beliefs associated with these traditions were far more potent and complex than we realized. In many cases, the power of these goddesses did not derive primarily (or solely) from the potency of the female reproductive system or reproductive energies. To reduce the power of the goddesses to their biological functions alone, is to diminish their stature, and to diminish the potential of mortal women as well.

In recent decades, thousands of people have been returning to these ancient principles and the veneration of the Divine Feminine. Numerous beliefs and ideas, old and new, have been combined in these resurging modern religions. The many attributes of the Feminine Divine are often referred to as facets or "guises" of a figure popularly referred to as "The Goddess." The archetypal energies or aspects of this new goddess figure are often categorized as a sacred triad consisting of "Maiden, Mother and Crone."

This innovative concept was created by the poet and novelist Robert Graves in 1948, during an attempt to creatively explore mythological elements of Celtic tradition (a culture he was not particularly familiar with). While his theory does not reflect the actual traditions of the past, his work inspired waves of enthusiasm for the Divine Feminine, particularly fueled during the Feminist movement of the 1970s. These new ideas, and the theological "wheels within wheels" they created, have continued to change and develop.[7]

As a result, the modern worship of this new Goddess archetype continues to grow at an exponential rate. Her veneration has been woven into many innovative spiritual traditions, including modern Goddess worship, Wicca, Neo-Paganism, and other new religious movements whose origins date back to the late 19th and early 20th centuries. Early occultists blended European folklore with reports of witchcraft trials and Victorian perceptions about the ancient religions of Greece, Rome, Egypt and the Near East. They focused on the veneration of a Goddess figure in an attempt to redress the imbalance of patriarchal religions and disconnection from nature and the wisdom of the past.[8]

One of the many impulses leading to the creation and expansion of modern Goddess theology, as well as the dramatic increase in other modern earth-honoring spiritualities, is the deeply felt but unspoken loss of tribal culture and native religion that we experience in Western society. The repercussions of this loss of connection with the earth, with community, and with the sacred is evident all around us.

Our collective soul loss is noted by indigenous peoples who still maintain native traditions. John Trudell, a famous A.I.M. (American Indian Movement) activist and artist speaks about the importance of remembering our ancestral wisdom:

> Every one of us has a tribal ancestry and we have a genetic memory. Encoded in that genetic memory is the experience of our individual and collective evolution.

You can follow it through the ancestry. The information is there, because we're human beings — the knowledge of all those experiences are with us.[9]

One of the terms used to describe the reconnection with ancestral knowledge and traditions is "re-nativization." Tirso Gonzales, a Peruvian scholar, consultant and activist of Aymara descent describes this important process:

Re-nativization means to regain the strength of who you are and how you want to be connected to this world and to your specific community. Re-nativization may mean for non–Indian people who I have met in the North, a beginning to reconnect themselves to Mother Earth and revisiting the past, their histories, their family stories, and how they want to procure balance and harmony among all living things in the world. This is a process in the making....[10]

Indigenous people all around the world have managed to preserve and maintain the traditional wisdom of their people, many times in spite of great struggles and through great dedication. Ancient wisdom is not considered just a part of the past, but an essential part of life in modern times as well.

In 2004, a group of thirteen indigenous women elders met in New York State to share their knowledge with each other and with non–Natives as well. They came from the Black Hills of South Dakota, the Amazon rainforest, the mountains of Tibet and the highlands of Central America; from the deserts of the American southwest, the rainforest of central Africa, the Arctic Circle, the Pacific Northwest and the Iroquois Confederacy.

Known as the International Council of Thirteen Indigenous Grandmothers, they formed an alliance focused on education, prayer and the healing of the earth, as well as the sacrality and power of women. These women elders believe that their ancestral ways of life — prayer, peacemaking and healing — are vitally important, and that the teachings of the ancestors will light a path to the future.[11] Yupik elder Rita Pitka Blumenstein comments on these important concepts:

I grew up with grandmothers, walked with grandmothers, and learned with grandmothers.... My urge to share their teachings is strong.... We forget who we are, and that is the cause of our illness.... It is essential to allow yourself to know what you know, instead of driving yourself to be. When there is so much striving to be and become, we don't often recognize what it is we really want when it's right there in front of us.[12]

Other indigenous councils have put forth a similar message. The Haudenosaunee Declaration of the Iroquois Confederacy includes these important words:

Brothers and Sisters — We point out to you the Spiritual Path of Righteousness and Reason. We bring to your thought and minds that right-minded human beings seek to promote above all else the life of all things....

> We point out to you that a Spiritual Consciousness is the Path to the Survival
> of Humankind... [We] are determined to take whatever action we can to halt the
> destruction of Mother Earth. In our territories, we continue to carry out our
> function as spiritual caretakers of the land....
> We will not stand idly by while the future of coming generations is being sys-
> tematically destroyed.... We must join hands with like-minded people and create
> a strength through unity."[13]

Thomas Banyacya, a spokesman for Hopi religious leaders, also sends an
urgent message to re-learn the ways of the past:

> Today people from this country, and from countries from all around the world,
> are coming together for peace bringing further realization of the Hopi prophe-
> cies.... Only through spiritual ways can we put aside the wrong action of the past
> and repair the damage done to our Mother Earth and the peoples of the Earth....
> Through religion we are going to find... the right way of living the truth and the
> peaceful way of harmony with each other and with nature all around, the clouds,
> the rain, the animals and the plant life. We are all a part of Mother Earth.... We
> are just like the trees out there — all different people with different languages,
> different colors and ways of expression. We are just like any other part of nature
> that is around us. This, we must understand.[14]

Part of our spiritual quest, and our responsibility as spiritual beings who
are part of the great web of life, is to recognize and honour the wisdom of
the past in its many historical and living forms. We must also find and embody
the roots of our own traditional knowledge in order to gain access to our true
spiritual potential, a power that can heal us, our society and our world.

Mary Leitka of the Hoh people of Washington State speaks about the
search for ancestral origins and tribal identity:

> Non-Indians are interested in Indian culture and medicine, but Indians are not
> unique in having this power. Every people on earth had this power in the begin-
> ning. We never lost ours; it is still being carried on. Every nationality and race
> must find their own, trace their roots.... People may be able to learn from us, but
> to really grow spiritually, they must find their own past. Ancestry is important. If
> they reached back to their ancestors, they would find out where they came from
> and a part of who they are.[15]

Tom Goldtooth, the national coordinator of the Indigenous Environmental
Network, describes the universality of indigenous wisdom, and its availability
to all:

> ... the traditional knowledge of Indigenous Peoples ... is no different from the
> knowledge of my *Diné* peoples of the Southwest or [my] Mdewakanton Dakota
> Oyate people.... This traditional knowledge is no different from the Aborigines
> of Australia or the Indigenous Peoples from Africa, or the Sami from the Arctic
> regions of Norway, Sweden, and Finland. This traditional knowledge has allowed
> our Indigenous Peoples to develop certain life ways, values, and cultural practices

that have given us knowledge to live in balance and in a sustainable way for thousands of years.[16]

Leon Shenandoah, Former Tadodaho Chief of the Iroquois, also spoke about the loss and restoration of tradition:

> The thing wrong with the world is that people don't have instructions.... A lot of people are searching for what they don't have.... They're searching for the wisdom of a whole way of life.... A lot of people have lost their way....
>
> People want to know who our medicine men and women are. They call them the holy ones. We are all holy and so are you. We still have our ceremonies to honor the Creator. You once had yours, too....
>
> You have to return to your circle. That will be hard because your ancestors covered your circle with confusion. Clear that away and there will be your ceremony.[17]

Remembering the Wisdom We Once Knew

Who are the goddesses of our inherited lineages? What powers and knowledge do they possess? They are guardians and personifications of nature, deified aspects of the land and the environment, protectors of wild creatures and patronesses of the hunt. They are associated with fertility, abundance, creation and childbirth, as well as conflict, challenges, destruction and rebirth. In some cases, they preside over the transitional points of the human life cycle, including the cycles and concerns of women's lives.

These goddesses are tribal matrons and ancestral spirits, spirits of the grain and the harvest, and deities of the earth and the waters. They are goddesses of wisdom, skill, prophesy, shapeshifting and magic, who decide the fate or destiny of living beings and play an important role in the cosmology of their people. They provide protection in times of conflict and have the power to choose and empower kings (and warrior queens). There seems to be no aspect of earthly or sacred existence in which the goddesses do not wield substantial power.

In the past, as the land and environment experienced upheaval and transformation, so did social and cultural realities. The land and our lives exist in an interconnected relationship, something we must never forget. As the land and the climate changed, we changed. And as we changed, the Divine Feminine took on new forms, for she is a powerful shapeshifter. Despite the challenges and innovations of the past, the powers of the Divine Feminine have always formed an important part of our cultural legacy. It is only in the last fifteen hundred years (or even less) that we have experienced a disconnection with that legacy. We are now beginning to realize the consequences of losing such an enormous part of our spiritual inheritance.

We are also beginning to understand that the roots of our culture and its spiritual foundations are not solely the product of Greek and Roman urban-based civilizations, nor are they the result of the imported religious traditions of the Near East. This deception has long been supported by the creators of empires (and hence of history books), and this upper class infrastructure has propagated male-dominated power structures for more than two thousand years. Instead, our authentic roots can be found in the myths and traditions of the indigenous people of ancient Europe (particularly those of the Bronze Age and afterwards), for these native belief systems have long supported and recognized the power of the Divine Feminine.

The goddesses of Europe possessed an enormous variety of attributes. Indeed, some of their power seems to derive from their diversity (a lesson that nature continues to try to instill within us). Many of the native religious traditions of Europe afforded special status to certain talismanic objects, including sacred vessels and blades. In some legends these objects were associated with female divinities or sacred women who performed divination, ceremony and ritual. But it is still difficult to say precisely what the pottery vessels and flint daggers of the Bronze Age signified.

Can we really support the outdated notion that they were just superstitious trappings offered to appease the angry gods, or assist the forlorn spirits of the deceased in their sepia-toned pagan afterlife? Given what we now know about the complexity and sophistication of ancient people, might these objects not have been imbued with a more refined and potent symbolism?

The vessel and blade appear in the archaeological record and in some of the earliest written sources as well, and have been sacral objects for thousands of years. From their earliest pottery and stone incarnations (many of which were extremely beautiful) they were transmuted into bronze daggers and copper vessels, and eventually into bronze and iron swords, and bronze, gold or silver cups or cauldrons. Over time, this imagery culminated in the sacred talismans of the Arthurian legends, Excalibur and the Grail, objects that were owned and empowered by powerful goddess figures who gifted them to the world of humans.

The image of the Goddess of Sovereignty is a powerful one, and she has existed over time in a variety of forms. One of her earliest manifestations in Europe may be as a reflection of the great goddess of the Scythians, who was the only member of their pantheon to be depicted in their vibrant artistic tradition. The goddess is depicted seated upon a throne while a male figure rides up before her to receive her blessing and approval. Elsewhere two men dismount from their horses (a symbol of the Goddess of Sovereignty) and sit in her presence. One of the men rests on the ground with his head in her lap.

Perhaps he is being healed by the goddess, or dreaming of his future destiny, a path chosen and empowered by her.

It is not difficult to see parallels between these images and later representations of the Sovereignty Goddess. In early Ireland, this divine figure was sometimes seated on a throne, where she was approached by heroic figures in search of their destiny, or by potential candidates for the stewardship of the land. They, too, must receive her approval and her blessings. When challenges arise, it is she who provides magic swords or shields as a form of protection. It is she who ferries the wounded back to the Otherworld realms to heal them, so that one day they will return to the world and restore its former glory.

We too, seek, the healing and empowerment of the Goddess. Our yearning for her presence and her blessings extends back to the origins of our being. We are hungry for a connection with the past, with ancient mysteries and the wisdom of lost cultures. This hunger stems from our own disconnection from relevant spiritual traditions, connection with the natural world, and with tribe and community. In searching for our lost roots, we must embark upon the hero or heroine's journey. This quest for knowledge and inspiration will ultimately connect us with Sovereignty, which can be defined as stewardship of the land and mastery of the self. It brings us into direct knowledge of self and source, in the internal sanctuary wherein the Divine Feminine has always dwelt.

In some ways, we have already begun the quest. We have wandered through the realms of archaeology and ritual, and explored ancient manuscripts and forgotten legends where we sought to decode the meaning of symbols, inscriptions, and prayers. Along the way we have encountered goddesses and warrior queens, and been guided by priestesses, seers and holy women who dedicated their lives to preserving the old ways and bringing to life the mysteries of these ancient traditions.

From Paleolithic rituals to Neolithic temples, from the Goddess of Sovereignty to the Maiden of the Grail, we have come to understand the importance of developing right relationship with the realms of the Divine. These sacred elements are part of our ancestral memory and serve as powerful tools for personal and cultural empowerment and transformation. When we finally encounter aspects of the sacred that have for so long formed part of our intuition and inner knowledge, a shift occurs inside us. In this moment of reconnection, we move towards a place of wholeness and the realization of our spiritual potential. The activation of this ancient knowledge has the power to connect us with our true path and our true self.

By remembering what we once knew, we reconnect with the most ancient parts of ourselves and realize the potency of our own divinity. The divine is numinous; it is inherent in all of creation. It is present in the earth and all its creatures, in all who have come before us, and in ourselves. All traditional cultures understand that the Divine is immanent in everything that exists. They also understand the connection between this world and the worlds of the Sacred, upon which we are dependent for our very being.

The Divine Feminine is an integral part of the Sacred, and without Her, any tradition or way of life is incomplete. The veneration of the Divine Feminine in Europe was more widespread and influential than we have previously realized, and took on many forms in different regions and eras. Reconnecting with this ancient wisdom is crucial for regaining balance in our world, in our communities and in our own lives. It is also important for re-empowering half of the world's people, and revitalizing native traditions.

The inherited legacy of these ancestral traditions can guide us towards our birthright — a spiritual connection with self, with others, with the earth, and the realms of the sacred. All of these exist within the great spiraling continuum of past, present and future. In that sacred place, the Divine Feminine stands at the center of the cosmos, wielding the sword of power and offering us the vessel of enlightenment. These are the gifts of the goddesses of the past and the future, and they are a testimony to her power, as well as our own. Take up the sword and drink from the cup, and remember all of who and what you are. This is the message of the Goddess, for to Remember is to Know.

Chapter Notes

Chapter 1

1. Carol Schaefer, *Grandmothers Counsel the World* (Boston: Trumpeter Books/Shambhala, 2006), 25.

2. Historical information for this narrative derived from: Donald Johanson and Blake Edgar, *From Lucy to Language* (New York: Simon and Shuster, 1996), 132–133.

3. *Ibid.*, 133, 162–164.

4. Randall White, *Dark Caves, Bright Visions: Life in Ice Age Europe* (New York: The American Museum of Natural History, in association with W.W. Norton and Co., 1986), 10–12.

5. *Ibid.*

6. Mircea Eliade, *The Sacred and the Profane: The Nature of Religion* (San Diego/New York: Harcourt Brace, 1987), 80–85, 104–107; Sean Kane, *Wisdom of the Mythtellers* (Peterborough Ontario: Broadview Press, 1994), 40–45, 65, 72, 79.

7. David Suzuki and Pater Knudtson, *Wisdom of the Elders — Honoring Sacred Native Visions of Nature* (New York: Bantam, 1992), 9–10, 18.

8. Johanson and Edgar, *From Lucy to Language*, 22–26, 30–31, 43–45.

9. *Ibid.*, 80–89.

10. *Ibid.*, 106–107.

11. Paul Mellars, "The Upper Paleolithic Revolution," in Barry Cunliffe, ed., *The Oxford Illustrated History of Prehistoric Europe* (Oxford: Oxford University Press, 2001), 42–78.

12. *Ibid.*, 30–31.

13. *Ibid.*, 97–99.

14. Chris Scarre, *Exploring Prehistoric Europe* (Oxford: Oxford University Press, 1998), 4–10; Jane McIntosh, *Handbook to Life in Prehistoric Europe* (New York: Facts on File, 2005), 1–38, 127–162.

15. Steven Mithen, *After the Ice: A Global Human History, 20,000– 5,000 BC* (Cambridge: Harvard University Press, 2004), 3–116; McIn-

tosh, *Handbook to Life in Prehistoric Europe*, 101–115.

16. Clive Gamble, "The Peopling of Europe 700,000— 40,000 Years before the Present," in Barry Cunliffe, ed., *The Oxford Illustrated History of Prehistoric Europe* (Oxford: Oxford University Press, 2001), 5–41.

17. Richard B. Lee and Richard Daly, *The Cambridge Encyclopedia of Hunters and Gatherers* (Cambridge University Press, New York, 1999), 399–410.

18. Randall White, *Prehistoric Art—The Symbolic Journey of Humankind* (New York: Harry N. Abrams, 2003), 10–12; McIntosh, *Handbook to Life in Prehistoric Europe*, 24–28; Johanson and Edgar, *From Lucy to Language*, 46–54.

19. White, *Prehistoric Art*, 14–15.

20. Richard Rudgley, *The Lost Civilizations of the Stone Age* (New York: Touchstone, 1999), 176–183.

21. Johanson and Edgar, *From Lucy to Language*, 100–101.

22. Paul G. Bahn and Jean Vertat, *Images of the Ice Age* (New York / Oxford: Facts on File, 1988), 17–54.

Chapter 2

1. Diane Bell, *Daughters of the Dreaming* (Minneapolis, University of Minnesota Press, 1997).

2. Historical information for this narrative derived from: Randall White, *Prehistoric Art—The Symbolic Journey of Humankind* (New York: Harry N. Abrams, 2003), 50–51; Paul Mellars, "The Upper Paleolithic Revolution," in Barry Cunliffe, ed., *The Oxford Illustrated History of Prehistoric Europe* (Oxford: Oxford University Press, 2001), 42–78.

3. *Ibid.*

4. White, *Prehistoric Art*, 74–80.

5. Steven Mithen, *After the Ice: A Global*

Human History 20,000— 5,000 BC (Cambridge: Harvard University Press, 2004), 3–4; Chris Scarre, *Exploring Prehistoric Europe* (Oxford: Oxford University Press, 1998), 4–10.

6. Paul G. Bahn and Jean Vertat, *Images of the Ice Age* (New York: Facts on File, 1988), 34–40, 54–64; White, *Prehistoric Art*, 26–31.

7. Bahn and Vertat, *Images of the Ice Age*, 163–165; Jean Clotter, *World Rock Art* (Los Angeles: Getty Conservation Institute, 2002), 73; White, *Prehistoric Art*, 102–104.

8. Bahn and Vertat, *Images of the Ice Age*, 99; White, *Prehistoric Art*, 83.

9. White, *Prehistoric Art*, 86–87.

10. *Ibid.*, 84; Bahn and Vertat, *Images of the Ice Age*, 163.

11. Bahn and Vertat, *Images of the Ice Age*, 140–141.

12. *Ibid.*, 163–165; Clotter, *World Rock Art*, 73; White, *Prehistoric Art*, 102–104.

13. Bahn and Vertat, *Images of the Ice Age*, 140–141; Clotter, *World Rock Art*, 73; White, *Prehistoric Art*, 102–104; André Leroi-Gourhan, *The Dawn of European Art* (Cambridge UK: Cambridge University Press, 1982), 50–54, 65–66.

14. Donald Johanson and Blake Edgar, *From Lucy to Language* (New York: Simon and Schuster, 1996), 102.

15. *Ibid.*, 103; Bahn and Vertat, *Images of the Ice Age*, 83, 115–134, 150–158; Leroi-Gourhan, *Dawn of European Art*, 28–45.

16. Bahn and Vertat, *Images of the Ice Age*, 86, 185.

17. White, *Prehistoric Art*, 50–56.

18. Bahn and Vertat, *Images of the Ice Age*, 83–86, 135–140; Margaret Beck, "Female Figurines in the European Upper Paleolithic: Politics and Bias in Archaeological Interpretation," in Allison Rautman, ed., *Reading the Body: Representations and Remains in the Archaeological Record* (Philadelphia: University of Pennsylvania, 2000), 203–214.

19. *Ibid.*

20. *Ibid.*

21. Bahn and Vertat, *Images of the Ice Age*, 136–137.

22. *Ibid.*, 138–140; Beck, "Female Figurines in European Upper Paleolithic," 205–214.

23. Bahn and Vertat, *Images of the Ice Age*, 138; Beck, "Female Figurines in European Upper Paleolithic," 208–212.

24. Beck, "Female Figurines in European Upper Paleolithic," 206–214.

25. *Ibid.*

26. Robert L. Kelly, *The Foraging Spectrum: Diversity in Hunter-Gatherer Lifeways* (Washington D.C.: Smithsonian Institution Press, 1995), 65–110, 205–206; Richard B. Lee and Richard Daly, *The Cambridge Encyclopedia of Hunters and Gatherers* (New York: Cambridge University Press, 1999), 419–425, 449–456.

27. *Ibid.*; Beck, "Female Figurines in European Upper Paleolithic," 206–214.

28. Beck, "Female Figurines in European Upper Paleolithic," 202–214; Bahn and Vertat, *Images of the Ice Age*, 135–140; Ruth Tringham and Margaret Conkey, "Rethinking Figurines: A Critical View from the Archaeology of Gimbutas," in Lucy Goodison and Christine Morris, eds., *Ancient Goddesses: The Myths and the Evidence* (Madison: University of Wisconsin Press, 1988), 22–45; David W., Anthony, ed., *The Lost World of Old Europe—The Danube Valley, 5000— 3500 BC* (Princeton NJ: Princeton University Press, 2002), 39–45, 113–127. See also: Alison E. Rautman and Lauren E. Talalay, "Diverse Approaches to the Study of Gender in Archaeology," in Allison Rautman, ed., *Reading the Body: Representations and Remains in the Archaeological Record* (Philadelphia: University of Pennsylvania, 2000).

29. Bahn and Vertat, *Images of the Ice Age*, 17–18, 33–34, 39–40, 53–54; White, *Prehistoric Art*, 50–56.

30. White, *Prehistoric Art*, 50–56.

Chapter 3

1. Carol Schaefer, *Grandmothers Counsel the World* (Boston: Trumpeter Books/Shambhala, 2006), 49.

2. Historical information for this narrative derived from: Steven Mithen, "The Mesolithic Age," in Barry Cunliffe, ed., *The Oxford Illustrated History of Prehistoric Europe* (Oxford: Oxford University Press, 2001), *passim*. This excellent study is utilized throughout this chapter. See pages 134–136 for antlered headdresses and ceremony.

3. Steven Mithen, *After the Ice: A Global Human History 20,000— 5000 BC* (Cambridge MA: Harvard University Press, 2004), 3–12, 110–116; J.G.D. Clark, *The Mesolithic Settlement of Northern Europe* (Cambridge: Cambridge University Press, 1936), 1–29.

4. Mithen, *After the Ice*, 110–132; Clark, *The Mesolithic Settlement*, 29–53.

5. Mithen, *After the Ice*, 113–132; M.C. Burkitt, *Our Early Ancestors: An Introductory Study of Mesolithic, Neolithic and Copper Age Cultures in Europe and Adjacent Regions* (Cambridge: Cambridge University Press, 1936), 8–41.

6. Mithen, *After the Ice*, 150–153.

7. *Ibid.*, 110–116; Jane McIntosh, *Handbook to Life in Prehistoric Europe* (New York: Facts on File, 2006), 112–115.

8. Mithen, *After the Ice*, 113–115; Clark, *The Mesolithic Settlement*, 46–53.

9. Mithen, *After the Ice*, 164, 187–188; Clark, *The Mesolithic Settlement*, 54–106; McIntosh, *Handbook to Life in Prehistoric Europe*, 127–162.

10. Clark, *The Mesolithic Settlement*, 107–123.

11. David Suzuki and Peter Knudtson, *Wisdom of the Elders* (New York: Bantam, 1992), xxxv.

12. Clark, *The Mesolithic Settlement*, 127–128; Burkitt, *Our Early Ancestors*, 95–96.

13. Mithen, *After the Ice*, 168–177; McIntosh, *Handbook to Life in Prehistoric Europe*, 281–282; Burkitt, *Our Early Ancestors*, 20–23, 43–44.

14. *Ibid.*

15. For more on egalitarianism in hunter-gather societies see: Christopher Boehm, *Hierarchy in the Forest: The Evolution of Egalitarian Behavior* (Cambridge: Harvard University Press, 1999), 1–42, 64–89; Robert L. Kelly, *The Foraging Spectrum: Diversity in Hunter-Gatherer Lifeways* (Washington D.C.: Smithsonian Institution Press, 1995), 293–332; David Riches, *Northern Nomadic Hunter-Gatherers* (London: Academic Press, 1982), 31–101.

16. Mithen, *After the Ice*, 181.

17. Mithen, *After the Ice*, 168–177; McIntosh, *Handbook to Life in Prehistoric Europe*, 281–282; Burkitt, *Our Early Ancestors*, 20–23, 43–44, 96.

18. *Ibid.*

19. *Ibid.*

20. Mithen, *After the Ice*, 170; Mithen, "*The Mesolithic Age*," 126.

21. *Ibid.*, Mircea Eliade, *Shamanism: Archaic Techniques of Ecstacy* (Princeton NJ: Princeton University Press, 1964), 3–145; Brian Hayden, *Shamans, Sorcerers and Saints: A Prehistory of Religion* (Washington D.C.: Smithsonian Books, 2003), 1–19, 46–87.

22. *Ibid.*, Sharon Paice MacLeod, *Celtic Myth and Religion: A Study of Traditional Belief* (Jefferson, N.C: McFarland, 2012), 65–67; James L. Pearson, *Shamanism and the Ancient Mind: A Cognitive Approach to Archaeology* (Walnut Creek: Altamira, 2002), 49–51, 65–76, 113–143.

23. Mithen, *After the Ice*, 143–145; Clark, *The Mesolithic Settlement*, 162–189; Burkitt, *Our Early Ancestors*, 33–43.

24. Steve Wall, *To Become a Human Being—The Message of Tadodaho Chief Leon Shenandoah* (Charlottesville VA: Hampton Roads Publishing, 2001), 40–41.

25. Mithen, *After the Ice*, 150–153.

26. *Ibid.*

27. Richard B. Lee and Richard Daly, *The Cambridge Encyclopedia of Hunters and Gatherers*, (Cambridge University Press, New York, 1999), 1.

28. *Ibid.*, 1.

29. *Ibid.*, 154.

Chapter 4

1. Steve Wall, *Wisdom's Daughters* (New York: Harper Perennial, 1993), 293.

2. Historical information for this narrative derived from: Barry Cunliffe, ed., *The Oxford Illustrated Encyclopedia of Prehistoric Europe* (Oxford: Oxford University Press, 2001); Robert L. Kelly, *The Foraging Spectrum: Diversity in Hunter-Gatherer Lifeways* (Washington D.C.: Smithsonian Institution Press, 1995); and Julien Ries, *The Origin of Religions* (Grand Rapids MI: William B. Eerdmans, 1994); Christopher Boehm, *Hierarchy in the Forest: The Evolution of Egalitarian Behavior* (Cambridge: Harvard University Press, 1999); Hugh Brody, *The Other Side of Eden: Hunters, Farmers and the Shaping of the World* (New York: North Point Press, 2000); and Randall White, *Prehistoric Art—The Symbolic Journey of Humankind* (2003, New York: Harry N. Abrams, 2003), pp. 50–56.

3. Bryan Sykes, *The Seven Daughters of Eve* (New York: W.W. Norton, 2001), 22–31; Donald Johanson and Blake Edgar, *From Lucy to Language* (New York: Simon and Schuster, 1996), 22–26, 43–45, 37–40.

4. Sykes, *Seven Daughters of Eve*, 52–62; Johanson and Edgar, *From Lucy to Language*, 38–40.

5. Sykes, *Seven Daughters of Eve*, 52–62; Johanson and Edgar, *From Lucy to Language*, 30–31.

6. Bryan Sykes, "Using genes to map population structure and origins," in Bryan Sykes, ed., *Human Inheritance* (Oxford: Oxford University Press, 1999), 93–117.

7. *Ibid.*, 99–105.

8. *Ibid.*, 93–117; Johanson and Edgar, *From Lucy to Language*, 46–50.

9. Sykes, *Seven Daughters of Eve*, 1–22, 32–51.

10. *Ibid.*, 108–115; Sykes, "*Using genes to map population structure*," 99–105.

11. *Ibid.*

12. *Ibid.*

13. Sykes, *Seven Daughters of Eve*, 202–212.

14. *Ibid.*, 213–220.

15. *Ibid.*, 221–233.

16. *Ibid.*, 243–251.

17. *Ibid.*, 234–242.

18. *Ibid.*, 252–259.

19. *Ibid.*, 260–270.

20. *Ibid.*, 271–286; Sykes, "Using genes to map population structure," 99–105.

21. Sykes, *Seven Daughters of Eve*, 185–194.

22. *Ibid.*, 131–145.

23. *Ibid.*, 271–286.

24. *Ibid.*; Johanson and Edgar, *From Lucy to Language*, 37–50.

25. Sykes, "Using genes to map population structure," 93–117; Sykes, *Seven Daughters of Eve*, 271–286.

26. David Suzuki and Peter Knudtson, *Wisdom of the Elders—Honoring Sacred Native Visions of Nature* (New York: Bantam, 1992).

27. Carl Jung, *The Archetypes and the Collective*

Unconscious (Princeton NJ: Princeton University Press, 1981).

28. Wall, *Wisdom's Daughters*, 2.

29. Carol Schaefer, *Grandmothers Counsel the World* (Boston: Trumpeter Books/Shambala, 2006), 136–137.

30. Wall, *Wisdom's Daughters*, 150–151.

31. Carl Jung, *The Structure and Dynamics of the Psyche* (New York: Pantheon Books, 1960), 432.

32. For more on this phenomenon see: Lucy Goodison and Christine Morris, "Exploring Female Divinity: From Modern Myth to Ancient Evidence" in Lucy Goodison and Christine Morris, eds., *Ancient Goddesses: The Myths and the Evidence* (Madison: University of Wisconsin Press, 1988), 6–21; Motz, Lotte, *The Faces of the Goddess* (New York: Oxford University Press, 1997); and Ruth Tringham and Margaret Conkey, "Rethinking Figurines: A Critical View from the Archaeology of Gimbutas," in Lucy Goodison and Christine Morris, eds., *Ancient Goddesses: The Myths and the Evidence* (Madison: University of Wisconsin Press, 1988), 22–45.

Chapter 5

1. Steve Wall, *To Become a Human Being— The Message of Tadodaho Chief Leon Shenandoah* (Charlottesville: Hampton Roads Publishing, 2001), 22.

2. Historical information for this narrative derived from: Alasdair Whittle, "The First Farmers" in Barry Cunliffe, ed., *The Oxford Illustrated History of Prehistoric Europe* (Oxford: Oxford University Press, 2001), 136–166; Andrew Sherratt, "The Transformation of Early Agrarian Europe: The Later Neolithic and Copper Ages 4500–2500 BC' in Barry Cunliffe, ed., *The Oxford Illustrated History of Prehistoric Europe* (Oxford: Oxford University Press, 2001), 167–201; Alasdair Whittle, *Neolithic Europe — A Survey* (Cambridge: Cambridge University Press, 1985), 29–32, 35–63. See also: Alasdair Whittle, *Europe in The Neolithic: The Creation of New Worlds* (Cambridge: Cambridge University Press, 1996); and Paul M. Dolukhanov, *Ecology and Economy in Neolithic Europe* (London: Duckworth, 1979).

3. Whittle, *Neolithic Europe — A Survey*, 29–32; Whittle, "*The First Farmers*," 136–137.

4. Steven Mithen, *After the Ice: A Global Human History 20,000— 5000 BC* (Cambridge: Harvard University Press, 2004), 158–167.

5. *Ibid.*

6. Whittle, "The First Farmers," 140–142; Jane M. Renfrew, *The Prehistoric Food Plants of the Near East and Europe* (New York: Columbia University Press, 1973), *passim*.

7. *Ibid.*

8. *Ibid.*

9. Whittle, *Neolithic Europe — A Survey*, 58–63; V. Gordon Childe, *The Dawn of European Civilization* (New York: Alfred A. Knopf, 1967), 203–212.

10. Whittle, "The First Farmers," 165–166; Whittle, *Neolithic Europe — A Survey*, 18–20; Sherratt, "The Transformation of Early Agrarian Europe," 177.

11. Sherratt, "The Transformation of Early Agrarian Europe," 200–201; M.C. Burkitt, *Our Early Ancestors: An Introductory Study of Mesolithic, Neolithic and Copper Age Cultures in Europe and Adjacent Regions* (Cambridge: Cambridge University Press, 1936), 50–64.

12. Jerry Mander, *In the Absence of the Sacred: The Failure of Technology and the Survival of the Indian Nations* (San Francisco: Sierra Club Books, 1992), 246–262.

13. *Ibid.*

14. Richard B. Lee and Richard Daly, *The Cambridge Encyclopedia of Hunters and Gatherers*, (New York: Cambridge University Press, 1999), 391–394, 406–407; Mander, *Absence of the Sacred*, 246–262.

15. Lee and Daly, *Cambridge Encyclopedia of Hunters and Gatherers*, 403–408; Mander, *Absence of the Sacred*, 228–230.

16. Mander, *Absence of the Sacred*, 246–262.

17. Lee and Daly, *Cambridge Encyclopedia of Hunters and Gatherers*, 3–6.

18. Ruth Tringham and Margaret Conkey, "Rethinking Figurines: A Critical View from the Archaeology of Gimbutas," in Lucy Goodison and Christine Morris, eds., *Ancient Goddesses: The Myths and the Evidence* (Madison: University of Wisconsin Press, 1988), 22–45. See also: Ruth Tringham and Margaret Conkey, "'The Goddess' and Popular Culture" in Lucy Goodison and Christine Morrison, eds., *Ancient Goddesses: The Myths and the Evidence* (Madison: University of Wisconsin Press, 1988) and Lotte Motz, *The Faces of the Goddess*, (New York: Oxford University Press, 1997).

19. Whittle, "The First Farmers," 145–165; Sherratt, "*The Transformation of Early Agrarian Europe*," 200–201; Whittle, *Neolithic Europe — A Survey*, 29–33; Childe, *Dawn of European Civilization*, 125–126, 198–201. See also Timothy Darvill, *Prehistoric Britain* (New York: Routledge, 1996), 73–74; Francoise Audouze and Olivier Buchenschutz, *Towns, Villages and Countryside of Celtic Europe* (Bloomington: Indiana University Press, 1992), 103; Christopher Scarre, *Ancient France: Neolithic Societies and Their Landscapes, 6,000–2,000 BC* (Edinburgh: Edinburgh University Press, 1983), 253–265.

20. *Ibid.*

21. Sherratt, "The Transformation of Early Agrarian Europe," 169.

22. Whittle, "The First Farmers," 143, -1449; 152–153, 161–162, Sherratt, "The Transformation

of Early Agrarian Europe," 169, 180–181, 186, 190–191.

23. Whittle,"The First Farmers," 144, 146, 151, 153, 161–162; Sherratt, "The Transformation of Early Agrarian Europe," 160–173, 182–184.

24. Sherratt, "The Transformation of Early Agrarian Europe," 170–176.

25. Whittle, "The First Farmers," 139, 143–149, 151, 153–154, 161–164; Sherratt, "The Transformation of Early Agrarian Europe," 169–175, 180–185, 190–191, 196.

26. Whittle, "The First Farmers," 139–140, 145, 150–151, 157–158, 162; Sherratt, "The Transformation of Early Agrarian Europe," 172–174.

27. Mircea Eliade, *The Sacred and the Profane: The Nature of Religion* (San Diego/New York: Harcourt Brace, 1987), 1–65.

28. Whittle, *Neolithic Europe—A Survey*, 32–34; Sherratt, "The Transformation of Early Agrarian Europe," 167–176; Childe, *Dawn of European Civilization*, 125–126, 198–201, 265–285.

29. Whittle, *Neolithic Europe—A Survey*, 33–34; Sherratt, "The Transformation of Early Agrarian Europe," 167–176.

30. David W. Anthony, *The Lost World of Old Europe—The Danube Valley, 5000—3500 BC* (Princeton: Princeton University Press, 2010), 39–45, 113–127; Whittle, *"The First Farmers,"*140, 145–148, 157–158, 161–162; Sherratt, "The Transformation of Early Agrarian Europe," 167,172–173, 177–178, 192, 200.

31. Anthony, *The Lost World of Old Europe*, 39–45, 113–127; Whittle, *Neolithic Europe—A Survey*, 68–70; Childe, *Dawn of European Civilization*, 90–91, 100–102, 109, 112, 125, 140–142; Ruth Tringham and Margaret Conkey, "Rethinking Figurines: A Critical View from the Archaeology of Gimbutas," in Lucy Goodison and Christine Morris, eds., *Ancient Goddesses: The Myths and the Evidence* (Madison: University of Wisconsin Press, 1988), 22–45.

32. *Ibid.*

33. Anthony, *Lost World of Old Europe*, 39–45, 113–127; Whittle, *Neolithic Europe—A Survey*, 63–70; Childe, *Dawn of European Civilization*, 90, 100–102; Burkitt, *Our Early Ancestors*, 64–67, 122–128.

34. Anthony, *Lost World of Old Europe*, 117–125; Whittle, *Neolithic Europe—A Survey*, 63–73; Childe, *Dawn of European Civilization*, 84–104; Burkitt, *Our Early Ancestors*, 86–94.

35. Anthony, *Lost World of Old Europe*, 122; Whittle, "The First Farmers," 144–149; Tringham and Conkey, "Rethinking Figurines,"22–45.

36. Anthony, *Lost World of Old Europe*, 39–45, 113–127; Whittle, "The First Farmers," 144, 146–148; Tringham and Conkey, "Rethinking Figurines,"22–45.

37. Anthony, *Lost World of Old Europe*, 39–45, 113–127; Whittle, "The First Farmers," 144, 146.

38. Tringham and Conkey, "Rethinking Figurines,"22–45.

39. Anthony, *Lost World of Old Europe*, 39–45, 113–127; Tringham and Conkey, *"Rethinking Figurines,"* 22–45. See also: Alison E. Rautman and Lauren E. Talalay, "Diverse Approaches to the Study of Gender in Archaeology," in Allison Rautman, ed., *Reading the Body: Representations and Remains in the Archaeological Record* (Philadelphia: University of Pennsylvania, 2000).

40. *Ibid.* See also Darvill, *Prehistoric Britain*, 73.

41. Lucy Goodison and Christine Morris, "Exploring Female Divinity: From Modern Myths to Ancient Evidence," in Lucy Goodison and Christine Morris, eds., *Ancient Goddesses: The Myths and the Evidence* (Madison: University of Wisconsin Press, 1988), 6–21.

42. *Ibid.*, 16–21.

43. Whittle, "The First Farmers," 145–148, 163–164; Sherratt, "The Transformation of Early Agrarian Europe," 167, 169, 176–177, 190, 200–201; Lee and Daly, *Cambridge Encyclopedia of Hunters and Gatherers*, 4, 394, 397, 400–404, 419–424.

44. David Suzuki and Peter Knudtson, *Wisdom of the Elders—Honoring Sacred Native Visions of Nature* (New York: Bantam, 1992), 197.

45. *Ibid.*, 242.

Chapter 6

1. Melissa K. Nelson, ed., *Original Instructions—Indigenous Teachings for a Sustainable Future* (Rochester VT: Bear and Company, 2008), 304–305.

2. Historical information for this narrative derived from: Michael J. O'Kelly, *Newgrange: Archaeology, Art and Legend* (London: Thames and Hudson, 1982); David Lewis-Williams and David Pearce, *Inside the Neolithic Mind* (London: Thames and Hudson, 2005); Brian Hayden, *Shamans, Sorcerers and Saints: A Prehistory of Religion* (Washington D.C.: Smithsonian Books, 2003); Brian Morris, *Religion and Anthropology—A Critical Introduction* (Princeton: Princeton University Press, 2006); Chris Scarre, *Exploring Prehistoric Europe* (Oxford: Oxford University Press, 1998).

3. Alasdair Whittle, *Neolithic Europe: A Survey* (Cambridge: Cambridge University Press, 1985), *passim*; Alasdair Whittle, *Europe in the Neolithic: The Creation of New Worlds* (Cambridge: Cambridge University Press, 1996), *passim*; Timothy Darvill, *Prehistoric Britain* (New York: Routledge, 1996), 73–74.

4. *Ibid.*

5. Andrew Sherratt, "The Transformation of Early Agrarian Europe: The Later Neolithic and Copper Ages 4500–2500 BC" in Barry Cunliffe,

ed., *The Oxford Illustrated History of Prehistoric Europe* (Oxford: Oxford University Press, 2001), 167–201.

6. Whittle, *Neolithic Europe—A Survey*, 196–263.

7. Christopher Scarre, ed. *Ancient France, 6000–2000 BC: Neolithic Societies and Their Landscapes* (Edinburgh: Edinburgh University Press, 1983), 6–270.

8. V. Gordon Childe, *The Dawn of European Civilization* (New York: Alfred A. Knopf, 1967), 303–340; Scarre, *Exploring Prehistoric Europe*, 11–13, 57–129; Whittle, *Neolithic Europe—A Survey*, 196–263.

9. *Ibid.*

10. Scarre, *Ancient France*, 47, 64–68, 116–117, 213–216, 230–233, 271–323, 309–312.

11. James Dyer, *Ancient Britain* (Philadelphia: University of Pennsylvania Press, 1990), 29–62; Darvill, *Prehistoric Britain*, 63–69, 85–86.

12. Michael Herity and George Eogan, *Ireland in Prehistory* (New York: Routledge, 1996), 31–36, 57–58, 67–69.

13. *Ibid.*, 58–61.

14. Jeffrey Gantz, *Early Irish Myths and Sagas* (Hammondsworth: Dorset , 1985), 41.

15. Michael J. O'Kelly, *Newgrange—Archaeology, Art and Legend* (London: Thames and Hudson, 1998), 13–23, 47, 93–100, 122–126.

16. P.J. Ashmore, *Neolithic and Bronze Age Scotland* (London: Batsford/Historic Scotland), 43–59.

17. *Ibid.*, Darvill, *Prehistoric Britain*, 43, 85.

18. O'Kelly, *Newgrange*, 123–127; Peter Harbison, *Pre-Christian Ireland—From the First Settlers to the Early Celts* (London: Thames and Hudson, 1988), 76–77; George Eogan, *Knowth and the passage-tombs of Ireland* (London: Thames and Hudson, 1986), 96–97; Andrew Sherratt, "The Transformation of Early Agrarian Europe: The Later Neolithic and Copper Ages 4500–2500 BC' in Barry Cunliffe, Barry, ed., *The Oxford Illustrated History of Prehistoric Europe* (Oxford: Oxford University Press, 2001), 195; Martin Brennan, *The Stones of Time— Calendars, Sundials and Stone Chambers of Ancient Ireland* (Rochester: Inner Traditions, 1994), 39, 70–89.

19. Eogan, *Knowth*, 61, 141–142, 176.

20. *Ibid.*

21. Darvill, *Prehistoric Britain*, 82, 88.

22. Lewis-Williams and Pearce, *Inside the Neolithic Mind*, 189–192.

23. *Ibid.*

24. Eogan, *Knowth*, 1986, 152–177; Brennan, *Stones of Time*, 127–177.

25. *Ibid.*

26. Lewis-Williams and Pearce, *Inside the Neolithic Mind*, 44–47, 69–72, 171–197, 260–271. See also Suzanne Carr, *Entoptic Phenomenon* (Master's Dissertation), www. oubliette.zetnet. co.uk.

27. Jean Clottes and David Lewis-Williams, *The Shamans of Prehistory—Trance and Magic in the Painted Caves* (New York: Harry N. Abrams, 1998), 31–35.

28. Lewis-Williams and Pearce, *Inside the Neolithic Mind*, 269–273.

29. *Ibid.*, 264–273. See also Eogan, *Knowth*, 1986, 122, 126–132, 187–195; O'Kelly, *Newgrange*, 154–159, 171, 181; Brennan, *Stones of Time*, 72–73, 80, 85, 89, 97, 106–107, 118, 130, 144–146, 150, 162, 168–169, 177, 181, 191–194.

30. Lewis-Williams and Pearce, *Inside the Neolithic Mind*, 264–269. See also J.D. Lewis-Williams and T.A. Dowson., "On Vision and Power in the Neolithic: Evidence from the Decorated Monuments" in *Current Anthropology* 34 (1), 1993; and J.D. Lewis-Williams, and T.A. Dowson, T.A., 'The Signs of All Times," in *Current Anthropology* 29 (2), 1988.

31. Joseph Campbell, *Historical Atlas of World Mythology: Volume 2—The Mythologies of the Great Hunt* (New York: Harper and Row, 1988), 57.

32. David Suzuki and Peter Knudtson, *Wisdom of the Elders—Honoring Sacred Native Visions of Nature* (New York: Bantam, 1992), 111.

33. *Ibid.*, 120.

34. Carol Schaefer, *Grandmothers Counsel the World—Women Elders Offer Their Vision for Our Planet* (Boston: Trumpeter Books/Shambala, 2006), 166.

35. I.H. Longworth, *Prehistoric Britain* (Cambridge: Harvard University Press, 1986), 20; D.V. Clarke, T.G. Cowie and A. Foxon, eds., *Symbols of Power at the Time of Stonehenge* (Edinburgh, National Museum of Antiquities of Scotland, 1985), 54, 59–60.

36. Lewis-Williams and Pearce, *Inside the Neolithic Mind*, 48–56, 82–85, 171–197; Francis Pryor, *Seahenge—New Discoveries in Prehistoric Britain* (London: Harper Collins, 2001), 135–150; James L. Pearson, *Shamanism and the Ancient Mind—A Cognitive Approach to Archaeology* (Walnut Creek: Altamira Press, 2002), 39–51, 115–117, 120–140.

37. O'Kelly, *Newgrange*, 15, 21, 73, 123; Eogan, *Knowth*, 111; Lewis-Williams and Pearce, *Inside the Neolithic Mind*, 256–260.

38. Lewis-Williams and Pearce, *Inside the Neolithic Mind*, 256–260; Mircea Eliade, *Shamanism—Archaic Techniques of Ecstasy* (Princeton: Princeton University Press, 1974), 47, 50, 52n, 125, 339, 350; Mircea Eliade, *Rites and Symbols of Initiation* (Woodstock: Spring Publications, 1995), 17, 99.

39. *Ibid.*

40. *Ibid.*

41. Pearson, *Shamanism and the Ancient Mind*, 73–75, 87–89, 95–107, 120–131; Lewis-Williams and Pearce, *Inside the Neolithic Mind*, 46–56, 67–69, 171–197, 253–256.

42. Pearson, *Shamanism and the Ancient Mind*,

97–105, 113–143; Sherratt, *"The Transformation
of Early Agrarian Europe,"* 175, 180, 184, 192; Herity and Eogan, *Ireland in Prehistory*, 68–69.
   43. Brian Morris, *Religion and Anthropology—
A Critical Introduction* (Cambridge: Cambridge
University Press, 2006), 19–22, 37–99; Pearson,
Shamanism and the Ancient Mind, 39–47, 49–51,
65–75, 97–107, 113–143; Lewis-Williams and
Pearce, *Inside the Neolithic Mind*, 40–47, 48–59,
67–69, 171–197, 253–256, 260–271; Hayden,
Shamans, Sorcerers and Saints, 7, 36–37, 48–87;
Clottes and Lewis-Williams, *Shamans of Prehistory*, 11–19, 92–99; Pryor, *Seahenge*, 135–150.
   44. V. Gordon Childe, *The Dawn of European
Civilization* (New York: Alfred A. Knopf, 1967),
112, 125, 272–278, 312–315; Lewis-Williams and
Pearce, *Inside the Neolithic Mind*, 113–115; Scarre,
Ancient France, 294–299; Elizabeth Shee Twohig,
"A 'Mother Goddess' in North-West Europe c.
4200–2500 BC?" in Lucy Goodison and Christine Morris, eds., *Ancient Goddesses: The Myths
and the Evidence* (Madison: University of Wisconsin Press, 1988), 164–197.
   45. *Ibid.*
   46. *Ibid.*
   47. Scarre, *Ancient France*, 294–297; Shee
Twohig, "A Mother Goddess?," 164–197.
   48. *Ibid.*
   49. *Ibid.*
   50. Jacob Taylor, *Matrilineal Descent in Contemporary Societies*, http:// explodie.org/writings
(5/20/2012)
   51. Shee Twohig, "A Mother Goddess?," 164–
197. See also Allision Rautman, ed., *Reading the
Body: Representations and Remains in the Archaeological Record* (Philadelphia: University of Pennsylvania, 2000); Lucy Goodison and Christine
Morris, eds., *Ancient Goddesses: The Myths and the
Evidence* (Madison: University of Wisconsin
Press, 1988).
   52. *Ibid.*
   53. *Ibid.*

Chapter 7

   1. Diane K. Osbon, ed., *A Joseph Campbell
Companion: Reflections on the Art of Living* (New
York: Harper Collins, 1991), 149, 198, 208.
   2. Historical information for this narrative
derived from: Andrew Sherratt, "The Transformation of Early Agrarian Europe: The Later Neolithic and Copper Ages, 4500–2500 BC" in
Barry Cunliffe, ed., *The Oxford Illustrated History
of Prehistoric Europe* (Oxford: Oxford University
Press, 2001), 167–201; J.P. Mallory, J.P, *In Search
of the Indo-Europeans — Language, Archaeology
and Myth* (New York: Thames and Hudson,
1999), *passim*; Andrew Sherratt, "The Emergence
of Élites: Earlier Bronze Age Europe, 2500–1300
BC," in Barry Cunliffe, ed., *The Oxford Illustrated

History of Prehistoric Europe* (Oxford: Oxford
University Press, 2001), 244–276; Anthony
Harding, "Reformation in Barbarian Europe,
1300–600 BC" in Barry Cunliffe, ed., *The Oxford
Illustrated History of Prehistoric Europe* (Oxford:
Oxford University Press, 2001), 304–335.
   3. Sherratt, "The Transformation of Early
Agrarian Europe," 167–201.
   4. Sherratt, *"The Emergence of Élites,"* 244–
276.
   5. *Ibid.*, 244–245; Harding, "Reformation
in Barbarian Europe," 309–315.
   6. Sherratt, "The Transformation of Early
Agrarian Europe," 177–180, 193–195; Pryor, Francis, *Seahenge — New Discoveries in Prehistoric
Britain* (London: Harper Collins, 2001), 80–107,
166–182.
   7. Pryor, *Seahenge*, 240–249, 267, 275.
   8. Sherratt, "The Transformation of Early
Agrarian Europe," 193–195; Pryor, *Seahenge*, 80–
107, 166–182; James Dyer, *Ancient Britain*
(Philadelphia: University of Pennsylvania, 1990),
63–78; Timothy Darvill, *Prehistoric Britain* (New
York: Routledge, 1996), 82–88, 92–97; Ashmore,
P.J., *Neolithic and Bronze Age Scotland* (London:
Batsford/Historic Scotland, 1997).
   9. *Ibid.*
   10. Darvill, *Prehistoric Britain*, 44, 46, 58, 85.
   11. Michael Herity and George Eogan, *Ireland
in Prehistory* (New York: Routledge, 1996), 124–
128.
   12. *Ibid.*, 117–123.
   13. Ken Osborne, ed., *Stonehenge and Neighbouring Monuments* (London: English Heritage,
2000), *passim*; Darvill, *Prehistoric Britain*, 14–15,
19, 80, 97–98, 117.
   14. *Ibid.*
   15. *Ibid.*
   16. Osborne, *Stonehenge*, 8–9.
   17. Sherratt, "The Emergence of Élites," 245–
250.
   18. Darvill, *Prehistoric Britain*, 85–86.
   19. K. Demakopoulou, C. Eluère, J. Jensen,
A. Jockenhovel, and J. Mohen, J., *Gods and Heroes
of the European Bronze Age* (London: Thames and
Hudson, 1999), 134, 261.
   20. Simon O'Dwyer, *Prehistoric Music of Ireland* (Stroud: Tempus, 2004), 27–54, 147–150.
   21. *Ibid.*, 59.
   22. Sherratt, "The Transformation of Early
Agrarian Europe," 189; Demakoupolou et al, *Gods
and Heroes of European Bronze Age*, 56–59.
   23. Demakopoulou et al, *Gods and Heroes of
European Bronze Age*, 247–249; D.V. Clarke, T.G.
Cowie and A. Foxon, A., eds., *Symbols of Power
at the Time of Stonehenge* (Edinburgh: National
Museum of Antiquities of Scotland, 1985), 120.
   24. V. Gordon Childe, *The Dawn of European
Civilization* (New York: Alfred A. Knopf, 1967),
287–302; Munro, Robert, *The Lake-Dwellings of
Europe* (London: Cassell and Co., 1890).

25. O'Dwyer, *Prehistoric Music of Ireland*, 54–56.

26. Demakopoulou et al, *Gods and Heroes of European Bronze Age*, 249–250.

27. *Ibid.*, 249.

28. Lisa Manniche, *Music and Musicians in Ancient Egypt* (London: British Museum Press, 1991), 24, 85–87, 109–110, 123, 126; Anne K. Capel and Glenn E. Markoe, eds., *Mistress of the House, Mistress of Heaven — Women in Ancient Egypt* (New York: Hudson Hills Press, 1996), 94–99; Bongioanni, A. and Croce, Maria S., *The Treasures of Ancient Egypt from the Egyptian Museum in Cairo* (New York: Rizzoli, 2003).

29. *Ibid.*

30. Capel and Markoe, *Mistress of the House*, 14–15, 41–43, 136, 162, 168–169; Manniche, *Music and Musicians in Ancient Egypt*, 24, 85–87, 109–110, 123, 126.

31. Michael Ryan, *The Illustrated Archaeology of Ireland* (Dublin: Country House, 1991), 73, 78–84; Peter Harbison, *Pre-Christian Ireland* (London: Thames and Hudson, 1994), 126–127.

32. Harbison, *Pre-Christian Ireland*, 125, 143–145; Demakopoulou et al, *Gods and Heroes of European Bronze Age*, 168–171.

33. Demakopoulou et al, *Gods and Heroes of European Bronze Age*, 172–181.

34. Clarke et al, *Symbols of Power at the Time of Stonehenge*, 120, 204–216.

35. Childe, *Dawn of European Civilization*, 287–302; Clarke *et al*, *Symbols of Power at the Time of Stonehenge*, 115.

36. Osborne, *Stonehenge*, 27.

37. Clarke et al, *Symbols of Power at the Time of Stonehenge*, 115, 117, 123.

38. *Ibid.*, 99, 110–112, 139, 148, 179, 221; Demakopoulou et al, *Gods and Heroes of European Bronze Age*, 238–240, 270–273; Ryan, *Illustrated Archaeology of Ireland*, 72, 86, 94–99.

39. Sherratt, "The Transformation of Early Agrarian Europe," 190–191; Sherratt, "*The Emergence of Élites*," 250–254.

40. Sherratt, "The Transformation of Early Agrarian Europe," 167–201; Sherratt, "The Emergence of Élites," 244–276.

41. Sherratt, "The Transformation of Early Agrarian Europe," 193; Sherratt, "The Emergence of Élites," 247–248, 259–260, 268–272; Demakopoulou et al, *Gods and Heroes of European Bronze Age*, 108–113; Darvill, *Prehistoric Britain*, 85–86.

42. Darvill, *Prehistoric Britain*, 103.

43. Sherratt, "The Transformation of Early Agrarian Europe," 190–191; Sherratt, "The Emergence of Élites," 250–254.

44. *Ibid.*

45. Sherratt, "The Emergence of Élites," 250–256.

46. Sharon Paice MacLeod, *Celtic Myth and Religion — A Study of Traditional Belief* (Jefferson

N.C.: McFarland, 2012), 15; Darvill, *Prehistoric Britain*, 132.

47. Sherratt, "The Emergence of Élites," 245, 250–251, 254, 262, 268–269; Demakopolou et al, *Gods and Heroes of European Bronze Age*, 31–34; Darvill, *Prehistoric Britain*, 98.

48. Demakopolou et al, *Gods and Heroes of European Bronze Age*, 88–97; Darvill, *Prehistoric Britain*, 132.

49. Demakopolou et al, *Gods and Heroes of European Bronze Age*, 106–107, 127–129; Sherratt, "The Emergence of Élites," 245, 254, 276; Darvill, *Prehistoric Britain*, 77, 86, 88–91, 108, 119–120, 122, 127.

50. Darvill, *Prehistoric Britain*, 127.

51. Darvill, *Prehistoric Britain*, 119–120, 122, 132; Sherratt, "The Emergence of Élites," 245, 250–256.

52. Demakopolou et al, *Gods and Heroes of European Bronze Age*, 79–82, 158.

53. *Ibid.*, 58, 79.

54. *Ibid.*, 86, 94, 123–124, 183.

55. *Ibid.*, 134–135.

56. Demakopolou et al, *Gods and Heroes of European Bronze Age*, 114–122, 137–141, 145–152; Sherratt, "The Transformation of Early Agrarian Europe," 197–198; J.P. Mallory, J.P., *In Search of the Indo-Europeans* (London: Thames and Hudson, 1989), 176, 204, 219–220.

57. *Ibid.*

58. Demakopolou et al, *Gods and Heroes of European Bronze Age*, 259; Scarre, *Ancient France*, 297–299.

59. Darvill, *Prehistoric Britain*, 98.

60. Sherratt, "The Transformation of Early Agrarian Europe," 190–192; Sherratt, "The Emergence of Élites," 250–256.

61. Mallory, *In Search of the Indo-Europeans*, 238–265.

62. *Ibid.*

63. 'Ancient DNA reveals Europe's dynamic genetic history,' 4/28/13. www.adelaide.edu.au/adelaidean/issues/14381/news14382.html

64. *Ibid.*

65. Mallory, *In Search of the Indo-Europeans*, 238–265.

66. Sherratt, "*The Emergence of Élites*," 250–256; Sherratt, "*The Transformation of Early Agrarian Europe*," 190–192, 201.

67. Mallory, *In Search of the Indo-Europeans*, 18–23, 66–109, 158–164; Calvert Watkins, ed., *Dictionary of Indo-European Roots* (Boston: Houghton Mifflin, 2000), *vii–xxi*.

68. Mallory, *In Search of the Indo-Europeans*, 262.

69. *Ibid.*, 263–264.

70. Watkins, *Dictionary of Indo-European Roots*, 23.

71. Mallory, *In Search of the Indo-Europeans*, 18–23, 66–109, 158–164; Watkins, *Dictionary of Indo-European Roots*, xxii–xxxv.

72. Mallory, *In Search of the Indo-Europeans*, 128–142.
73. *Ibid.*, 128–130.
74. *Ibid.*
75. *Ibid.*, 130–135.
76. *Ibid.*, 135–142.
77. *Ibid.*, 257–261.
78. Carol Schaefer, *Grandmothers Counsel the World* (Boston: Trumpeter/Shambhala, 2006), 95, 184.

Chapter 8

1. Theodore Levin, *Where Rivers and Mountains Sing: Sound, Music, and Nomadism in Tuva and Beyond* (Bloomington: Indiana University Press, 2006), 180–181.
2. Carol Schaefer, *Grandmothers Counsel the World* (Boston: Trumpeter Books/Shambhala, 2006), 138. This quote is from a recounting of the message of the White Buffalo Calf Woman to the women of the Lakota nation, as spoken by Lakota elders Rita and Beatrice Long Visitor Holy Dance.
3. Historical information for this narrative derived from: Timothy Taylor, "Thracians, Scythians and Dacians, 800 BC – AD 300" in Barry Cunliffe, ed., *The Oxford Illustrated History of Prehistoric Europe* (Oxford: Oxford University Press, 2001); Tamara Talbot Rice, *The Scythians* (New York: Frederick A. Praeger, 1957); Frank Trippett, ed., *The First Horsemen* (New York: Time Life Books, 1974); Jeannine, Davis-Kimball, *Warrior Women— An Archaeologist's Search for History's Hidden Heroines* (New York: Warner Books, 2002); David W. Anthony, *The Horse, The Wheel and Language— How Bronze Age Riders from the European Steppes Shaped the Modern World* (Princeton: Princeton University Press, 2007).
4. Sherratt, Andrew, "The Emergence of Élites: Earlier Bronze Age Europe, 2500–1300 BC" in Barry, Cunliffe, ed., *The Oxford Illustrated History of Prehistoric Europe* (Oxford: Oxford University Press, 2001), 256–270; Anthony Harding, "Reformation in Barbarian Europe, 1300–600 BC" in Barry Cunliffe, ed., *The Oxford Illustrated History of Prehistoric Europe* (Oxford: Oxford University Press, 2001), 304–315.
5. Sherratt, "The Emergence of Élites," 244–245, 251–256; Harding, "*Reformation in Barbarian Europe*," 306–314.
6. Barry Cunliffe, "Iron Age Societies in Western Europe and Beyond, 800–140 BC," in Barry Cunliffe, ed., *The Oxford Illustrated History of Prehistoric Europe* (Oxford: Oxford University Press, 2001), 367–369.
7. Rice, The Scythians, 33–55; Trippett, *The First Horsemen* 9–18; Taylor, "Thracians, Scythians and Dacians," 373–377, 380–384.

8. Rice, The Scythians, 33–55; Trippett, *The First Horsemen* 9–18; Taylor, "Thracians, Scythians and Dacians," 373–384.
9. Rice, The Scythians, 58–70; Taylor, "Thracians, Scythians and Dacians," 379–380.
10. Rice, The Scythians, 58–70, 158–189.
11. Rice, The Scythians, 58–70; Trippett, *The First Horsemen* 9–18; Taylor, "*Thracians, Scythians and Dacians*," 381–384.
12. Rice, The Scythians, 70–76, 26–133; Taylor, "Thracians, Scythians and Dacians," 381, 383.
13. Trippett, *The First Horsemen* 18; Rice, The Scythians, 58–70.
14. Rice, The Scythians, 58–70, 79, 87–89; Trippett, *The First Horsemen*,15, 18, 98, 106, 115.
15. Rice, *The Scythians*, 76–79.
16. *Ibid.*, 64–65, 68.
17. *Ibid.*, 76–79.
18. *Ibid.*, 87–89; Trippett, *The First Horsemen*, 117–125.
19. Rice, *The Scythians*, 87–89; Trippett, *The First Horsemen*, 99–116.
20. Rice, *The Scythians*, 81–83, 92–123., Trippett, *The First Horsemen*, passim.
21. Rice, *The Scythians*, 81–83.
22. *Ibid.*, 94–95.
23. *Ibid.*, 81–83, 92–123, 135–140, 141–143.
24. Rice, *The Scythians*,147–196; Trippett, *The First Horsemen*, passim.
25. *Ibid.*, 158–189.
26. Davis-Kimball, *Warrior Women*, 108–111.
27. *Ibid.*, 110.
28. Trippett, *The First Horsemen* 54–55; Rice, *The Scythians*, 118–119.
29. Rice, *The Scythians*, 158–189; Mircea Eliade, *Shamanism— Archaic Techniques of Ecstasy* (Princeton: Princeton University Press, 1974), 88–95, 148–157.
30. Rice, *The Scythians*, 85; Trippett, *The First Horsemen*, 22.
31. Jaan Puhvel, *Comparative Mythology* (Baltimore: Johns Hopkins University Press, 1984), 113–114.
32. Puhvel, *Comparative Mythology*, 114; Trippett, *The First Horsemen*, 128.
33. Rice, *The Scythians*, 158–189; Trippett, *The First Horsemen*, 87–97, 113.
34. Rice, *The Scythians*, 158–189.
35. Eliade, *Shamanism*, 5–11.
36. Rice, *The Scythians*, 86.
37. Rice, *The Scythians*, 85–87.
38. *Ibid.*
39. *Ibid.*
40. Trippett, *The First Horsemen*, 132–133.
41. Rice, *The Scythians*, 85–87.
42. Trippett, *The First Horsemen*, 68–69.
43. Taylor, "Thracians, Scythians and Dacians," 394–397.
44. *Ibid.*
45. *Ibid.*, 396–397.

46. Davis-Kimball, *Warrior Women*, 13, 21; Trippett, *The First Horsemen*, 10, 30, 51.
47. Taylor, "Thracians, Scythians and Dacians," 395; Davis-Kimball, *Warrior Women*, 115–117; Trippett, *The First Horsemen*, 80–81.
48. *Ibid.*
49. Taylor, "Thracians, Scythians and Dacians," 395.
50. *Ibid.*, 395; Davis-Kimball, *Warrior Women*, 115–117; Trippett, *The First Horsemen*, 80–81.
51. *Ibid.*
52. Davis-Kimball, *Warrior Women*, 232.
53. Taylor, "Thracians, Scythians and Dacians," 395; Davis-Kimball, *Warrior Women*, 118; Calvert Watkins, ed., *Dictionary of Indo-European Roots* (Boston: Houghton Mifflin, 2000), 50.
54. Davis-Kimball, *Warrior Women*, 114–115.
55. *Ibid.*, 115–116.
56. *Ibid.*, 116.
57. *Ibid.*
58. *Ibid.*, 116–117.
59. *Ibid.*, 118–119.
60. *Ibid.*, 117.
61. *Ibid.*, 44, 51, 99–100, 238.
62. *Ibid.*
63. *Ibid.*, 44.
64. Taylor, "Thracians, Scythians and Dacians," 395; Davis-Kimball, Jeannine, "Chieftain or Warrior-Priestess?" in *Archaeology*, Sept/Oct. 1997, 44–48.
65. Taylor, "Thracians, Scythians and Dacians," 395; Davis-Kimball, *Warrior Women*, 54–58.
66. *Ibid.*
67. Davis-Kimball, *Warrior Women*, 70, 236.
68. *Ibid.*, 73, 77–79, 103–107, 239.
69. *Ibid.*, 135, 225, 230.
70. *Ibid.*, 73–74.
71. *Ibid.*, 77–79.
72. Taylor, "Thracians, Scythians and Dacians," 394–396; Davis-Kimball, *Warrior Women*, 70–72, 58–60, 84–88, 136–137, 144–145, 236–237.
73. Davis-Kimball, *Warrior Women*, 58–61, 70–72.
74. *Ibid.*

Chapter 9

1. Sharon Paice MacLeod, *Celtic Myth and Religion: A Study of Traditional Belief* (Jefferson N.C.: McFarland, 2012), 8.
2. Historical information for this narrative derived from: Proinsias MacCana, "Celtic Religion and Mythology" in Venceslas Kruta, ed., *The Celts* (New York: Rizzoli, 1991), 616–627; Anne Ross, "Ritual and the Druids," in Miranda Green, ed., *The Celtic World* (New York: Routledge, 1996), 423–444; Jane Webster, "Sanctuaries and sacred places," in Miranda Green, ed., *The Celtic World* (New York: Routledge, 1996), 445–464; T.G.E. Powell, *The Celts* (London: Thames and Hudson, 1980), 143–186; Stuart Piggott, *The Druids* (New York: Thames and Hudson, 1993), 100–119; MacLeod, *Celtic Myth and Religion*, 5, 9–15, 22–24, 25–33, 36–37.
3. Barry Cunliffe, *The Celtic World* (New York: McGraw-Hill, 1979), 18–19; MacLeod, *Celtic Myth and Religion*, 18–19.
4. Ruth and Vincent Megaw, *Celtic Art: From Beginnings to the Book of Kells* (London: Thames and Hudson, 1989), *passim.*
5. Timothy Bridgman, "Names and Naming Conventions Concerning Celtic Peoples in Some Early Ancient Greek Authors," *CSANA Yearbook* 7, 113–127; S.A. Handford, ed., *Caesar: The Conquest of Gaul* (London: Penguin, 1982), 28; Bridgman, Timothy, "Keltoi, Galatai, Galli: Were They All One People?," *Proceedings of the Harvard Celtic Colloquium*, Vol. XXV, 2005, 155–162.
6. Cunliffe, *The Celtic World*, 18–19; Powell, *The Celts*, 18–24.
7. MacLeod, *Celtic Myth and Religion*, 19–21.
8. Cunliffe, *The Celtic World*, 44–47; MacLeod, *Celtic Myth and Religion*, 19–22.
9. Cunliffe, *The Celtic World*, 42–44; MacLeod, *Celtic Myth and Religion*, 19–22; Powell, *The Celts*, 61–142.
10. Cunliffe, *The Celtic World*, 28–67; Powell, *The Celts*, 61–142; Duval, Alan, "Celtic Society in the First Century BC" in Venceslas Kruta, ed., *The Celts* (New York: Rizzoli, 1997), 509–515.
11. Martin J. Ball, *The Celtic Languages* (New York: Routledge, 2002), 64–98.
12. Powell, *The Celts*, 182–186; MacLeod, *Celtic Myth and Religion*, 22–24.
13. Piggott, *The Celts*, 100–118; MacLeod, *Celtic Myth and Religion*, 23–26.
14. *Ibid.*
15. MacLeod, *Celtic Myth and Religion*, 34–47.
16. Powell, *The Celts*, 150–181; Cunliffe, *The Celtic World*, 88–95.
17. Powell, *The Celts*, 176–179; MacLeod, *Celtic Myth and Religion*, 15.
18. Stanley Ireland, *Roman Britain: A Sourcebook* (New York: Routledge, 1986), 15–16.
19. Ireland, *Roman Britain*, 23.
20. *Ibid.*, 19.
21. Fergus Kelly, *A Guide to Early Irish Law* (Dublin: Dublin Institute for Advanced Studies, 1995), 3–16.
22. *Ibid.*, 8, 12–13, 19, 27; Powell, *The Celts*, 78–88.
23. Kelly, *Guide to Early Irish Law*, 17–21.
24. Phillip Freeman, *War, Women and Druids: Eyewitness Reports and Early Accounts of the Ancient Celts* (Austin: University of Texas Press, 2002), 59.
25. *Ibid.*, 55.

26. *Ibid.*

27. John T. Koch and John Carey, ed., *The Celtic Heroic Age — Literary Sources for Ancient Celtic Europe and Early Ireland and Wales* (Aberystwyth: Celtic Studies Publications, 2003), 42.

28. Koch and Carey, *Celtic Heroic Age*, 43–44; Freeman, *War, Women and Druids*, 58–59; Ireland, *Roman Britain*, 59–70.

29. *Ibid.*, 61.

30. *Ibid.*, 64–67.

31. *Ibid.*, 66–67.

32. Kelly, *Guide to Early Irish Law*, 77–78.

33. Patrick K. Ford, *The Celtic Poets* (Belmont: Ford and Bailie, 1999), *xv-xxix*; Kelly, *Guide to Early Irish Law*, 43–50, 137–138.

34. *Ibid.*

35. Kelly, *Guide to Early Irish Law*, 49.

36. Kelly, *Guide to Early Irish Law*, 49, 68–78; MacLeod, *Celtic Myth and Religion*, 185–193.

37. Kelly, *Guide to Early Irish Law*, 49, 68–78.

38. *Ibid.*

39. *Ibid.*

40. *Ibid.*

41. *Ibid.*, 78–79, 134.

42. *Ibid.*, 68–69, 77.

43. MacLeod, *Celtic Myth and Religion*, 30–31.

44. Koch and Carey, *Celtic Heroic Age*, 44–45.

45. MacLeod, *Celtic Myth and Religion*, 26–28.

46. *Ibid.*, David Rankin, *Celts and the Classical World* (New York: Routledge, 1996), 235, 292–293.

47. Ireland, *Roman Britain*, 58–59; Rankin, *Celts and Classical World*, 291–292.

48. *Ibid.*

49. MacLeod, *Celtic Myth and Religion,* 28–29.

50. Rankin, *Celts and Classical World*, 47, 110, 258, 292; MacLeod, *Celtic Myth and Religion*, 28–29.

51. *Ibid.*

52. Cunliffe, *The Celtic World*, 91; Miranda Green, *Celtic Goddesses* (New York: George Braziller, 1996), 16, 141, 144.

53. http:// ancientweb. org / images / explore / Spain; for the Woman of Elche and Dama de Baza.

54. *Ibid.*

55. MacLeod, *Celtic Myth and Religion*, 11–12, 34–38.

56. *Ibid.*

57. *Ibid.*, 34–38.

58. Green, *Celtic Goddesses*, 36, 38–51, 112, 166, 172, 184–187.

59. *Ibid.*

60. *Ibid.*, 36, 196–197.

61. *Ibid.*, 90–99, 133.

62. *Ibid.*, 102–104, 125, 134–135, 169–170, 178.

63. *Ibid.*, 89–104.

64. *Ibid.*, 165–167.

65. *Ibid.*, 161–164; Cunliffe, 78–79.

66. Ross, Anne, *Pagan Celtic Britain* (New York: Academy, 1996), 179.

67. Ross, *Pagan Celtic Britain*, 66, 192, 277, 286, 420.

68. Koch and Carey, *Celtic Heroic Age*, 266.

69. Gwynn, Edward, *The Metrical Dindshenchas* (Dublin: Dublin Institute for Advanced Studies, 1991), Part III, 26–39.

70. *Ibid.*, 286–297.

71. Donncha Ó hAodha, *Bethu Brigte*, (Dublin: Dublin Institute for Advanced Studies, 1978); Green, *Celtic Goddesses*, 25, 143, 182, 192, 195–202; MacLeod, *Celtic Myth and Religion*, 51.

72. *Ibid.*

73. Sharon Paice MacLeod, "*Mater Deorum Hibernensium*: Identity and Cross-Correlation in Early Irish Myths," in *Proceedings of the Harvard Celtic Colloquium*, Vol. XIX, 1999, 340–384.

74. *Ibid.*

75. *Ibid.*

76. *Ibid.*, Green, *Celtic Goddesses*, 40–41; Gwynn, *Metrical Dindshenchas*, Part IV, 308–311.

77. MacLeod, "*Mater Deorum Hibernensium*," 340–384; Ross, *Pagan Celtic Britain*, 219–285.

78. MacLeod, "*Mater Deorum Hibernensium*," 379–380.

79. *Ibid.*, 340–384.

80. Proinsias MacCana, "Celtic Goddesses of Sovereignty" in Elisabeth Benard and Beverly Moon, eds., *Goddesses Who Rule* (Oxford: Oxford University Press, 2000); Ross, *Pagan Celtic Britain*, 265–289; MacLeod, *Celtic Myth and Religion*, 10, 49–50.

81. *Ibid.*

82. MacLeod, *Celtic Myth and Religion*, 123–131.

83. Gwynn, *Metrical Dindshenchas*, Part III, 310.

84. Joan Halifax, *The Fruitful Darkness* (New York: Harper San Francisco, 1993), 187–191.

Chapter 10

1. Carol Schaefer, *Grandmothers Counsel the World* (Boston: Trumpeter Books/Shambhala, 2006), 58.

2. H.R. Ellis Davidson, *Myths and Symbols of Pagan Europe* (Syracuse: Syracuse University Press, 1988), 92.

3. Historical information for this narrative derived from: Barry Cunliffe, "Iron Age Societies in Western Europe and Beyond, 800–140 BC" in Barry Cunliffe, ed., *The Oxford Illustrated History of Prehistoric Europe* (Oxford: Oxford University Press, 2001), 336–372; Davidson, *Myths and Symbols of Pagan Europe*; H.R. Ellis Davidson, *Gods and Myths of Northern Europe* (New York: Penguin, 1964); Malcolm Todd, "Barbarian Eu-

rope, AD 300–700" in Barry Cunliffe, ed., *The Oxford Illustrated History of Prehistoric Europe* (Oxford: Oxford University Press, 2001), 447–482; Lotte Motz, *The Faces of the Goddess* (New York: Oxford University Press, 1997); Jordan Paper, *Through the Earth Darkly: Female Spirituality in Comparative Perspective* (New York: Continuum, 1997); Alexander Carmichael, ed., *Carmina Gadelica* (Hudson: Lindisfarne, 1994).

4. Cunliffe, Barry, "The Impact of Rome on Barbarian Society, 140 BC-AD 300" in Cunliffe, Barry, ed., *The Oxford Illustrated History of Prehistoric Europe* (Oxford: Oxford University Press, 2001), 411–446.

5. *Ibid.*, 423–425.
6. *Ibid.*
7. *Ibid.*, 411–446.
8. Piggott, Stuart, *The Druids* (New York: Thames and Hudson, 1993), 123–191.
9. *Ibid.*
10. Clark, Elizabeth, *The First Christians*, www.pbs.org/wgbh/pages/frontline/shows/religion/first/roles.html; Pagels, Elaine H., *Women in the Early Church*, www.pbs.org/wgbh/pages/frontline/shows/religion/first/roles.html. See also: Pagels, Elaine, *The Gnostic Gospels* (New York: Vintage, 1989); Pagels, Elaine, *Beyond Belief: The Secret Gospel of Thomas* (New York: Vintage, 2004); Pagels, Elaine, *Reading Judas: The Gospel of Judas and the Shaping of Christianity* (New York: Viking Adult, 2007).

11. Gershoy, Leo, ed., *A Survey of European Civilization* (Boston: Houghton Mifflin, 1969), 311–324; Butler, Hazel, "The Cult of Isis and Early Christianity" historyoftheancientworld. com, from *Hohonu: A Journal of Academic Writing*, Vol. 7 (2005); "The Cults of Magna Mater and Mithras," courses.ttu.edu/gforstyh/3302cp/20.htm; "Eastern Religions in the Roman World," www.netmuseum.org.

12. *Ibid.*
13. *Ibid.*
14. Gershoy, 301–342; Clark and Pagels, www.pbs.org/wbgh/pages/frontline/shows/religion/first/roles.html.

15. Thomas, Charles, *Celtic Britain* (London: Thames and Hudson, 1986), 121–150; Ó Croinín, Daibhi, "The Irish Missions," in Kruta, Venceslas, ed., *The Celts* (New York: Rizzoli, 1991), 687–691; Davidson, 1988, 2, 8, 11, 132–133, 168, 173, 183, 193, 219; Paper, 1997, *passim*; Puhvel, Jaan, *Comparative Mythology* (Baltimore: Johns Hopkins University Press, 1988), 190.

16. Shutova, Nadezhda, "Woman and Man in Udmurt and Berermian Religious Practice in the Late Nineteenth and Early Twentieth Century," in *Cosmos: The Journal of the Traditional Cosmology Society*, The Ritual Year 4: The Ritual Year and Gender (Edinburgh: School of Celtic and Scottish Studies, University of Edinburgh, Vol. 25, 2009), 3–21.

17. Ruotsala, Helena, "The Flower Festival as an Example of Mari Women Maintaining Rituals," in *Cosmos: The Journal of the Traditional Cosmology Society*, The Ritual Year 4: The Ritual Year and Gender (Edinburgh: School of Celtic and Scottish Studies, University of Edinburgh, Vol. 25, 2009), 23–33.

18. Joseph O'Meara, ed., *Gerald of Wales — The History and Topography of Ireland* (London: Penguin, 1982), 110–111; Thomas, *Celtic Britain*, 121–181.

19. Todd, "Barbarian Europe," 447–482; Puhvel, *Comparative Mythology*, 189–221; Davidson, *Myths and Symbols in Pagan Europe*, 16, 24, 117, 120, 150, 157, 159.

20. Handford, S.A., transl., *Caesar — The Conquest of Gaul* (London: Penguin, 1982), 143–146.

21. Todd, "Barbarian Europe," 448–449, 486–471.

22. *Ibid.*, 449–450, 463–467.
23. *Ibid.*
24. *Ibid.*
25. *Ibid.*, 460–463.
26. *Ibid.*
27. *Ibid.*, 451–452.
28. *Ibid.*
29. *Ibid.*, 477–478.
30. *Ibid.*, 472–474.
31. *Ibid.*, 459, 475–477.
32. *Ibid.*, 453–457.
33. *Ibid.*
34. Davidson, *Myths and Symbols in Pagan Europe*, 16, 24, 117, 120, 150, 157, 159.
35. *Ibid.*, 16.
36. *Ibid.*, 17, 44, 62, 90, 120, 200, 204, 208, 214.
37. *Ibid.*, 24, 174, 190, 193, 200, 208, 215, 226.
38. *Ibid.*, 119–120.
39. *Ibid.*, 24, 117, 157.
40. Tacitus' *Germania* in English and Latin, Chapter 40: www. northvegr. org / history. See also: J.C.G. Anderson, *Tacitus: Germania* (London: Bristol Classical Press, 1988).
41. Gale Owen, *Rites and Religions of the Anglo-Saxons* (New York: Barnes and Noble, 1981).
42. *Ibid.*
43. Davidson, *Myths and Symbols in Pagan Europe*, 39, 110–111.
44. *Ibid.*, 108–110.
45. Jesse L. Byock, transl., *Snori Sturluson — The Prose Edda* (London: Penguin, 2005), 42–44, 111–112, 142.
46. Davidson, *Myths and Symbols in Pagan Europe*, 2–3, 8–10.
47. Gwyn Jones, *A History of the Vikings* (Oxford: Oxford University Press, 2001).
48. Davidson, *Myths and Symbols in Pagan Europe*, 170, 172.
49. Puhvel, *Comparative Mythology*, 193–200; Davidson, *Myths and Symbols in Pagan Europe*.
50. Puhvel, *Comparative Mythology*, 194. See

also: Byock re: Poetic Edda — Hávamál 138, *xvii-xxviii*, 30–42; Hávamál — www.pitt.edu /~dash havamal/html.
51. Puhvel, *Comparative Mythology*, 194–201. See also: Byock, *Snorri Sturluson*, 30–42; Davidson, *Gods and Myths of Northern Europe*.
52. Byock, *Snorri Sturluson*, 30–42.
53. *Ibid.*
54. *Ibid.*
55. Davidson, *Myths and Symbols in Pagan Europe*, 119–120; Byock, *Snorri Sturluson*, 42–44, 111–112, 142.
56. Byock, *Snorri Sturluson*, 33–35, 81–83, 141; Davidson, *Myths and Symbols in Pagan Europe*, 111, 175, 213.
57. Davidson, *Myths and Symbols in Pagan Europe*, 110, 120–121.
58. Byock, *Snorri Sturluson*, 45; Davidson, *Myths and Symbols in Pagan Europe*, 1, 45, 58, 85, 96, 107, 122–123, 152, 163, 194.
59. Davidson, *Myths and Symbols in Pagan Europe*, 96, 164.
60. *Ibid.*, 42, 50, 58, 105, 120–121, 133, 162, 202, 222.
61. *Ibid.* See also Byock, *Snorri Sturluson*, 35, 141.
62. Davidson, *Myths and Symbols in Pagan Europe*, 160–164.
63. *Ibid.*, 130; Byock, *Snorri Sturluson*, 35, 141.
64. Jaan Puhvel, "Indo-European Structure of the Baltic Pantheon," in Gerald J. Larson, Scott C. Littleton, and Jaan Puhvel, eds., *Myth in Indo-European Antiquity* (Berkeley: University of California Press, 1974), 75–86; Puhvel, *Comparative Mythology*, 222–238.
65. *Ibid.*
66. *Ibid.*
67. *Ibid.*
68. *Ibid.*
69. Puhvel, *Comparative Mythology*, 224, 226.
70. Motz, *Faces of the Goddess*, 72–73, 78–79, 80–83.
71. *Ibid.*, 80–83.
72. *Ibid.*, 77–78.
73. *Ibid.*
74. *Ibid.*, 73–77.
75. *Ibid.*
76. *Ibid.*
77. Puhvel, *Comparative Mythology*, 228–231. Regarding Ossetians and Scytho-Sarmations see: ossetians.com.
78. Tamara Talbot Rice, *The Scythians* (New York: Frederick A. Praeger, 1957), 180–184.
79. *Ibid.*
80. *Ibid.*
81. Shutova, "Woman and Man in Udmurt and Berermian Religious Practice," 9.
82. Louise Bachman, "Pre-Christian Saami Religion" in Jordan Paper, *Through the Earth Darkly: Female Spirituality in Comparative Perspective* (New York: Continuum, 1997), 15–27.

83. *Ibid.*
84. *Ibid.*

Chapter 11

1. Medieval Welsh poem *Preideu Annwfn* attributed to the legendary poet-seer Taliesin; translated from Middle Welsh by Sharon Paice MacLeod. Quotation from Joseph Campbell: Diane K. Osbon, ed., *A Joseph Campbell Companion: Reflections on the Art of Living* (New York: Harper Collins, 1991), 161.
2. Historical information for this narrative derived from: Roger S. Loomis, ed., *Arthurian Literature in the Middle Ages* (Oxford: Oxford University Press, 2001); Oliver, J. Padel, *Arthur in Medieval Welsh Literature* (Cardiff: University of Wales Press, 2000); James J. Wilhelm, ed., *The Romance of Arthur: An Anthology of Medieval Texts in Translation* (New York: Garland Publishing, 1994); John B. Coe and Simon Young, ed., *The Celtic Sources for the Arthurian Legend* (Felinfach: Llanerch, 1995); Anne Ross, *The Folklore of Wales* (Stroud: Tempest, 2001); Leslie Alcock, *Arthur's Britain: History and Archaeology, AD 367–634* (Harmondsworth: Penguin, 1971); Richard L. Brengle, ed., *Arthur, King of Britain: History, Chronicle, Romance and Criticism* (New York: Meredith Publishing, 1964); Roger S. Loomis, *The Development of Arthurian Romance* (New York: Norton and Company, 1963); Roger S. Loomis, *The Grail: From Celtic Myth to Christian Symbol* (Princeton: Princeton University Press, 1991); Thelma S. Fenster, S., ed., *Arthurian Women* (New York: Routledge, 2000).
3. P.C. Bartrum, *Early Welsh Genealogical Tracts* (Cardiff: University of Wales Press, 1996).
4. John J. Parry, and Robert A. Caldwell, "Geoffrey of Monmouth" in Loomis, *Arthurian Literature in the Middle Ages*, 72–93.
5. Lewis Thorpe transl., *Geoffrey of Monmouth: The History of the Kings of Britain* (Hammondsworth: Penguin, 1982); Richard M. Loomis "Arthur in Geoffrey of Monmouth" in Wilhelm, *The Romance of Arthur*, 59–94; James J. Wilhelm "Wace: *Roman de Brut* (Merlin Episodes and "The Birth and Rise of Arthur" in Wilhelm, *The Romance of Arthur*, 95–108; James J. Wilhelm, "Layamon: *Brut* ('The Death of Arthur')" in Wilhelm, *The Romance of Arthur*, 109–120; William K. Kibler, "Chrétien De Troyes: *Lancelot*, or *The Knight of the Cart*" in Wilhelm, *The Romance of Arthur*, 121–201; Roger Sherman Loomis, "The Oral Diffusion of the Arthurian Legend," in Loomis, *Arthurian Literature in the Middle Ages*, 52–63; Charles Foulon, "Wace" in Loomis, *Arthurian Literature in the Middle Ages*, 94–1–3; Roger Sherman Loomis, "Layamon's *Brut*" in Loomis, *Arthurian Literature in the Middle Ages*, 104–111;

6. *Ibid.*

7. Loomis, "The Oral Diffusion of the Arthurian Legend," 52–63.

8. Thomas Charles-Edwards, "The Arthur of History" in Rachel Bromwich, A.O.H. Jarman, and Brynley F. Roberts, *The Arthur of the Welsh: The Arthurian Legend in Medieval Welsh Literature* (Cardiff: University of Wales Press, 1991), 15–32; Kenneth H. Jackson, "The Arthur of History," in Loomis, *Arthurian Literature in the Middle Ages*, 1–11; Charles Thomas, *Celtic Britain* (London: Thames and Hudson, 1986), 37–52, 69–76; Barry Cunliffe, *Iron Age Britain* (London: Batsford, 1997), 59–70, 76–80, 115–118; Nora Chadwick, *Celtic Britain* (North Hollywood: Newcastle, 1989), 35–51.

9. *Ibid.*

10. *Ibid.*

11. Padel, *Arthur in Medieval Welsh Literature*, 3–13; James J. Wilhelm, "Arthur in the Latin Chronicles," in Wilhelm, *The Romance of Arthur*, 1–10; Charles-Edwards, '*The Arthur of History*," 15–32; Coe and Young, *The Celtic Sources for the Arthurian Legend*, 2–5.

12. Charles-Edwards, "The Arthur of History," 15–32; Jackson, "The Arthur of History," 1–10.

13. *Ibid*; Coe and Young, *The Celtic Sources for the Arthurian Legend*, 6–11.

14. *Ibid*; Coe and Young, *The Celtic Sources for the Arthurian Legend*, 12–13.

15. Brynley F. Roberts, "*Culhwch ac Olwen*, The Triads, Saints' Lives,' in Bromwich, Jarman and Roberts, *The Arthur of the Welsh*, 73–96; Loomis, "*The Oral Diffusion of the Arthurian Legend*," 52–63; Wilhelm, *The Romance of Arthur*, 6; Padel, *Arthur in Medieval Welsh Literature*, 38–45; Coe and Young, *The Celtic Sources for the Arthurian Legend*, 14–47.

16. Roger S. Loomis, "The Legend of Arthur's Survival," in Loomis, *Arthurian Literature in the Middle Ages*, 64–71; Sims-Williams, Patrick, "*The Early Welsh Arthurian Poems*," in Bromwich, Jarman and Roberts, *The Arthur of the Welsh*, 49–50; Wilhelm, *The Romance of Arthur*, 6–7.

17. Wilhelm, "Arthur in the Latin Chronicles," 7.

18. Roger S. Loomis, "The Legend of Arthur's Survival," in Loomis, *Arthurian Literature in the Middle Ages*, 64–71; Sims-Williams, '*The Early Welsh Arthurian Poems*,'in Bromwich, Jarman and Roberts, *The Arthur of the Welsh*, 49–50; Wilhelm, *The Romance of Arthur*, 6–7.

19. Sims-Williams, "The Early Welsh Arthurian Poems," 33–72.

20. *Ibid.*, Coe and Young, *The Celtic Sources for the Arthurian Legend*, 99–101.

21. Brynley F. Roberts, "*Culhwch ac Olwen*, The Triads, Saints' Lives," 73–96.

22. Charles-Edwards, '*The Arthur of History*," 15–32; Jackson, "The Arthur of History," 1–10.

23. Bromwich, Jarman and Roberts, *The Arthur of the Welsh*, 3–6; Jackson, "*The Arthur of History*," 3; Bollard, John K., "Arthur in the Early Welsh Tradition," in Wilhelm, *The Romance of Arthur*, 11–24; Padel, *Arthur in Medieval Welsh Literature*, 6–10; Coe and Young, *The Celtic Sources for the Arthurian Legend*, 156–159; A.O.H. Jarman and Gwilym Rees Hughes, *A Guide to Welsh Literature*, Vol I (Cardiff: University of Wales Press, 1992), 68–80.

24. *Ibid.*

25. Sims-Williams, "*The Early Welsh Arthurian Poems*," 33–72; Kenneth H. Jackson, "Arthur in Early Welsh Verse," in Loomis, *Arthurian Literature in the Middle Ages*, 12–19; Coe and Young, *The Celtic Sources for the Arthurian Legend*, 135–139; Marged Haycock, *Legendary Poems from the Book of Taliesin* (Aberystwyth: CMCS Publications, 2007), 433–451.

26. Sioned Davies, transl., *The Mabinogion* (Oxford: Oxford University Press, 2007), 179–213; Idris L. Foster, "*Culhwch and Olwen* and *Rhonabwy's Dream*," in Loomis, *Arthurian Literature in the Middle Ages*, 31–42; Brynley F. Roberts, "*Culhwch ac Olwen*, The Triads, Saints' Lives," 73–96.

27. *Ibid.*; Daphne Brooke, *Saints and Goddesses: The Interface with Celtic Paganism* (Wigtownshire: Friends of the Whithorn Trust, 1999).

28. Thorpe, "Geoffrey of Monmouth," 237, 257.

29. Rachel Bromwich, *Trioedd Ynys Prydain* (Cardiff: University of Wales Press, 1978), 147.

30. *Ibid.*, 381–382; Brynley F. Roberts, "*Culhwch ac Olwen*, The Triads, Saints' Lives," in Bromwich, Jarman and Roberts, *The Arthur of the Welsh*, 110.

31. Davies, *The Mabinogion*, 207.

32. Bromwich, *Trioedd Ynys Prydain*, 380–381.

33. *Ibid.*, 154, 196–206.

34. Whitley Stokes, ed., *Sanas Chormaic* (Calcutta: Irish Archaeological and Celtic Society, 1868), 23; Sharon Paice MacLeod, "*Mater Deorum Hibernensium*: Identity and Cross-Correlation in Early Irish Myth," in *Proceedings of the Harvard Celtic Colloquium*, Vol. XIX, 1999, 377, 380.

35. Proinsias MacCana, "Celtic Goddesses of Sovereignty," in Elisabeth Benard and Beverly Moon, eds., *Goddesses Who Rule* (Oxford: Oxford University Press, 2000).

36. Sharon Paice MacLeod, "Abduction, Swordplay, Monsters and Mistrust: Findabair, Gwenhwyfar and the Restoration of Honour," in *Proceedings of the Harvard Celtic Colloquium*, Vol. XXVIII, 2008.

37. Thorpe, "*Geoffrey of Monmouth*," 200–201.

38. *Ibid.*

39. *Ibid.*, 205–208.
40. *Ibid.*
41. *Ibid.*, 209, 221. For references concerning Gawain (or *Gwalchmai*, the Welsh version of his name) refer to the index in Bromwich, Jarman and Roberts, *The Arthur of the Welsh.* For Mordred (or *Medrawt / Medraut*), see Bromwich, *Trioedd Ynys Prydain*, 385, 455; MacLeod, "Abduction, Swordplay, Monsters and Mistrust," 192 n27.
42. Joseph Stevenson, *Gerald of Wales on The Instruction of Princes* (Felinfach: Llanerch Press, 1991); Roger Sherman Loomis, "The Legend of Arthur's Survival," in Loomis, *Arthurian Literature in the Middle Ages*, 64–71
43. Parry and Caldwell, *"Geoffrey of Monmouth,"* 72–93.
44. Wilhelm, *"Layamon: Brut,"* 109–120; Loomis, "Layamon's *Brut*" in Loomis, *Arthurian Literature in the Middle Ages*, 104–111.
45. Samuel N. Rosenberg, "The Prose Merlin and The Suite du Merlin (Episodes)," in Wilhelm, *The Romance of Arthur*, 305–364.
46. Jean Frappier, "The Vulgate Cycle," in Loomis, *Arthurian Literature in the Middle Ages*, 295–318.
47. *Ibid.*
48. Tom P. Cross and Clark H. Slover, *Ancient Irish Tales* (Totowa: Barnes and Noble, 1969), 588–595.
49. Robin Gwyndaf, *Welsh Folk Tales* (Cardiff: National Museums and Galleries of Wales, 1999), 78.
50. *Ibid.*
51. MacLeod Estate Office, *Dunvegan Castle* (Isle of Skye: MacLeod Estate Office, 2003), 35–42.
52. Thorpe, "Geoffrey of Monmouth," 217, 225, 255.
53. Wilhelm, "Wace: Roman de Brut," 106.
54. John Carey, *Ireland and The Grail* (Aberystwyth: Celtic Studies Publications, 2007), *xiv-xvi*, 74, 79–82, 87–88, 90, 265–267, 339–340, 356–357.
55. *Ibid.*, 3, 11–14, 67–77, 137–138, 319, 343. Loomis, Roger S. Loomis, *The Development of Arthurian Romance* (New York: Norton, 1963).
56. Carey, *Ireland and the Grail*, 67–77.
57. *Ibid.*, 43–66, 67–77, 79–80, 133–149.
58. *Ibid.*
59. Frappier, "The Vulgate Cycle," 184–191; Carey, *Ireland and the Grail*, 1–8.
60. *Ibid.*
61. Carey, *Ireland and the Grail*, 15–26.
62. Philip Freeman, *War, Women and Druids: Eyewitness Reports and Early Accounts of the Ancient Celts* (Austin: University of Texas Press, 2002), 53–54.
63. Michael J. Enright, *Lady with a Mead Cup: Ritual, Prophecy and Lordship in the European Warband from La Tène to the Viking Age*

(Dublin: Four Courts Press, 1996), 34–35, 80, 82, 170–175, 185–187, 262–268, 273–277, 281, 286–287.
64. Proinsias MacCana, "Aspects of the Theme of King and Goddess in Irish Literature," in *Études Celtiques* VII, 1995.
65. J.P. Mallory, *In Search of the Indo-Europeans— Language, Archaeology and Myth* (New York: Thames and Hudson, 1999), 108, 136, 264, 275; K. Demakopoulou, C. Eluère, J. Jensen, A. Jockenhovel, and J. Mohen, J., *Gods and Heroes of the European Bronze Age* (London: Thames and Hudson, 1999), 6, 39, 40, 45, 127–129, 169, 257–258, 265, 268–273; Enright, *Lady with a Mead Cup*, 134–136; Andrew Sherratt, 'The Transformation of Early Agrarian Europe: The Later Neolithic and Copper Ages 4500–2500 BC' in Barry Cunliffe, ed., *The Oxford Illustrated History of Prehistoric Europe* (2001, Oxford: Oxford University Press), 190–193; Andrew Sherratt, "The Emergence of Élites: Earlier Bronze Age Europe, 2500–1300 BC," in Barry Cunliffe, ed., *The Oxford Illustrated History of Prehistoric Europe* (Oxford: Oxford University Press, 2001), 245, 250–256, 265, 273; Barry Cunliffe, "Iron Age Societies in Western Europe and Beyond, 800–140 BC," in Barry Cunliffe, ed., *The Oxford Illustrated History of Prehistoric Europe* (Oxford: Oxford University Press, 2001), 344–349; Peter Harbison, *Pre-Christian Ireland— From the First Settlers to the Early Celts* (London: Thames and Hudson, 1988), 104–110, 133–139; Ruth and Vincent Megaw, *Celtic Art: From Beginnings to the Book of Kells* (London: Thames and Hudson, 1989), 27–28, 32–33, 44, 46–47, 174, 185; Ian Armit, *Celtic Scotland* (London: Batsford, 1997), 23, 90, 92–93; Barry Cunliffe, *The Celtic World* (New York: McGraw-Hill, 1979), 22–23, 34–37, 42, 104, 109.
66. Mallory, *In Search of the Indo-Europeans*, 122, 244–245, 264; Sherratt, *"The Emergence of Élites,"* 256–261, 262, 269, 273; Demakopoulou et al, *Gods and Heroes of the European Bronze Age*, 31–34, 88–97, 103–107, 116, 127–129, 148, 234–239, 250, 256–257; Cunliffe, "Iron Age Societies in Western Europe and Beyond," 361, 364, 368; Harbison, *Pre-Christian Ireland*, 133–139, 161–163; Megaw, *Celtic Art*, 45, 59, 80–81, 126–135, 166, 195, 214–215, 219; Armit, *Celtic Scotland*, 23, 48, 85, 90, 92–93; Cunliffe, *The Celtic World*, 22, 33–37, 46–47, 58, 129, 134.
67. Osbon, *A Joseph Campbell Companion: Reflections on the Art of Living* (New York: Harper Collins, 1991)
10–1, 22, 72–82, 208–209.
68. David Suzuki and Peter Knudtson, *Wisdom of the Elders— Honoring Sacred Native Visions of Nature* (New York: Bantam, 1992); Mircea Eliade, *Shamanism: Archaic Techniques of Ecstasy* (Princeton: Princeton University Press, 1964), 88–95, 99–107.
69. Osbon, *A Joseph Campbell Companion*, 72.

Chapter 12

1. Melissa K. Nelson, ed., *Original Instructions — Indigenous Teachings for a Sustainable Future* (Rochester: Bear and Company, 2008), 63.

2. Carol Schaefer, *Grandmothers Counsel the World* (Boston: Trumpeter Books/Shambhala, 2006), 19.

3. David Suzuki and Peter Knudtson, *Wisdom of the Elders — Honoring Sacred Native Visions of Nature* (New York: Bantam, 1992), 20.

4. Information for this narrative has been drawn from the following news sources: BBC News Europe, http://www.bbb.co.uk/news/world-europe "Princess sheds new light on early Celts," 5/1/2011; DW Top Stories / Culture, http://www.dw.de/archaeologists-revise-image-of-ancient-celts, 1/19/2013; The Guardian, August 31, 2008, 'Greece: Pagans call on Athena to protect the Acropolis,' 9/1/2008; htttp://www.guardian.co.uk/world/ 2008/sep/01/acropolis-museum; USA Today, 8/28/2008, 'After 1,500 years, pagans plan Acropolis prayer,' http://usatoday30.usatoday.com/news/world/2008-08-28; Smithsonian.com, March 2009, 'Ireland's Endangered Cultural Site,' http://www.smithsonianmag.com/travel/-Endangered-Cultural-Treasures-The-Hill-of-Tara-Ireland.html; Irish Independent, 'Five arrested during protest against M3 at Hill of Tara,' July 18, 2007; *http://www.m3motorway.ie;* The Nordic Page, 'Shamanism Approved as a Religion in Norway,' 3/15/2012, *www.tnp.no/2792-shamanism-approved-as-a-religion-in-Norway.*

5. Material in this summary derived from sources listed in the bibliographies of previous chapters.

6. For more on this topic, see: Lucy Goodison and Christine Morris, "Exploring Female Divinity: From Modern Myth to Ancient Evidence" in Lucy Goodison and Christine Morris, eds., *Ancient Goddesses: The Myths and the Evidence* (Madison: University of Wisconsin Press,1988), 6–21; Lotte Motz, *The Faces of the Goddess* (New York: Oxford University Press, 1997); and Ruth Tringham and Margaret Conkey, "Rethinking Figurines: A Critical View from the Archaeology of Gimbutas," in Lucy Goodison and Christine Morris, eds., *Ancient Goddesses: The Myths and the Evidence* (Madison: University of Wisconsin Press, 1988), 22–45.

7. The work in question is Robert Graves, *The White Goddess* (New York: Creative Age Press, 1948). For a detailed exploration of the formation of modern Goddess worship, Wicca, and other Neo-Pagan Earth Religions during the last few centuries see: Ronald Hutton, *The Triumph of the Moon* (Oxford: Oxford University Press, 2001).

8. Hutton, *The Triumph of the Moon, passim.*

9. Nelson, *Original Instructions*, 318.

10. *Ibid.*, 302.

11. Schaefer, *Grandmothers Counsel the World,* 3–12.

12. *Ibid.*, 43–47.

13. Suzuki and Knudtson, *Wisdom of the Elders*, 238–241.

14. Thomas Banyacya, "The Hopi Message to the UN General Assembly," December 11, 1992. http:// nativenet. uthscsa.edu / archive / nl / 9301 / 0164. html.

15. Steve Wall, *Wisdom's Daughters — Conversations with Women Elders of Native America* (New York: Harper Perennial, 1993), 202.

16. Nelson, *Original Instructions*, 221–222.

17. Steve Wall, *To Become a Human Being — The Message of Tadodaho Chief Leon Shenandoah* (Charlottesville: Hampton Roads Publishing, 2001), 29.

Bibliography

Alcock, Leslie. *Arthur's Britain: History and Archaeology, AD 367–634.* Harmondsworth: Penguin, 1971.

Anderson, J.C.G.. *Tacitus: Germania.* London: Bristol Classical Press, 1988.

Anthony, David W. *The Lost World of Old Europe—The Danube Valley, 5000—3500 BC.* Princeton: Princeton University Press, 2010.

_____. *The Horse, The Wheel and Language—How Bronze Age Riders from the European Steppes Shaped the Modern World.* Princeton: Princeton University Press, 2007.

Armit, Ian. *Celtic Scotland.* London: Batsford, 1997.

Ashmore, P.J. *Neolithic and Bronze Age Scotland.* London: B.T. Batsford Ltd. / Historic Scotland, 1997.

Audouze, Francoise and Buchenschutz, Olivier. *Towns, Villages and Countryside of Celtic Europe.* Bloomington: Indiana University Press, 1992.

Bachman, Louise. "Pre-Christian Saami Religion." In Paper, Jordan, *Through the Earth Darkly: Female Spirituality in Comparative Perspective.* New York: Continuum, 1997.

Bahn, Paul G. and Vertat, Jean. *Images of the Ice Age.* New York/Oxford: Facts on File, 1988.

Ball, Martin J. *The Celtic Languages.* New York: Routledge, 2002.

Banyacya, Thomas. "The Hopi Message to the UN General Assembly." December 11, 1992. http://nativenet.uthscsa.edu/archive/nl/9301/0164.html.

Bartrum, P.C. *Early Welsh Genealogical Tracts.* Cardiff: University of Wales Press, 1996.

Beck, Margaret. "Female Figurines in the European Upper Paleolithic: Politics and Bias in Archaeological Interpretation." In Rautman, Allison, ed., *Reading the Body: Representations and Remains in the Archaeological Record.* Philadelphia: University of Pennsylvania Press, 2000.

Bell, Diane. *Daughters of the Dreaming.* Minneapolis: University of Minnesota Press, 1997.

Benard, Elisabeth and Moon, Beverly, eds. *Goddesses Who Rule.* Oxford: Oxford University Press, 2000.

Bitel, Lisa M. "Ekphrasis at Kildare: The Imaginative Architecture of a Seventh-Century Hagiographer." In *Speculum: A Journal of Medieval Studies*, Volume 79. No. 3. Cambridge: The Medieval Academy of America, 2004.

_____. *Land of Women: Tales of Sex and Gender from Early Ireland.* Ithaca: Cornell University Press, 1996.

Boehm, Christopher. *Hierarchy in the Forest: The Evolution of Egalitarian Behavior.* Cambridge: Harvard University Press, 1999.

Bollard, John K. "Arthur in the Early Welsh Tradition." In Wilhelm, James J., ed., *The Romance of Arthur: An Anthology of Medieval Texts in Translation.* New York: Garland, 1994.

Bongioanni, A. and Croce, Maria S. *The Treasures of Ancient Egypt from the Egyptian Museum in Cairo.* New York: Rizzoli, 2003.

Brengle, Richard L. ed. *Arthur, King of Britain: History, Chronicle, Romance and Criticism.* New York: Meredith Publishing, 1964.

Brennan, Martin. *The Stones of Time—Calendars, Sundials and Stone Chambers of Ancient Ireland.* Rochester: Inner Traditions, 1994.

Bridgman, Timothy. "Names and Naming Conventions Concerning Celtic Peoples in Some Early Ancient Greek Authors." In *CSANA Yearbook 7.*

Bridgman, Timothy. "Keltoi, Galatai, Galli: Were They All One People?" In *Proceedings of the Harvard Celtic Colloquium*, Vol. XXV, 2005.

Brody, Hugh. *The Other Side of Eden: Hunters, Farmers and the Shaping of the World*. New York: North Point Press, 2000.

Bromwich, Rachel; Jarman, A.O.H.; and Roberts, Brynley F., *The Arthur of the Welsh: The Arthurian Legend in Medieval Welsh Literature*. Cardiff: University of Wales Press, 1991.

_____. *Trioedd Ynys Prydain*. Cardiff: University of Wales Press, 1978.

Brooke, Daphne. *Saints and Goddesses: The Interface with Celtic Paganism*. Wigtownshire: Friends of the Whithorn Trust, 1999.

Burkitt, M.C. *Our Early Ancestors: An Introductory Study of Mesolithic, Neolithic and Copper Age Cultures in Europe and Adjacent Regions*. Cambridge: Cambridge University Press, 1936.

Butler, Hazel. "The Cult of Isis and Early Christianity." historyoftheancientworld.com, from *Hohonu: A Journal of Academic Writing*, Vol. 7, 2005.

Byock, Jesse L. transl. *Snori Sturluson—The Prose Edda*. London: Penguin, 2005.

Campbell, Joseph. *Historical Atlas of World Mythology: Volume 2—The Mythologies of the Great Hunt*. New York: Harper and Row, 1988.

Capel, Anne K. and Markoe, Glenn E., eds. *Mistress of the House, Mistress of Heaven—Women in Ancient Egypt*. New York: Hudson Hills Press, 1996.

Carey, John. *Ireland and The Grail*. Aberystwyth: Celtic Studies Publications, 2007.

Carmichael, Alexander, ed. *Carmina Gadelica*. Hudson: Lindisfarne, 1994.

Carr, Suzanne. *Entoptic Phenomenon* (Master's Dissertation. www.oubliette.zetnet.co.uk.

Chadwick, Nora K. *Celtic Britain*. North Hollywood: Newcastle Publishing, 1989.

Charles-Edwards, Thomas. "The Arthur of History" in Bromwich, Rachel; Jarman, A.O.H.; and Roberts, Brynley F., *The Arthur of the Welsh: The Arthurian Legend in Medieval Welsh Literature*. Cardiff: University of Wales Press, 1991.

Childe, V. Gordon. *The Dawn of European Civilization*. New York: Alfred A. Knopf, 1967.

Clark, Elizabeth. *The First Christians*. www.pbs.org/wgbh/pages/frontline/shows/religion/first/roles.html

Clarke, D.V., Cowie, T.G., and Foxon, A., eds.

Symbols of Power at the Time of Stonehenge. Edinburgh: National Museum of Antiquities of Scotland, 1985.

Clark, J.G.D. *The Mesolithic Settlement of Northern Europe*. Cambridge: Cambridge University Press, 1936.

Clottes, Jean and Lewis-Williams, David. *The Shamans of Prehistory—Trance and Magic in the Painted Caves*. New York: Harry N. Abrams, 1998.

Coe, John B. and Young, Simon, ed. *The Celtic Sources for the Arthurian Legend*. Felinfach: Llanerch, 1995.

Cross, Tom P. and Slover, Clark H. *Ancient Irish Tales*. Totowa: Barnes and Noble, 1996.

Cunliffe, Barry. "The Impact of Rome on Barbarian Society, 140 BC-AD 300." In Cunliffe, Barry, ed., *The Oxford Illustrated History of Prehistoric Europe*. Oxford: Oxford University Press, 2001.

_____. "Iron Age Societies in Western Europe and Beyond, 800–140 BC." In Cunliffe, Barry, ed., *The Oxford Illustrated History of Prehistoric Europe*. Oxford: Oxford University Press, 2001.

_____. *The Ancient Celts*. Oxford: Oxford University Press, 1997.

_____. *Iron Age Britain*. London: Batsford, 1997.

_____. *The Celtic World*. New York: McGraw-Hill, 1979.

Cunliffe, Barry, ed. *The Oxford Illustrated History of Prehistoric Europe*. Oxford: Oxford University Press, 2001.

Darvill, Timothy. *Prehistoric Britain*. New York: Routledge, 1996.

Davidson, H.R. Ellis. *Myths and Symbols in Pagan Europe*. Syracuse: Syracuse University Press, 1988.

Davidson, H.R. Ellis. *Gods and Myths of Northern Europe*. New York: Penguin, 1964.

Davies, Sioned, transl. *The Mabinogion*. Oxford: Oxford University Press, 2007.

Davis-Kimball, Jeannine. *Warrior Women—An Archaeologist's Search for History's Hidden Heroines*. New York: Warner Books, 2002.

_____. "Chieftain or Warrior-Priestess?" In *Archaeology*, Sept/Oct. 1997.

Demakopoulou, K., Eluère, C., Jensen, J., Jockenhovel, A., and Mohen, J. *Gods and Heroes of the European Bronze Age*. London: Thames and Hudson, 1999.

Dillon, Myles. *Early Irish Literature*. Dublin: Four Courts Press, 1994.

Dolukhanov, Paul M. *Ecology and Economy in Neolithic Europe*. London: Duckworth, 1979.

Duval, Alan. "Celtic Society in the First Century BC." In Kruta, Venceslas, ed., *The Celts*. New York: Rizzoli, 1997.

Dyer, James. *Ancient Britain*. Philadelphia: University of Pennsylvania Press, 1990.

Eliade, Mircea. *Rites and Symbols of Initiation*. Woodstock: Spring Publications, 1995.

_____. *The Sacred and The Profane: The Nature of Religion*. San Diego/New York: Harcourt Brace, 1987.

_____. *Shamanism — Archaic Techniques of Ecstacy*. Princeton: Princeton University Press, 1974.

Enright, Michael J. *Lady with a Mead Cup: Ritual, Prophecy and Lordship in the European Warband, From La Tène to the Viking Age*. Dublin: Four Courts Press, 1996.

Eogan, George. *Knowth and the passage-tombs of Ireland*. London: Thames and Hudson, 1986.

Fenster, Thelma S., ed. *Arthurian Women*. New York: Routledge, 2000.

Ford, Patrick K. *The Celtic Poets*. Belmont: Ford and Bailie, 1999.

_____. "Celtic Women: The Opposing Sex." In *Viator: Medieval and Renaissance Studies*, Volume 19. Berkeley: University of California Press, 1988.

Foster, Idris L. "*Culhwch and Olwen* and *Rhonabwy's Dream*." In Loomis, Roger S., ed., *Arthurian Literature in the Middle Ages*. Oxford: Oxford University Press, 2001.

Foulon, Charles. "Wace." In Loomis, Roger S., ed., *Arthurian Literature in the Middle Ages*. Oxford: Oxford University Press, 2001.

Frappier, Jean. "The Vulgate Cycle." In Loomis, Roger S., ed., *Arthurian Literature in the Middle Ages*. Oxford: Oxford University Press, 2001.

Freeman, Philip. *War, Women and Druids: Eyewitness Reports and Early Accounts of the Ancient Celts*. Austin: University of Texas Press, 2002.

Gamble, Clive. "The Peopling of Europe 700,000 — 40,000 Years before the Present." In Cunliffe, Barry, ed., *The Oxford Illustrated History of Prehistoric Europe*. Oxford: Oxford University Press, 2001.

Gantz, Jeffrey. *Early Irish Myths and Sagas*. Hammondsworth: Dorset Press, 1985.

Gershoy, Leo, ed. *A Survey of European Civilization*. Boston: Houghton Mifflin, 1969.

Goodison, Lucy and Morris, Christine, eds. *Ancient Goddesses: The Myths and the Evidence*. Madison: University of Wisconsin Press, 1988.

Goodison, Lucy and Morris, Christine. "Exploring Female Divinity: From Modern Myth to Ancient Evidence." In Goodison, Lucy and Morris, Christine, eds., *Ancient Goddesses: The Myths and the Evidence*. Madison: University of Wisconsin Press, 1988.

Green, Miranda. *Celtic Goddesses*. New York: George Braziller, 1996.

Gwyndaf, Robin. *Welsh Folk Tales*. Cardiff: National Museums and Galleries of Wales, 1999.

Gwynn, Edward. *The Metrical Dindshenchas*. Dublin: Dublin Institute for Advanced Studies, 1991.

Halifax, Joan. *The Fruitful Darkness*. New York: Harper San Francisco, 1993.

Handford, S.A., ed. *Caesar: The Conquest of Gaul*. London: Penguin, 1982.

Harbison, Peter. *Pre-Christian Ireland — From the First Settlers to the Early Celts*. London: Thames and Hudson, 1988.

Harding, Anthony. "Reformation in Barbarian Europe, 1300–600 BC." In Cunliffe, Barry, ed., *The Oxford Illustrated History of Prehistoric Europe*. Oxford: Oxford University Press, 2001.

Haycock, Marged. *Legendary Poems from the Book of Taliesin*. Aberystwyth: CMCS Publications, 2007.

Hayden, Brian. *Shamans, Sorcerers and Saints: A Prehistory of Religion*. Washington, D.C.: Smithsonian Books, 2003.

Herity, Michael and Eogan, George. *Ireland in Prehistory*. New York: Routledge, 1996.

Hutton, Ronald. *The Triumph of the Moon*. Oxford: Oxford University Press, 2001.

Ireland, Stanley. *Roman Britain: A Sourcebook*. New York: Routledge, 1986.

Jackson, Kenneth H. "The Arthur of History." In Loomis, Roger S., ed., *Arthurian Literature in the Middle Ages*. Oxford: Oxford University Press, 2001.

_____. "Arthur in Early Welsh Verse." In Loomis, Roger S., ed., *Arthurian Literature in the Middle Ages*. Oxford: Oxford University Press, 2001.

Jarman, A.O.H. and Hughes, Gwilym Rees. *A Guide to Welsh Literature*, Vol I. Cardiff: University of Wales Press, 1992.

Johanson, Donald and Edgar, Blake. *From Lucy to Language*. New York: Simon and Schuster, 1996.

Jones, Gwyn. *A History of the Vikings*. Oxford: Oxford University Press, 2001.

Jung, Carl. *The Archetypes and the Collective*

Unconscious. Princeton: Princeton University Press, 1981.

_____. *The Structure and Dynamics of the Psyche*. New York: Pantheon Books, 1960.

Kane, Sean. *Wisdom of the Mythtellers*. Peterborough: Broadview Press, 1994.

Kelly, Fergus. *A Guide to Early Irish Law*. Dublin: Dublin Institute for Advanced Studies, 1995.

Kelly, Robert L. *The Foraging Spectrum: Diversity in Hunter-Gatherer Lifeways*. Washington, D.C.: Smithsonian Institution Press, 1995.

Kibler, William K. "Chrétien De Troyes: *Lancelot*, or *The Knight of the Cart*." In Wilhelm, James J., ed., *The Romance of Arthur: An Anthology of Medieval Texts in Translation*. New York: Garland, 1994.

Koch, John T. and Carey, John, eds. *The Celtic Heroic Age — Literary Sources for Ancient Celtic Europe and Early Ireland and Wales*. Aberystwyth: Celtic Studies Publications, 2003.

Koch, John T. "Some Suggestions and Etymologies Reflecting on the Mythology of the Four Branches." In *Proceedings of the Harvard Celtic Colloquium*, Volume IX, 1989.

Kruta, Venceslas, ed. *The Celts*. New York: Rizzoli, 1997.

Larson, Gerald J., Littleton, C. Scott., and Puhvel, Jaan, eds. *Myth in Indo-European Antiquity*. Berkeley: University of California Press, 1974.

Lee, Richard B. and Daly, Richard. *The Cambridge Encyclopedia of Hunters and Gatherers*. New York: Cambridge University Press, 1999.

Leroi-Gourhan, André. *The Dawn of European Art*. Cambridge: Cambridge University Press, 1982.

Levin, Theodore. *Where Rivers and Mountains Sing: Sound, Music, and Nomadism in Tuva and Beyond*. Bloomington: Indiana University Press, 2006.

Lewis-Williams, David and Pearce, David. *Inside the Neolithic Mind*. London: Thames and Hudson, 2005.

Lewis-Williams, J.D. and Dowson, T.A. "On Vision and Power in the Neolithic: Evidence from the Decorated Monuments." In *Current Anthropology* 34 (1), 1993.

_____. "The Signs of All Times." In *Current Anthropology* 29 (2), 1988.

Lincoln, Bruce. *Myth, Cosmos and Society: Indo-European Themes of Creation and Destruction*. Cambridge: Harvard University Press, 1986.

Longworth, I.H. *Prehistoric Britain*. Cambridge: Harvard University Press, 1986.

Loomis, Richard M. "Arthur in Geoffrey of Monmouth." In Wilhelm, James J., ed., *The Romance of Arthur: An Anthology of Medieval Texts in Translation*. New York: Garland, 1994.

Loomis, Roger S., ed. *Arthurian Literature in the Middle Ages*. Oxford: Oxford University Press, 2001.

_____. "The Oral Diffusion of the Arthurian Legend." In Loomis, Roger S., ed., *Arthurian Literature in the Middle Ages*. Oxford: Oxford University Press, 2001.

_____, "The Legend of Arthur's Survival," in Loomis, Roger Sherman, "The Oral Diffusion of the Arthurian Legend," in Loomis, Roger S., ed., *Arthurian Literature in the Middle Ages*. Oxford: Oxford University Press, 2001.

_____. *The Grail: From Celtic Myth to Christian Symbol*. Princeton: Princeton University Press, 1991.

_____. *The Development of Arthurian Romance*. New York: Norton and Company, 1963.

MacCana, Proinsius. "Celtic Goddesses of Sovereignty." In Benard, Elisabeth and Moon, Beverly, eds., *Goddesses Who Rule*. Oxford: Oxford University Press, 2000.

_____. "Aspects of the Theme of King and Goddess in Irish Literature." In *Études Celtiques* VII, 1995.

_____. *The Mabinogi*. Cardiff: University of Wales Press, 1992.

_____. "Celtic Religion and Mythology." In Kruta, Venceslas, ed., *The Celts*. New York: Rizzoli, 1991.

MacLeod Estate Office. *Dunvegan Castle*. Isle of Skye: MacLeod Estate Office, 2003.

MacLeod, Sharon Paice. *Celtic Myth and Religion: A Study of Traditional Belief*. Jefferson, N.C.: McFarland, 2012.

_____. "Abduction, Swordplay, Monsters and Mistrust: Findabair, Gwenhwyfar and the Restoration of Honour." In *Proceedings of the Harvard Celtic Colloquium*, Vol. XXVIII, 2008.

_____. "*Mater Deorum Hibernensium*: Identity and Cross-Correlation in Early Irish Myths." In *Proceedings of the Harvard Celtic Colloquium*, Vol. XIX, 2008.

Mallory, J.P. *In Search of the Indo-Europeans — Language, Archaeology and Myth*. New York: Thames and Hudson, 1999.

Mander, Jerry. *In the Absence of the Sacred: The Failure of Technology and the Survival of the*

Indian Nations. San Francisco: Sierra Club Books, 1992.

Manniche Lise. *Music and Musicians in Ancient Egypt.* London: British Museum Press, 1991.

McIntosh, Jane. *Handbook to Life in Prehistoric Europe.* New York: Facts on File, 2006.

Megaw, Ruth and Vincent. *Celtic Art: From Beginnings to the Book of Kells.* London: Thames and Hudson, 1989.

Mellars, Paul. "The Upper Paleolithic Revolution." In Cunliffe, Barry, ed., *The Oxford Illustrated History of Prehistoric Europe.* Oxford: Oxford University Press, 2001.

Mithen, Steven. *After the Ice: A Global Human History, 20,000–5000 BC.* Cambridge: Harvard University Press, 2004.

_____. "The Mesolithic Age." In Cunliffe, Barry, ed., *The Oxford Illustrated History of Prehistoric Europe.* Oxford: Oxford University Press, 2001.

Morford, Mark P.O. and Lenardon, Robert J. *Classical Mythology.* New York: Oxford University Press, 2002.

Morris, Brian. *Religion and Anthropology—A Critical Introduction.* Princeton: Princeton University Press, 2006.

Motz, Lotte. *The Faces of the Goddess.* New York: Oxford University Press, 1997.

Munro, Robert. *The Lake-Dwellings of Europe.* London: Cassell, 1890.

Nelson, Melissa K., ed. *Original Instructions—Indigenous Teachings for a Sustainable Future.* Rochester: Bear and Company, 2008.

Ó Croinín, Daibhi. "The Irish Missions." In Kruta, Venceslas, ed., *The Celts.* New York: Rizzoli, 1991.

O'Dwyer, Simon. *Prehistoric Music of Ireland.* Stroud: Tempus, 2004.

Ó hAodha, Donncha. *Bethu Brigte.* Dublin: Dublin Institute for Advanced Studies, 1978.

O'Kelly, Michael J. *Newgrange: Archaeology, Art and Legend.* London: Thames and Hudson, 1982.

O'Meara, Joseph, ed. *Gerald of Wales—The History and Topography of Ireland* London: Penguin, 1982.

Osbon, Diane K., ed. *A Joseph Campbell Companion: Reflections on the Art of Living.* New York: Harper Collins, 1991.

Osborne, Ken, ed. *Stonehenge and Neighbouring Monuments.* London: English Heritage, 2002.

Owen, Gale R. *Rites and Religions of the Anglo-Saxons.* New York: Barnes and Noble, 1981.

Padel, Oliver J. *Arthur in Medieval Welsh Literature.* Cardiff: University of Wales Press, 2000.

Pagels, Elaine. *Reading Judas: The Gospel of Judas and the Shaping of Christianity.* New York: Viking Adult, 2007.

_____. *Beyond Belief: The Secret Gospel of Thomas.* New York: Vintage, 2004.

_____. *The Gnostic Gospels.* New York: Vintage, 1989.

Pagels, Elaine H. *Women in the Early Church,* www. pbs. org / wgbh / pages / frontline / shows / religion / first / roles. html.

Paper, Jordan. *Through the Earth Darkly: Female Spirituality in Comparative Perspective.* New York: Continuum, 1997.

Parry, John J., and Caldwell, Robert A. "Geoffrey of Monmouth." In Loomis, Roger S., ed., *Arthurian Literature in the Middle Ages.* Oxford: Oxford University Press, 2001.

Patterson, Nerys. *Cattle Lords and Clansmen: The Social Structure of Early Ireland.* Notre Dame: University of Notre Dame Press, 1994.

Pearson, James L. *Shamanism and the Ancient Mind: A Cognitive Approach to Archaeology.* Walnut Creek: Altamira, 2002.

Piggott, Stuart. *The Druids.* New York: Thames and Hudson, 1993.

Powell, T.G.E. *The Celts.* London: Thames and Hudson, 1980.

Pryor, Francis. *Seahenge—New Discoveries in Prehistoric Britain.* London: Harper Collins, 2001.

Puhvel, Jaan. *Comparative Mythology.* Baltimore: Johns Hopkins University Press, 1984.

_____. "Indo-European Structure of the Baltic Pantheon." In Larson, Gerald J., Littleton, C. Scott., Puhvel, Jaan, eds., *Myth in Indo-European Antiquity.* Berkeley: University of California Press, 1974.

Quin, E.G., et al., eds. *Dictionary of the Irish Language, Based Mainly on Old and Middle Irish Materials.* Dublin: Royal Irish Academy, 1913–1980.

Rankin, David. *Celts and the Classical World.* New York: Routledge, 1996.

Rautman, Allison, ed. *Reading the Body: Representations and Remains in the Archaeological Record.* Philadelphia: University of Pennsylvania Press, 2000.

Rautman, Alison E. and Talalay, Lauren E. "Diverse Approaches to the Study of Gender in Archaeology." In Rautman, Allison, ed., *Reading the Body: Representations and Remains in the Archaeological Record.* Philadelphia: University of Pennsylvania Press, 2000.

Rees, Alwyn and Brinley. *Celtic Heritage*. New York: Thames and Hudson, 1978.

Renfrew, Colin. "Reflections on the Archaeology of Linguistic Diversity." In Sykes, Bryan, ed., *The Human Inheritance: Genes, Language and Evolution*. Oxford: Oxford University Press, 1999.

Renfrew, Jane M. *The Prehistoric Food Plants of the Near East and Europe*. New York: Columbia University Press, 1973.

Rice, Tamara Talbot. *The Scythians*. New York: Frederick A. Praeger, 1957.

Riches, David. *Northern Nomadic Hunter-Gatherers: A Humanistic Approach*. London: Academic Press, 1982.

Ries, Julien. *The Origin of Religions*. Grand Rapids: Wm. B. Eerdmans, 1994.

Roberts, Brynley F. "*Culhwch ac Olwen*, The Triads, Saints' Lives." In Bromwich, Rachel; Jarman, A.O.H.; and Roberts, Brynley F., *The Arthur of the Welsh: The Arthurian Legend in Medieval Welsh Literature*. Cardiff: University of Wales Press, 1991.

Roberts, Brynley F. "Geoffrey of Monmouth, *Historia Regum Brittaniae*." In Bromwich, Rachel; Jarman, A.O.H.; and Roberts, Brynley F., *The Arthur of the Welsh: The Arthurian Legend in Medieval Welsh Literature*. Cardiff: University of Wales Press, 1991.

Rosenberg, Samuel N. "The Prose Merlin and The Suite du Merlin (Episodes)." In Wilhelm, James J., ed., *The Romance of Arthur: An Anthology of Medieval Texts in Translation*. New York: Garland, 1994.

Ross, Anne. *The Folklore of Wales*. Stroud: Tempest, 2001.

_____. "Ritual and the Druids." In Green, Miranda, ed., *The Celtic World*. New York: Routledge, 1996.

_____. *Pagan Celtic Britain*. New York: Academy, 1996.

Rudgeley, Richard. *The Lost Civilizations of the Stone Age*. New York: Touchstone, 1999.

Ruotsala, Helena. "The Flower Festival as an Example of Mari Women Maintaining Rituals." In *Cosmos: The Journal of the Traditional Cosmology Society*, The Ritual Year 4: The Ritual Year and Gender. Edinburgh: School of Celtic and Scottish Studies, University of Edinburgh, Vol. 25, 2009.

Ryan, Michael, ed. *The Illustrated Archaeology of Ireland*. Dublin: Country House, 1991.

Scarre, Chris. *Exploring Prehistoric Europe*. Oxford: Oxford University Press, 1998.

Scarre, Christopher, ed. *Ancient France—6000–2000 BC: Neolithic Societies and Their Landscapes*. Edinburgh: Edinburgh University Press, 1983.

Schaefer, Carol. *Grandmothers Counsel the World—Women Elders Offer Their Vision for Our Planet*. Boston: Trumpeter Books/Shambala, 2006.

Shee Twohig, Elizabeth. "A 'Mother Goddess' in Northwest Europe c. 4200–2500 BC?" In *Ancient Goddesses: The Myths and the Evidence*, Goodison, Lucy and Morris, Christine, eds. Madison: University of Wisconsin Press, 1988.

Sherratt, Andrew. "The Transformation of Early Agrarian Europe: The Later Neolithic and Copper Ages 4500–2500 BC." In Cunliffe, Barry, ed., *The Oxford Illustrated History of Prehistoric Europe*. Oxford: Oxford University Press, 2001.

_____. "The Emergence of Élites: Earlier Bronze Age Europe, 2500–1300 BC." In Cunliffe, Barry, ed., *The Oxford Illustrated History of Prehistoric Europe*. Oxford: Oxford University Press, 2001.

Shutova, Nadezhda. "Woman and Man in Udmurt and Besermian Religious Practice in the Late Nineteenth and Early Twentieth Century." In *Cosmos: The Journal of the Traditional Cosmology Society*, The Ritual Year 4: The Ritual Year and Gender. Edinburgh: University of Edinburgh, Vol. 25, 2009.

Sims-Williams, Patrick. "The Early Welsh Arthurian Poems." In Bromwich, Rachel; Jarman, A.O.H.; and Roberts, Brynley F., *The Arthur of the Welsh: The Arthurian Legend in Medieval Welsh Literature*. Cardiff: University of Wales Press, 1991.

Stevenson, Joseph. *Gerald of Wales on The Instruction of Princes*. Felinfach: Llanerch Press, 1991.

Stringer, Chris. "The Fossil Record and the Evolution of *Homo Sapiens* in Europe and Australasia." In Sykes, Bryan, ed. *The Human Inheritance: Genes, Language and Evolution*. Oxford: Oxford University Press, 1999.

Suzuki, David and Knudtson, Peter. *Wisdom of the Elders—Honoring Sacred Native Visions of Nature*. New York: Bantam, 1992.

Sykes, Bryan. *The Seven Daughters of Eve—The Science That Reveals Our Genetic Ancestry*. New York: W.W. Norton, 2001.

Sykes, Bryan, ed. *The Human Inheritance: Genes, Language and Evolution*. Oxford: Oxford University Press, 1999.

Taylor, Timothy. "Thracians, Scythians and Dacians, 800 BC – AD 300." In Cunliffe, Barry, ed., *The Oxford Illustrated History of Prehistoric Europe*. Oxford: Oxford University Press, 2001.

Thomas, Charles. *Celtic Britain*. London: Thames and Hudson, 1986.

Thorpe, Lewis, transl. *Geoffrey of Monmouth: The History of the Kings of Britain*. Hammondsworth: Penguin, 1982.

Todd, Malcolm. "Barbarian Europe, AD 300–700." In Cunliffe, Barry, ed., *The Oxford Illustrated History of Prehistoric Europe*. Oxford: Oxford University Press, 2001.

Tringham, Ruth and Conkey, Margaret. "Rethinking Figurines: A Critical View from the Archaeology of Gimbutas." In Goodison, Lucy and Morrison, Christine, eds., *Ancient Goddesses: The Myths and the Evidence*. Madison: University of Wisconsin Press, 1988.

_____. "'The Goddess' and Popular Culture." In Goodison, Lucy and Morrison, Christine, eds., *Ancient Goddesses: The Myths and the Evidence*. Madison: University of Wisconsin Press, 1988.

Trippett, Frank, ed. *The First Horsemen*. New York: Time Life Books, 1974.

Wall, Steve. *To Become a Human Being: The Message of Tadodaho Chief Leon Shenandoah*. Charlottesville: Hampton Roads, 2001.

_____. *Wisdom's Daughters — Conversations with Women Elders of Native America*. New York: Harper Perennial, 1993.

Watkins, Calvert, ed. *Dictionary of Indo-European Roots*. Boston: Houghton Mifflin, 2000.

Webster, Jane. "Sanctuaries and sacred places." In Green, Miranda, ed., *The Celtic World*. New York: Routledge, 1996.

White, Randall. *Prehistoric Art—The Symbolic Journey of Humankind*. New York: Harry N. Abrams, 2003.

_____. *Dark Caves, Bright Visions: Life in Ice Age Europe*. New York: The American Museum of Natural History/W.W. Norton and Co., 1986.

Whitley Stokes, ed. *Sanas Chormaic*. Calcutta: Irish Archaeological and Celtic Society, 1868.

Whittle, Alasdair. "The First Farmers." In Cunliffe, Barry, ed., *The Oxford Illustrated History of Prehistoric Europe*. Oxford: Oxford University Press, 2001.

_____. *Europe in The Neolithic: The Creation of New Worlds*. Cambridge: Cambridge University Press, 1996.

_____. *Neolithic Europe: A Survey*. Cambridge: Cambridge University Press, 1985.

Wilhelm, James J., ed. *The Romance of Arthur: An Anthology of Medieval Texts in Translation*. New York: Garland, 1994.

Wilhelm, James J. "Wace: *Roman de Brut* (Merlin Episodes and "The Birth and Rise of Arthur"). In Wilhelm James J., ed., *The Romance of Arthur: An Anthology of Medieval Texts in Translation*. New York: Garland, 1994.

_____. "Layamon: *Brut* ("The Death of Arthur")." In Wilhelm, James J., ed., *The Romance of Arthur: An Anthology of Medieval Texts in Translation*. New York: Garland, 1994.

_____. "Arthur in the Latin Chronicles." In Wilhelm, James J., ed., *The Romance of Arthur: An Anthology of Medieval Texts in Translation*. New York: Garland, 1994.

Young, Jean I., tr. *Snorri Sturluson — The Prose Edda*. Berkeley: University of California Press, 1964.

Recommended Reading

David W. Anthony. *The Horse, The Wheel and Language — How Bronze Age Riders from the European Steppes Shaped the Modern World*.

Paul G. Bahn and Jean Vertat. *Images of the Ice Age*.

Elisabeth Benard and Beverly Moon. *Goddesses Who Rule*.

Rachel Bromwich, A.O.H. Jarman and Brynley F. Roberts, eds. *The Arthur of the Welsh: The Arthurian Legend in Medieval Welsh*.

D.V. Clarke, T.G. Cowie and A. Foxon, eds. *Symbols of Power at the Time of Stonehenge*.

Jean Clottes and David Lewis-Williams. *The Shamans of Prehistory — Trance and Magic in the Painted Caves*.

Barry Cunliffe. *The Celtic World*.

Barry Cunliffe, ed. *The Oxford Illustrated History of Prehistoric Europe*.

H.R. Ellis Davidson. *Myths and Symbols in Pagan Europe*.

K. Demakopoulou, C. Eluère, J. Jensen, A. Jockenhovel, and J. Mohen, J., eds. *Gods and Heroes of the European Bronze Age*.

Lucy Goodison and Christine Morris, eds. *Ancient Goddesses: The Myths and the Evidence*.

Ronald Hutton. *The Triumph of the Moon*.

Donald Johanson and Blake Edgar. *From Lucy to Language*.

Richard B. Lee and Richard Daly. *The Cam-*

bridge Encyclopedia of Hunters and Gatherers.

David Lewis-Williams and David Pearce. Inside the Neolithic Mind.

Roger S. Loomis. The Development of Arthurian Romance.

Sharon Paice MacLeod. Celtic Myth and Religion: A Study of Traditional Belief.

J.P. Mallory. In Search of the Indo-Europeans—Language, Archaeology and Myth.

Jerry Mander. In the Absence of the Sacred: The Failure of Technology and the Survival of the Indian Nations.

Steven Mithen. After the Ice: A Global Human History, 20,000–5000 BC.

Lotte Motz. The Faces of the Goddess.

Melissa K. Nelson. Original Instructions—Indigenous Teachings for a Sustainable Future.

Jordan Paper, ed. Through the Earth Darkly: Female Spirituality in Comparative Perspective.

Stuart Piggott. The Druids.

T.G.E. Powell The Celts.

Jaan Puhvel. Comparative Mythology.

Allison Rautman, ed. Reading the Body: Representations and Remains in the Archaeological Record.

Carol Schaefer. Grandmothers Counsel the World—Women Elders Offer Their Vision for Our Planet.

David Suzuki and Peter Knudtson. Wisdom of the Elders—Honoring Sacred Native Visions of Nature.

Bryan Sykes. The Seven Daughters of Eve—The Science That Reveals Our Genetic Ancestry.

Steve Wall. Wisdom's Daughters—Conversations with Women Elders of Native America.

Randall White. Dark Caves, Bright Visions: Life in Ice Age Europe.

James J. Wilhelm, ed. The Romance of Arthur: An Anthology of Medieval Texts in Translation.

Index